*Essays in Jewish
Social and Economic
History*

Arcadius Kahan, with Vilna in the background

Essays in Jewish Social and Economic History

Arcadius Kahan

Edited by
Roger Weiss

With an introduction by
Jonathan Frankel

The University of Chicago Press
Chicago and London

ARCADIUS KAHAN taught at the University of
Chicago from 1958 until his death in 1982. His
many publications include *The Plow, the
Hammer, and the Knout*, published by the
University of Chicago Press.

ROGER W. WEISS is professor of social sciences
at the University of Chicago.

The frontispiece is from the film *Image before My Eyes*
(courtesy of YIVO Institute for Jewish Research, New York).

The University of Chicago Press, Chicago 60637
The University of Chicago Press, Ltd., London

© 1986 by The University of Chicago
All rights reserved. Published 1986
Printed in the United States of America
95 94 93 92 91 90 89 88 87 86   5 4 3 2 1

Library of Congress Cataloging-in-Publication Data

Kahan, Arcadius.
    Essays in Jewish social and economic history.

    Includes index.
    1. Jews—Soviet Union—Economic conditions—Addresses,
essays, lectures.   2. Jews, East European—United States—
Economic conditions—Addresses, essays, lectures.
3. Jews—United States—Economic conditions—Addresses,
essays, lectures.   4. Jews—Lithuania—Vilnius—Addresses, essays, lectures.   5. Jews—Soviet Union—
Identity—Addresses, essays, lectures.   6. Soviet Union—
Ethnic relations—Addresses, essays, lectures.
7. United States—Ethnic relations—Addresses, essays,
lectures.   8. Vilnius (Lithuania)—Ethnic relations—Addresses, essays, lectures.   I. Weiss, Roger, 1930–   .
II. Title.
DS140.5.K33   1986   330.947'0089924   86-1427
ISBN 0-226-42240-2

Contents

Preface

Arcadius Kahan's untimely death interrupted his plan to write a comprehensive statement on the transformation of the Eastern European Jewish community. He had written papers dealing with demography, migration, urbanization, the impact of industrialization, and the growth of Jewish entrepreneurship during the last hundred years, and he had plans to extend these studies to other European countries. The essays gathered in this volume would not have appeared in their present form if he had lived, but some of them would have been the studies on which, as in his work on the economic history of Russia, he would have built a definitive book. They may lack a certain consistency of style and of scholarly apparatus, but they have a remarkable coherence, perspective, and continuity of theme for the great variety of occasions that prompted their composition.

The editor's task has been to smooth out the English, to check some references, to impose a more uniform transliteration of Russian and Yiddish place-names, and it called for familiarity with Hebrew, Yiddish, Russian, Polish, and German, and the sources in those languages on which Kahan drew. Much help has been provided by Pearl Kahan, Richard Hellie, Jonathan Frankel, and other colleagues and friends, but there will be errors remaining for which the author is not to be blamed. When Kahan's friend, the late Alexander Erlich, was unable to complete the introduction to this volume, the difficult task was generously undertaken by Professor Jonathan Frankel of the Hebrew University, Jerusalem, and completed with distinction, so that we can better understand the significance of Kahan's studies and his personal relationship to this work. In these essays Kahan stated his profound attachment to the fate of the Eastern European Jewish community, to the ideals of the Bund, and to the scholarship that was inspired by YIVO. Not only was this side of his work an expression of filial piety but it was a profound completion of the scholarly and political debates of his father's generation. In this quest for understanding the continuity of the experience of his community and of his participation in the attempt at solutions, he was joined by his wife Pearl, and it is the editor's certain judgment that the author would have dedicated this work to her. Gathering the material and translating from the Yiddish could not have been done without her.

Acknowledgment and thanks are due the publishers of the essays who have given permission for their inclusion in this volume. Such acknowledgment and thanks are noted below together with information on the other chapters regarding the occasion for their composition.

1. "The Impact of Industrialization Process in Tsarist Russia on the Socioeconomic Conditions of the Jewish Population." 1980. Unpublished.
2. "The Urbanization Process of the Jews in Nineteenth Century Europe" (paper delivered at Conference on the Legacy of Jewish Migration, sponsored by the Center for Jewish Studies of the Graduate Center, CUNY; Brooklyn College Conference on Society in Change; and the YIVO Institute for Jewish Research, New York, 1981). Unpublished.
3. "Notes on Jewish Entrepreneurship in Tsarist Russia," Occasional Paper no. 57, Wilson Center, Kennan Institute for Advanced Russian Studies, 1978. Published in G. Guroff and F. Carstensen, eds., *Entrepreneurship in Imperial Russia and the Soviet Union* (Princeton, N.J., Princeton University Press, 1983).
4. "Economic Opportunities and Some Pilgrims' Progress: Jewish Immigrants from Eastern Europe in the United States, 1890–1914," *Journal of Economic History* 38, no. 1 (March 1978). Copyright © The Economic History Association. Reprinted with permission.
5. "The First Wave of Jewish Immigration from Eastern Europe to the United States" (paper delivered at YIVO Institute Conference on Jewish Immigration, New York, 1980). Unpublished.
6. "Jewish Life in the United States: Perspectives from Economics," in Joseph B. Gittler, ed., *Jewish Life in the United States: Perspectives from the Social Sciences* (New York: New York University Press, 1981). Copyright © 1981 by New York University. Reprinted by permission of New York University Press.
7. "Vilna—The Socio-Cultural Anatomy of a Jewish Community in Interwar Poland," YIVO Institute. Unpublished.
8. "Introduction of Czeslaw Milosz, YIVO and the American Jewish Committee, 1981. Unpublished.
9. "The University of Vilna" (paper delivered at American Association

for the Advancement of Slavic Studies, New Haven, 1979). Unpublished.

10. "A Day in the Ghetto" (paper delivered at Northwestern University, Evanston, Ill., 1978). Unpublished.
11. "Forces for and against Jewish Identity in the USSR" (paper delivered at Symposium on Jewish Culture in the Soviet Union, Spertus College of Judaica, Chicago, 1976). Unpublished.
12. "Religion and Soviet Policy: The Case of Judaism" (paper delivered at International Slavic Conference, Garmisch, 1980). Unpublished.
13. "The Soviet Jews" (paper delivered at Jewish Federation Council General Assembly, Dallas, 1977). Unpublished.

"On Edom" (quoted here p. 150, Chapter 9) was originally published in Hal Draper, ed., *The Complete Poems of Heinrich Heine.* (Boston: Suhrkamp/Insel Publishers, Boston, 1982). Reprinted with permission.

Introduction

Arcadius Kahan was born and grew up in Vilna, which had been the ancient capital of Lithuania but found itself included in independent Poland during the years 1920–39. The Second World War totally disrupted his life. It was only in 1959 at the age of almost forty, living in Chicago, that he received his doctoral degree and began to establish his reputation as one of the leading authorities in the West on Russian economic history.

The articles and lectures collected here, however, all deal with aspects of Jewish history, particularly with the economic development of East European Jewry both in the Tsarist Empire and in the new centers established by the great emigrations to the West. For the most part, they were written in the 1970s when Kahan began to devote much of his time and energy to this area of research.

Nobody reading this book can fail, I believe, to conclude that, in taking up these themes, Kahan was moved by some profound sense of obligation to his own self, by a need to bridge the chasm that had so abruptly broken his life in two in 1939–40. He was reaching back to the world of his youth which had been destroyed, most of its inhabitants killed, the remnant scattered across the globe. And he was taking up the threads of a historiographical tradition which had developed over a span of some four decades before the war, reaching heights of real achievement until it too had been overtaken by catastrophe.

An enterprise of this kind can easily fall into the traps set by nostalgia and filial piety, but Arcadius Kahan was by temperament utterly averse to anything that smacked of sentimentality. In this respect, he was much more the Litvak, the *misnaged,* in the Vilna manner, than the *khosed* of his family's origins (but then Hasidism was always more restrained in its emotionalism in Lithuania than elsewhere). His chosen language was that of statistics, inputs and outputs, costs and benefits, the calculations made by rational economic man. He understood that some of the most dramatic chapters in modern Jewish history can best be told precisely through the objective analysis of the figures which sum up the lives lived and decisions made by hundreds of thousands, millions, of individuals. Gershom Scholem talked much of what he termed "neutralized messianism"; Kahan's work can be seen, perhaps, as a kind of "neutralized romanticism," the poetry of the epic conveyed through the terminology of mathematics.

The impact of modernity on the highly traditional and culturally enclosed world of Russian Jewry released extraordinary energies of the most varied kind and with the most explosive effect. And as a result, Jewish society, thought, and politics were transformed with a rapidity and on a scale without precedent since the destruction of the Second Temple in 70 C.E. Arcadius Kahan was fascinated by this grand upheaval, which had been mirrored in the remarkable story of his own family. Indeed, his family's saga can be seen not so much as typical, although in many ways it was that, but even more as archetypal.

His great-great-grandfather, Zvi Cohen, was a *khosed* from the town of Shklov and was a relatively wealthy merchant and contractor. Shklov in the first half of the nineteenth century was an important commercial center with two its annual fairs, a link between Moscow and Central Asia in the east and Prussia in the west. And it is permissible, perhaps, to ask whether the family fortune was not made, in part at least, by that foreign trade which Kahan came to see as the most important source of the entrepreneurial capital accumulated by the emergent Jewish bourgeoisie under Alexander I and Nicholas I.

Shklov's prosperity proved to be short-lived as trade routes shifted elsewhere and Zvi Cohen moved a short way to the south to Mohilev on the upper reaches of the Dnieper. Following the accession of Alexander II in 1855, new regulations were introduced permitting wealthier Jewish merchants (those in the First and Second Guilds) and others in select categories to live outside the Pale of Settlement. Among those exploiting the new opportunities was Zvi's son, Hillel, who now spent most of his time in St. Petersburg, returning home only once or twice a year. He was a wholesale dealer in gold and silver, and his wife supplemented the family income by running a shop in Mohilev. He remained an observant *khosed,* and his children were brought up in their grandfather's home, which stood, together with the family prayer and study house (*bes ha-medresh*), in an enclosed court. A series of tutors (*melamdim*) were brought in to teach the sons (among them Yitskhok and Mordkhe) Talmud, Hebrew, Bible, and the rabbinic commentaries. But since the times were changing fast they also had private teachers to give them a good grounding in Russian and German.

Arcadius's grandfather, Yitskhok, chose to live his life and bring up his children in the town of his birth, Mohilev. In contrast, his brother, Mordkhe (Arcadius's great-uncle), was from the first swept into the Sturm und Drang phase of nascent Jewish nationalism. Mordekhai Ben Hillel Ha-Cohen, as he usually chose to call himself, had begun while still in his teens to publish articles in the Hebrew journals which then, in the 1870s, were growing in number and circulation. He even managed to place an article in Peretz Smolenskin's *Ha-Shahar*. During the extraordinary upheaval in the Russian-Jewish world, which followed the pogroms of 1881, he was on the editorial board of *Razsviet,* a Jewish weekly in the Russian language, published in St. Petersburg, which then became the most militant champion of the emigrationist camp and of proto-Zionism.

After having made a number of visits to Palestine over the years, he settled there in 1907. He was by then a well-known writer and memoirist in Hebrew and Yiddish, and he became a leading figure in the group that presided over the establishment of the new city of Tel Aviv.

Like many others in the first generation of Russian Zionists (or more exactly, Hoveve Zion), he was highly critical of the young socialists who had begun arriving in Palestine in 1904. He saw them as nihilistic, blinkered by abstract ideologies. ("Real workers," he wrote in 1908, "would not stay until after midnight to hear speeches and statements . . . when they have to get up the next morning to work. They have filled their bellies with Marxist doctrine.") All this, however, did not stop his own son, David Ha-Cohen, from joining the Histadrut and the Haganah nor from rising to prominence in Mapai, the most important political party in the Palestinian Jewish labor movement. After the creation of Israel in 1948 he served for many years as a member of Knesset and for a time as chairman of its Foreign Affairs and Defense Committee. (It should not go without mention that one of David Ha-Cohen's sisters became the wife of Arthur Ruppin; another, the daughter-in-law of Ahad Ha-Am.)

The next generation in Mohilev likewise supplied a new recruit to the burgeoning workers' movement in Palestine. Yitskhok's daughter, Rosa, was a member of the wave of young immigrants who arrived in that country following the Bolshevik Revolution and the subsequent Civil War. She, too, eventually made her mark in the Histadrut, where she was known as a formidably strong-willed organizer. Her son, Arcadius's first cousin, is Yitshak Rabin, who served as Chief of Staff at the time of the June War in 1967, as Prime Minister in the years 1874–77, and is now, in 1985, Minister of Defense.

How this succession of writers, politicians, and soldiers emerged, almost without transition, from the self-contained culture of Hasidic piety must always remain a source of sheer astonishment. And in no case, perhaps, was this phenomenon more fully exemplified than in the life of Arcadius's own father, Borekh Mordkhe Cohen, who as a revolutionary in Russia found himself acting variously as political journalist, party activist, and fighter in the armed underground movement.

Born in Mohilev in 1883, he was sent to study in the renowned *yeshives* of Brisk (where he lived in the home of its spiritual leader, the famous Rabbi Haim Soloveichik) and of Volozhin. But while still in his teens he joined the Bund, a Jewish socialist movement founded in 1897, Marxist, revolutionary, committed to the idea of Jewish national autonomy in the Diaspora, totally opposed to Zionism. For eight years he lived the life of a professional revolutionary, forever on the move, called upon to demonstrate endless improvisation in organizing strikes, clandestine printing presses, illegal journals, armed fighting units.

In 1901, we find him in Homel editing, together with Yosef Chaim Brenner (then a Bundist), the paper *Der Kamf.* In April 1905, he led the self-defense forces in Zhitomir in a fierce and effective fight against a major pogrom (some thirty Jews were killed, about a hundred wounded). In June, he was on the barricades in the street fighting in Lodz; wounded, he was taken for dead. (He had the unusual experience of reading his own obituary.)

As a party activist, Virgily, as he now came to be known, tended toward the moderate wing of the Bund, seeking with mainstream Menshevism a broad anti-Tsarist coalition as against the social revolution à outrance demanded by the Bolsheviks. This was his position during the 1905 revolution and again in 1917 when he was a member of the St. Petersburg Soviet. And following the Bolshevik seizure of power, he was among those leaders of the Bund who chose the path of emigration rather than of cooperation with Communism. He settled in Vilna where, still a Bundist (a member of the right-wing opposition to the Warsaw leadership), he played an active role in an amazing number of political, cultural, educational, and philanthropic institutions: the secular Yiddish school movement, ORT, YIVO, the Bundist youth movement, the town council—to name just a few.

In his essay on Vilna (Chapter 7), Kahan attributes what he termed the "excess or hypertrophy of organization" primarily to "the aggressive and competitive existence of the various ideologies and the zealous spirit of their adherents." All in all, he concludes, despite the conflicts and waste involved, the net result was an enormous and positive investment of effort in the public good. Virgily died in 1936; his funeral was attended by some twenty thousand people.

As a young man, Arcadius, who had been born in 1920, also became an active member of the Bund. It fell to him, as a student in the Law Faculty of the Stefan Batory University, to lead the struggle against the regulation of 1937 which forced segregation on the Jewish students (separate seating in the lecture halls, for example). In his essay on the university, he described the depths of disappointment and anguish which he and his fellow Jewish students felt at this exclusionist policy. ("We were saddened and cried out of our helplessness and because we felt betrayed.") But he did have the satisfaction at least of being able to negotiate an agreement by which the Bund and the Polish Socialist Party (PPS) undertook to organize a general strike of the workers of Vilna in protest.

In 1940, Vilna (now once again part of the Lithuanian state) was annexed by the USSR; and the new Soviet authorities in pursuit of their policy of "atomization" (to use a term considered most apt by Kahan) rounded up the leadership of the various Jewish parties. Among those arrested was Arcadius Kahan, who ended up in a labor camp in Vorkuta. Eventually, he was able to join the Polish Division of the Red Army and marched with it across Eastern Europe to Germany. In the postwar period, he returned to Poland and renewed his activity in the Bund, now like Polish Jewry as a whole— decimated beyond recognition. He edited the *Yugnt-veker* for the party in Lodz and in 1947 was a delegate to the world conference of the Bund in Brussels. It was only when the regime stepped up its policy of *Gleichschaltung,* forcing the Bund toward absorption into the Communist party, that he, like his father thirty years earlier, chose to emigrate rather than acquiesce. He reached the United States in 1950 and served from 1952 to 1954 (while studying at Rutgers University) as director of the Bund Archives in New York.

In 1955, still a Ph.D. candidate, he moved to Chicago to work as a research assistant with Professor D. Gale Johnson, and in 1958 he joined the faculty of the University of Chicago, where he soon established himself as a highly respected colleague of both the economists and the historians. His work on the Russian economy of the eighteenth century was marked by a characteristic refusal to take for granted any of the accepted assumptions, however hallowed by time. In particular, he came to the conclusion that the economic advances made in the period of Peter I did not constitute a passing episode; and that the Russian economy, including the agriculture of the serf-owning and westernizing nobility remained buoyant throughout the eighteenth century.

When he turned to the economic history of Russian Jewry, he brought to bear the same determination to go over ground others had already traversed, to see how far-established conclusions would stand up under critical scrutiny, and only then to push beyond the frontiers of previous research. The difference is that in this area he was isolated. In the interwar period, many scholars had worked on the problems that fascinated Kahan, but even those who had survived the war and found refuge in Israel or the United States had belonged to a much older age group. By the 1970s, there was hardly anybody left (Simon Kuznets and Dov Weinryb being notable exceptions).

Intense interest in the social and economic transformation of Russian Jewry had first been stimulated by the competitive needs of the rival Jewish socialist parties at the turn of the century. A fierce faith in Marxism became the hallmark of the young recruits drawn into politics on the eve of the 1905 revolution. And the theoreticians of each party set out to demonstrate that the dynamics of economic change were leading with iron logic, stage by stage, to the final end; that is, to the fulfillment of the given party program.

Thus, the Bund, which rejected Zionism and other territorialist strategies, sought out evidence of the essential normality of Jewish economic life in the Russian Empire. True, the Jewish proletariat was made up for the most part of craft rather than industrial workers, but the overall numbers were on the rise. And what deviations there were from the general norm had to be explained by transient political factors, by the tsarist policies of discrimination, which would be eliminated by the revolution.

As against this, the young ideologists of the various Zionist and territorialist parties argued that the forces that pushed Jewish masses to the margins of the economy were rooted in inexorable socioeconomic processes at work not only in Eastern Europe but also in the West. The future, still more than the present, belonged to the sweatshop. Eventually, the great emigration—in itself the most significant phenomenon—would be forced toward an underdeveloped territory where alone a normal Jewish economy could develop.

Of course, the conflicting theses then developed, for all their claims to be strictly "scientific," were shaped by the spirit of engagé research, of *partiinost*. Nonetheless, theoreticians such as Jacob Lestschinsky or Ber Borokhov studied the available statistics and economic trends with the enthusiasm of total commitment and with an impressive determination to examine the microcosmic as the key to the macrocosmic.

By the 1920s, the veterans of 1905 had had to live through the World War, two more revolutions, a Civil War, and the accompanying terror of the pogroms. Some were in Vilna and Warsaw; others under Soviet rule; still others in Germany or the United States. Their faith in their ability to extrapolate accurate prognoses both short- and long-term from the socioeconomic facts had, in many cases, been cooled by the passage of time. What remained was a belief in the centrality of the Jewish masses, in the *folk,* its history, culture, and future; and their dedication to the study of the *folk* in objective terms.

The group which founded YIVO (the Jewish Scientific Institute) in 1925 was drawn for the most part from the generation of 1905: Elias Tcherikower, Abraham Menes, Max Weinreich, Nahum Shtif, Jacob Lestschinsky, Resach Liebman Hersch, Samuel Niger (Charny), Ben Adir (Abraham Rozin), and, of course, Virgily Cohen. It was conceived as an international body, its center in Vilna, but with branches in Warsaw, Berlin, and New York; and with close links to Minsk and Kiev. (Communication with colleagues in the USSR was still thriving in the mid-1920s.) The research conducted under the auspices of YIVO bore the stamp of its origins, with the emphasis placed on Yiddish literature and philosophy; modern history, particularly of revolutionary and mass movements; folklore; and, most important from our point of view here, the statistical and demographic study of socioeconomic development.

A steady stream of work in this latter field was published in the 1920s and 1930s by such associates of YIVO as Lestschinsky, Hersch, and Menes. While their concerns were still very much those of their youth (proletarianization, industrialization, emigration), there was no trace left of the narrow party line. And they were able to find a common language with specialists of a nonsocialist background such as Arthur Ruppin and Boris Brutzkus. Across many frontiers and in increasingly difficult circumstances, they developed a vigorous school of research and intellectual enquiry.

In the essays on economic history which make up the bulk of this book, Arcadius Kahan was, as it were, opening up a dialogue with this group of men. He recognized their importance; and their names are to be found in acknowledgments and notes. But he was very much an active partner in this dialogue, forever ready to find new answers to old questions—and even more, to ask new questions.

What is most striking is that Kahan had clearly come to regard the entire subject from his own perspective. In 1905, the pivotal point of the research was proletarianization and the class struggle; during the interwar period it had shifted to the broader category of the *folk*, the Yiddish-speaking masses. For Kahan, writing in the 1970s, the true center of the drama had become the struggle of the Jewish people as a whole, in Eastern Europe and beyond, for economic survival. And he argued that exclusive concern with the working classes and the poor had hitherto made it impossible to see the full range of historical reality. Above all, how was the wealth produced which had permitted so rapid, so extraordinary a growth in population?

There were, perhaps, 1–1½ million Jews in the Russian Empire at the beginning of the nineteenth century; by the end of the century, there were over 5,200,000. This number continued to rise, albeit more slowly, until

1914. But over and beyond this, during the period 1880–1914, some 2 million Jews emigrated from the Tsarist Empire to the United States, South America, Canada, South Africa, Western Europe, and Palestine. Among them, too, the growth rate was high. Thus, all in all, in the space of just over one hundred years there was a population increase of some eightfold, perhaps more. This was a change of extraordinary dimensions. By the end of the century the number of Jews in the Tsarist Empire (or originating from it) alone had surpassed by far the total population of world Jewry in 1800.

All this was the more remarkable given the fact that the tsarist government sought myriad ways to restrict the economic possibilities open to its Jewish subjects. They were confined (with few exceptions) to the Pale of Settlement; forbidden to live in villages; not permitted to own land (except in their relatively few agricultural colonies); effectively excluded from government service; and (after 1887) limited in their educational opportunities. Moreover, their traditional areas of concentration included in the Northwest region particularly some of the most underdeveloped and infertile areas in Europe (marshland, forests, poor agricultural soil). Again, the Jewish people by the time of its annexation to Russia with the partitions of Poland was largely impoverished, had few sources of capital, and was not rich in technological or craft skills.

How were these obstacles overcome and the population explosion sustained? This was the question that fascinated Kahan. In contrast to so many of his predecessors, he was not interested in impoverishment and marginalization or proletarianization and industrialization as phenomena in their own right. He saw them, rather, as parts of a larger totality—the entire economic effort of the Jewish community, or people.

Thus, for example, he took a new look at the two primary sources which had been constantly quarried since the period of the 1905 revolution: the government census of 1897, and the two-volume research report published between 1906 and 1908 by the Jewish Colonization Association. By comparing the information in the two works (an arduous and complex task given the nature of the data), he concluded that the census had seriously underestimated the extent of employment among the Jewish population within the Pale of Settlement. He estimated the figure to be approximately 1½ million as against the census figure of close to 1.3 million. The number of those working in crafts and industry within the Pale at the turn of the century, according to his estimate, was not the 660,000 stated by the Census but closer to 750,000. (He put the number of Jewish factory workers at that time as 50,000, again higher than generally assumed.)

Piecing together the fragmentary statistics available for the prewar years, 1910–14, Kahan argued that there was a steady rise in the number of

Jews working as craftsmen and artisans, both employers and employees. And he even concluded that the influx more than compensated for "the huge losses of craftsmen" caused by emigration.

In turn, he saw this trend as a natural by-product of two other related developments: internal migration, and urbanization. The number of Jews migrating from one place to another within Eastern Europe (mainly the Russian Empire) between 1881–1914 was probably, in his estimate, well above the minimal estimate of 1 or 1.2 million. And the number of Jews living in cities grew in the period 1897–1910 by almost 40 percent. Only the move to urban centers from the smaller settlements made possible the acquisition of new skills and the development of new forms of employment.

The "most revealing indicator," in this context as he saw it, was that the number of Jewish communities with a total population of at least five thousand had risen by 1910 from 173 to 256. Given the enormous economic handicaps facing the Russian Jews, they were left with no choice but to depend increasingly on each other for employment, help, education. There was a measure of security in numbers.

Kahan's interest in the Jewish entrepreneur stemmed from this general conception. There was no room here for the traditional hostility displayed by the radical intelligentsia against the capitalist and oligarch. Most obviously, Jewish manufacturers employed tens of thousands of Jewish workers in their factories. But beyond that, there was a vast network of economic relationships: putting out for domestic manufacture; subcontracting; purchase from, and sale to, wholesalers; links from wholesalers to retailers; and all this tied together by the grant of credit and loans which, in turn, required a high degree of trust. To describe this type of multilevel interdependency, Kahan constantly returned to the term "vertical integration," a phenomenon that reached its highest degree of development in the textile and clothing industries.

The impact of the Jewish entrepreneurs was felt, however, far beyond textiles, timber, and transportation (areas in which the Jews were highly concentrated). Even outside the Pale, as Kahan describes, they were active in Baku oil wells, Siberian gold mines, fisheries on the Volga, cotton plantations in Central Asia. Their success contributed not only to the development of Russia but also, by ways direct and indirect, to that of the Jewish people within the Pale.

It was characteristic of Kahan's approach that he assigned positive importance to educational efforts that had often been regarded as mere palliatives or self-serving philanthropy. He concluded that the voluntary organizations which took upon themselves the teaching of technical and other skills were acting logically given the high degree of impoverishment and semi-literacy prevailing within the Jewish community. But he likewise emphasized that without personal investment in the acquisition of new skills, often at great sacrifice to the individual, no institutional aid would have made much difference.

In his eyes, the vitality of the Russian Jewish people found its purest expression in the great emigration overseas, especially—but not only—to the United States. He emphasized the high percentage of the emigrants who declared themselves craftsmen or skilled laborers. While treating these statistics with due skepticism, he still argued that they reflected a mass determination to integrate into a dynamic and industrial economy, leaving behind forever the "culture of poverty."

The essay on Central European Jewry in this collection should not be seen as peripheral. Kahan had no time for the widely held view of a basic divide separating the *Ostjuden* from the German Jews. The same processes of modernization which had so thoroughly transformed the Jewish way of life in the West were proceeding apace in the Tsarist Empire by the mid-nineteenth century. And those Russian Jews who emigrated westward to a large extent adapted themselves to the preexisting models they found there—even while rebelling against them. "The emerging pattern was one of integration of both groups," he concludes, "and the formation of larger, concentrated settlements of what was becoming a German Jewry, or French, British or American Jewry."

Kahan's concept of the Jewish community as a living organism struggling to survive against the odds finds its most direct expression, perhaps, in the remarkable essay on the interwar Vilna in which he grew up (see Chapter 7). There, too, he uses his chosen medium of statistical and strictly factual analysis. But he also allows another voice to be heard: "I personally know now that in the period between both World Wars . . . the Shekhinah rested in the narrow streets of the Jewish Quarter of Vilna." The same theme, with its Hasidic resonance, was taken up in the words of welcome he gave Czeslaw Milosz on his visit to YIVO in New York: "For myself, I must admit, when the Shekhinah, the Divine Presence, abandoned its resting place in the narrow streets of the Jewish Quarter and left on the road to Ponary to join the Jews on their last journey, Vilna ceased to exist except only in the Platonic sense of Vilna *shel maale*."

Jonathan Frankel

Jerusalem
November 1985

The Impact of Industrialization in Tsarist Russia on the Socioeconomic Conditions of the Jewish Population

The point of departure for our inquiry is the halfway mark in Russia's intensive industrialization under the Tsarist regime, 1897–98. The choice is not arbitrary but is primarily dictated by the availability of two sets of evidence generated by the first All-Empire Population Census of January 28 (February 11), 1897, and by an 1898 study commissioned, directed, and subsequently published by the Jewish Colonization Association (JCA).[1] These two studies provide an opportunity for a cross-sectional analysis of the social structure of the Jewish population within the Pale of Settlement in Russia and permit inferences both about the prior and subsequent impact of industrialization in Russia upon the social structure of the Jewish population.

The inquiry is limited to the Pale of Settlement, a territory that included fifteen Western districts of Russia and the ten districts of the former kingdom of Poland, and does not cover the Russian Empire as a whole, although what took place outside the Pale was obviously also of consequence to the inhabitants of the Pale. In dealing with the subject, it was impossible to distill and separate the effects of political, administrative, and other decisions by the Russian authorities and set them apart from the purely economic decisions and actions that affected the Jews, nor was it possible to explain some economic decisions by individuals and groups without reference to the legal or administrative framework. Perhaps a few examples will suffice to illustrate the above contention. The existence of the Pale of Settlement itself provides a major problem for economic analysis

Drawing on documents and data long in the public domain, this essay is directed at interpretation. I avoid drawing attention to differences with previous treatments of the subject, and the reader will have to reach his own conclusions about the differences he finds. My intellectual debts to the work of Arthur Ruppin, B. Brutskus, Jacob Lestschinsky, and Simon Kuznets are gratefully acknowledged. I would also like to thank Miss Any Crumpacker for her able assistance in working through the available sources.

since it is difficult to calculate the costs imposed by this limitation upon mobility and to estimate the decrease of opportunities resulting from the preservation of the Pale. It would also be incomprehensible and difficult to understand why, for example, Jewish lumber merchants exported timber rather than processed wood products, and why they used river transport rather than railroads, without the knowledge that by the decrees of 1882 Jews were prohibited from residing in rural areas in the districts of European Russia (with the exception of Poland). They could not, therefore, establish saw mills close to the sources of supply and, according to the decrees of 1887, they were limited in the use of government property and could not establish warehouses near government-owned railroads. A further problem, pertains to the mass migration of Russian Jews abroad. It is not at all clear to what extent the migration process contributed to the changes in the social structure of the remaining Jewish population, especially since not all of the migration was for economic reasons.

Among the various topics under consideration in the inquiry, the following will be singled out for special discussion: (1) demographic characteristics of the Jewish population, (2) the occupational structure of the Jewish population, (3) the occupational structure and its socioeconomic corollary, (4) the process of urbanization, (5) internal migration and emigration abroad, (6) discrimination and the response.

Industrialization in Russia, beginning with the 1860s and 1870s, proceeded along two main lines. On the one hand, the emancipation of the serfs in 1861 and the relaxation of impediments to mobility of the peasants helped capital accumulation and the use of available labor resources to carry Russia along the road of factory-type production by relying upon private efforts to change the structure of the Russian economy in a gradual manner. On the other hand, the policy of the government providing overhead capital investment, a modern transportation network, developing an indigenous capital goods industry, attracting foreign capital for the development of Russian natural resources, especially in coal mining, metallurgy, oil, etc., created a pattern as described by Professor Gerschenkron of spurts of economic activity in particular sectors, thus making Russian industrial development overly dependent upon governmental investment and monetary and fiscal policies. The spurtlike pattern of Russian industrialization also found its expression in the setting up of new industries (railroad equipment is one of many examples) to produce import substitutes, and thus required within relatively short periods huge initial outlays of capital and relatively speedy adjustments and responses on the part of the labor force. And while the level of technical training of the labor force was low, along with very labor-intensive factory operations, there were placed enterprises with a high degree of mechanization, a capital-intensity designed to save on labor, because of the scarcity of certain skills.

It is the spurtlike feature of Russian industrialization that required government subsidies, foreign investment, or the ability to mobilize substantial amounts of domestic capital on short notice in an underdeveloped money market.

Given the relative scarcity of capital within the Jewish community, or competing opportunities for investment (e.g., residential housing), Jewish entrepreneurs found themselves at a disadvantage. Did industrialization narrow their areas of choice? The available evidence indicates the contrary, with one important caveat. While it is true that the direct participation of Jewish entrepreneurs in the growth of heavy, capital-goods industries was limited owing to some of the characteristics of industrialization mentioned above, the ongoing process actually widened the areas of choice for Jewish entrepreneurs. If few of them actually built railroads, many established subcontracting enterprises that supplied the railroad industry. If very few could enter oil production, many could establish themselves in oil processing, transportation, and marketing. If the basic chemicals required large capital outlays, smaller-size operations and more specialized enterprises using basic chemicals were open for Jewish entrepreneurship. Thus a large area for Jewish entrepreneurial activity was made available and was stimulated by Russian industrialization. And although two major geographic areas most affected by the industrialization process, the St. Petersburg-Moscow region and the Southern region, were totally or predominantly outside the Jewish Pale of Settlement, the impact of a less spectacular growth of industry in the Pale was deeply felt in the Jewish milieu.

Industrialization in Russia affected economic opportunities and the distribution of employment of the Jewish population through the relatively slow growth of the internal market for manufactured consumer goods. The savings ratio was relatively high; capital formation was directed toward investments in buildings (nonresidential as well as residential), in factory equipment, in stocks of raw materials, and in railroads; but consumption grew slowly. The increased earnings stimulated population growth, yet consumption expenditures remained limited to what were conventionally described as "necessities." Thus, purchasing power earmarked for manufactured consumer goods, after high taxes, a relatively high rate of savings, food expenditures, and housing, increased sluggishly and did not provide the necessary stimulus for a rapid growth of the consumer goods industries.

Since the bulk of Jewish employment was concentrated in consumer goods, this characteristic of Russian industrialization put severe constraints

3

upon the growth of employment and income of the majority of the Jewish population.

Population

The Population Census provided two sets of data (see Appendix, table A1): one for the Jewish religion, and a second for the population that spoke a Jewish language or considered Yiddish to be its mother tongue.[2] The difference between the two is less important in terms of absolute numbers than because the data on occupations grouped according to the mother tongue other than Yiddish[3] were incorporated in the employment groups of other nationalities. This means a "loss" of 99,830 individuals, a reduction for the Jewish population of the Pale from 4,910,327 to 4,810,497 Jews.[4] However, a substantial part of the total non-Yiddish-speaking Jews was concentrated in a few big cities, among which were Warsaw (34,335), Odessa (14,589), Lodz (6,234), and Kiev (2,256). Such individuals, with above-average education, probably had above-average income. Although we have no knowledge about this group with respect to its employment distribution, we may assume that it included a higher-than-proportionate share of members of the liberal professions, perhaps also merchants, bankers, and industrial entrepreneurs.[5] In what follows, I will use data from the first set, the Population Census, according to religion.

Two characteristic features of the rate of population increase have to be noted. One is the higher rate of population increase throughout the whole period in the smaller towns and semi-rural areas than in big cities; the second is the secular decline of the death rate, which during the second half of the century was coupled with a stable birthrate, thus resulting in an increase of the population growth rate. In the first decade of the twentieth century the birthrate began to decline, causing a decrease of the rate of population growth. Among factors influencing the birthrate, such elements as mass emigration, urbanization, and the general uncertainty caused by the wave of revolution and pogroms played the most important role. That urbanization affected the birthrate, or the rate of survivors during childhood, can be seen from the census data on the age distribution of the total population of the provinces of European Russia. Urban residence itself might not be the only reason for the behavior of the birthrate; acculturation of the Jews with other population groups in the cities, income rise, or income decline might all explain changes in the observed birthrate. Generalizations at this stage would be hazardous to offer beyond noting the trend of a decline in the birthrate in cities.[6] Since the vast majority of those involved in migration were in the 15–45-year age group, their departure could have affected the rate of population increase only in one direction, downward.

The sex distribution of the Jewish population (see Appendix, table A1) points to a larger percentage of females in the total population both for the empire and for the Pale (51.5 percent). The most important regional variations in the sex distribution are between the Northwest region with the highest percentage of women in the population (51 percent) and the Southern region with the lowest (50 percent). Obviously, the data for particular districts reveal even greater extremes than the totals for the major regions. At the one extreme, there is the district of Kovno with 53 percent women and, at the other, the district of Tavria with 48 percent women. The most likely explanation for the extreme differences is to be sought in the consequences of the process of migration (both internal and overseas), in which the Northwest was a source of out-migration and the South was still absorbing an influx of population of many national groups in Russia, Jews included. As far as the sex distribution of the population is concerned, the age groups in which the male population dominated were at both ends of the age distribution, below 10 years and above 60 years of age (see Appendix, table A2). We must hope more research would be forthcoming from demographers to explain these variations. There are several implications of the prevalence of women in the intermediate age groups. We find, for example, considerably more widows than widowers; we find a significantly lower median age for women entering into marriage than among men, a larger potential supply of women in the labor force, and, by the same token, a higher rate of dependents per male employed among the Jewish population by comparison with other ethnic groups.

The age distribution of the Jewish population reflected in the Population Census of 1897 is heavily weighted toward the young age groups to the disadvantage of the groups in the age category most suitable for employment (see table 1).

This above data and the other available evidence suggest at least two

Table 1   Age Distribution of Jewish Population (1897)

Years	Empire	European Russia	Districts of Poland	Urban European Russia	Urban Polish Districts
Below 10	28.4	27.9	29.7	26.2	28.8
10–19	23.9	24.0	23.9	24.4	24.6
20–59	42.4	42.6	41.0	44.1	41.8
60–	5.3	5.4	5.2	5.4	5.0

Source: Census of 1897.

propositions. First, that the areas primarily affected by industrialization, the cities, exhibited a higher percentage of population of working age (20–59); internal migration that made this possible would have continued for some time in the following period.[7] Second, the data on employment of the Jewish population and the employment pattern indicate that the income of the members of the "working-age" groups was insufficient to meet the income requirements of the Jewish population, and one would have to assume that a sizable portion of the age group 10–19 was also employed.[8]

The Occupational Structure

The occupational distribution of the Jewish population in the Pale of Settlement reported by the Population Census of 1897 represents a society in flux. Some of the occupations were typical for a traditional, preindustrial society with its preponderance of nonspecialized general services (e.g., unspecified trading activities, a huge labor supply of unskilled labor—domestic servants, day laborers, etc.), with emphasis on trade in foodstuffs and beverages. Other occupations arose in order to meet the needs of an industrializing society for ready-to-wear clothing, for housing, for new forms of distribution of goods, etc. Glancing over the list of occupations, with hindsight of course, one can see the degree of social obsolescence or usefulness, and the future shrinkage or expansion of particular occupations.

There are a few problems to which I would like to address myself in the discussion of the occupational structure. One of the problems is the size of employment, the other is the degree of concentration within what appears to be a very broad occupational distribution; the third problem is the one of interdependence of occupational or employment categories.

I will therefore start with a scrutiny of the available evidence about the size of the labor force and argue that the available data represent an underestimate of the actual employment.

The economically active Jewish population in the Pale can be distributed, according to the census data of 1897, among the major regions (see table 2).

On the basis of noncensus evidence, one could state that the above totals represent an underestimate of the economically active (employed). The major omission perhaps of up to 100,000 employed workers is in female employment.[9] While the percentage of female employment varied between 26 percent in the northwest and 19 percent in the South, the percentage of employed women in the Pale was probably closer to 27–28 percent than to the reported 22 percent, according to the census.[10]

After the exclusion of such employment categories as agriculture, for-

Table 2 Economically Active Jewish Population in the Pale (1897)

Region	Including Armed Forces[1]			Excluding Armed Forces		
	Males	Females	Total	Males	Females	Total
Northwest	324,937	109,406	434,343	315,442	109,406	424,848
Southwest	322,430	78,394	400,824	315,138	78,394	393,532
South	184,190	41,729	225,919	178,398	41,729	220,127
Polish districts	285,031	77,509	362,540	272,861	77,509	350,370
Total Pale	1,116,588	307,038	1,423,626	1,081,839	307,038	1,388,877

[1]The number of Jews in the armed forces includes only those who were stationed within the Pale. In view of the bias of sending many Jewish soldiers to serve outside the Pale (almost 23,000), the total exhibits a somewhat lower estimate than if the recruits would be distributed in terms of their place of origin.

estry, ownership of money capital and real estate, we are left with a census figure of about 1,290,000 employed, which can be classified in major employment categories. The vast majority could be divided in the following groups:[11]

Employment in the production of goods	495,395
Employment in transportation	43,976
Employment in private services	189,546
Employment in trade	412,568
Employment in communal services	55,690
Total	1,197,175

Still another way of classifying the census data on employment would be to divide the total in three major categories: manual labor, trade, and the liberal professions.

By using the above figures we can estimate that the number engaged in manual labor in the production of goods was about 475,000 (out of 495,395); in transportation about 44,000; in private services about 140,000; a total of about 660,000 for manual labor; 412,000 for trade; and about 125,000 for white-collar workers, salaried employees and liberal professions, owners and managers of enterprises. In terms of the categories of hired employees and workers versus self-employed, we can estimate the self-employed as about 700,000 and the hired employees at 500,000.

The census and the JCA data show the same pattern of employment in four major branches of employment (see table 3). The total employment figures for the selected branches yield about 450,000 reported by the census, and 467,000 reported by the JCA of which 440,000 were craftsmen and over 27,000 factory workers. The close agreement of the JCA data with the census indicates a serious underreporting on the part of the census, since only 78 percent of the Jewish population in the Pale lived in places

Table 3   Comparison of Census Employment Data and JCA Data for Industry

	Census Employment	JCA Craft Employment	JCA Factory Employment
Textiles	33,309	21,623	8,503
Hides, leather, and furs	20,446	17,639	5,542
Clothing and footwear	235,993	234,828	n.a.
Total	289,748	274,090	14,045
Construction, ceramics, wood, furniture	82,489	77,500	7,883
Metals and metalworking	40,304	39,578	2,553
Food and beverages	44,797	48,459	2,997
Total	167,590	165,537	13,433

Note: n.a. = not available.

covered by the JCA study. In addition, since the JCA study was clearly deficient in reporting employment in such major cities as Warsaw, Lodz, Odessa, and Kiev with a large factory and craft employment, one would expect the employment data of the census to be higher than that reported by the JCA, which is not the case if we are to judge from table 3. The historian Abraham Menes in his note[12] attempted to estimate the deficiencies of the JCA study.[13]

While these adjustments would go some way toward improving the results of the JCA study, it is necessary to note that Menes did not draw any conclusions from two examples of deficient census data known to him.[14]

My view would raise the census data on employment of Jews in the Pale in craft and industry to about 750,000, trade to about 450,000, while the total employment would reach 1.5 million.

When one turns from the problem of size of gainful employment to the variety of occupations, one's first impression is of the degree of concentration in particular sectors of the economy, primarily crafts and trade, and in both cases the emphasis on the consumer goods sector, rather than the capital goods sector. In the area of trade we find a preponderance in foodstuffs, in agricultural products, and in undifferentiated retail (and also some wholesale) trade. The role of the Jewish trader as the middleman for rural clients and for the lower classes of the urban areas is still very much in evidence, dominating the picture, while Jewish traders in manufactured consumer goods were fewer and were concentrated in the larger cities. The sector of crafts is interesting because it portrays the broad spectrum of occupations as well as the areas of concentration to an extent unparalleled by the other employment sectors.[15]

But any discussion on the role of craft employment with relation to the industrialization process cannot avoid two basic issues. One issue is whether, under the impact of industrialization, craft employment was expanding, stationary, or declining. The available evidence points to an absolute increase of craft employment in Russia prior to World War I. Roughly comparable data for 1900 and 1910 for the territory of the Pale of Settlement indicate an increase of craft employment in small shops (master craftsman with one hired worker) of 35 percent and an increase of 36 percent in the number of shops employing two workers and more.[16] Scattered evidence from some of the districts of the Pale of Settlement for various years tends to support the impression of craft employment still expanding until World War I.[17] I would assume that the Jewish artisans participated in the growth of Jewish urban population, a growth which I have estimated for the period 1897–1910 of 38.5 percent in the Pale.[18] The consequence of the latter assumption would be to suggest that Jewish employment in crafts during the first decade of the century increased by comparison with 1897 and that the huge losses of craftsmen sustained by the Jewish population as a result of migration were more than compensated by the influx of newcomers into craft occupations. The other issue is the size distribution of employment in the craft establishments. One can observe the tendency of craft establishments, especially in the larger cities, to grow in size. The data of the JCA reflected the years 1898–99[19] and point to the relationship between the size of the craft establishment and the degree of urbanization. The size of craft shops within a particular branch of production seems to depend upon the size of the city. Thus, we find a much higher percentage of hired journeymen and apprentices per master craftsman in larger cities than in the smaller towns. We could conclude that the process of urbanization of the Jewish population tended to increase the average size of the labor force per craftshop, thus increasing the capital endowment per shop and leading toward a higher degree of concentration of the labor force. But one has to consider also the interoccupational differences among the various craft occupations with respect to size of the shops. In other words, did the crafts with a high concentration of Jewish artisans exhibit a higher- or lower-than-average size of employment per craft establishment.[20] The available data for a number of districts (mostly of the northwest) suggest that such occupations as weaving, tailoring, shoemaking, tanning, and cabinet making, all occupations in which the percentage of Jewish artisans was relatively high, had a higher-than-average employment per shop.

Just a few comments might be in order to put the employment distribution of the Jewish population in a proper historical perspective. One need not mention the virtual absence of Jews employed in government service, or in the offices of local self-government, because the state's discriminatory policies can be taken for granted. The same governmental attitudes caused almost complete exclusion of the Jews from employment in railroad transportation. Around the turn of the century, not less than 480,000 people were employed on the railroads with only about 1,800 Jews among them. The acquisition of private railroads by the state probably threatened the employment security of the few Jews they employed. It is, therefore, no wonder that the employment of Jews in transportation was concentrated in the most backward sector, that of short-haul services for freight and passengers.

The preindustrial period in Russia as well as in a number of other countries was marked by a lesser division of labor and by more direct and closer contacts between producers and consumers. The demand for final goods, or even for intermediary goods in the local or regional markets, determined to a very large extent the supply of commodities in those markets and the employment and income of the producers. It would not be wrong to assume that the employment and income, and probably the pattern of settlement (except for external prohibitions), depended upon the absorption capacity or demand for goods produced or services rendered by the Jewish population in the local markets. One would be correct to emphasize the direct dependence of the size and variety of Jewish employment on the conditions of the local or narrow regional markets. Preindustrial society was marked by the interdependence of groups or types of employment within a relatively close geographical range, and the welfare of the Jews in the Russian Empire depended largely upon the relative incomes of the general population within the particular regions inhabited by the Jews or, if we may say it, upon a "horizontal" relationship. The process of industrialization brought some fundamental changes in the scope and structure of the markets and in the relationships between the Jews and their immediate surroundings. If prior to industrialization and the development of a railroad network the volume of production was determined by the purchases of local consumers or perhaps by the purchases at a regional fair, it subsequently was determined by a wider market. The process of industrialization and commercialization of agriculture, as well as urbanization, created new wants, a demand for new kinds of goods and thereby for new skills, for new types of services. New opportunities arose which made the employment of large groups less dependent upon the local markets and more dependent upon the organization of the national market.

The existence of a high rate of participation of the Jews in a particular area of trade might have served as a stimulus to enter into craft production or industrial entrepreneurship in order to benefit from the fact that Jewish traders might be willing to distribute goods produced by Jewish industrial entrepreneurs or artisans. One might, however, question the validity of such reasoning and expectations of discrimination on the part of Jews in favor of other Jews within an economic (not cultural) context. Since the whole problem of discrimination is discussed in much greater detail at a later point in this essay, I would at this point argue that the costs of discrimination of some Jews in favor of other Jews were most likely very small. Perhaps a few examples will illustrate some of the conditions under which the costs of discrimination could be examined. In considering the cases of credit operations—even if we assume that the scarcity of capital within the Jewish community was greater than in the general economy and we would expect interest rates to be higher—in cases when credit was extended by Jewish entrepreneurs to traders and artisans, or by Jewish wholesale merchants to retail traders, the risks involved in credit operations within the Jewish community were usually smaller than in the credit transactions between a Jewish lender and a non-Jewish borrower. The force and influence of the Jewish community tended to diminish the risk of default by comparison with the cumbersome and costly legal procedures of the Russian courts which habitually poorly protected the lender. Thus, the scarcity of capital resulting in a high rate of interest was counteracted by diminished risks. This was so to such an extent that Jews lending money to Jews did not involve additional costs to the lender, while many of the Jewish borrowers found no other outside sources of loanable funds and turned to the Jewish lenders, even if it was at a higher rate of interest. If we take the case of employment (or contract) of Jewish artisans by a Jewish wholesale merchant for the production (or delivery) of a certain volume of goods, again the costs of discrimination to the merchant were small. Given the rate of underemployment within the Jewish communities or within Jewish crafts (as witnessed by both the seasonal variations in employment and the widespread secondary or auxiliary employment even among skilled craftsmen), and the existence of a downward wage flexibility, it is likely that the labor costs of many goods or in many (by no means all) services were lower within the Jewish community than within the general market. If one were to add the adaptability of the artisans in increasing their volume of employment by the use of family labor, etc., and the scarcity of other employment opportunities, it would become clear that in many cases the costs of discrimination were nonexistent. Obviously the list of examples could be extended, but they would in numerous cases support the contention that in purely economic terms the costs of discrimination in establishing a vertical structure among Jews engaged at various stages of the production and distribution process were probably negligible. In fact, I

11

would claim that not only were the initial expectations about the feasibility of "vertical integration" correct but that this type of arrangement was crucial for the economic survival of the Jewish population in Russia during the period under investigation. This was the only viable alternative to either the abolition of the Pale of Settlement or emigration of another huge number of Jews, over and above the impressive figures of actual out-migration.

Unfortunately, the only data which provide some insight into the problem and are readily available are those of the Population Census of 1897. From the census data I have selected the ones that pertain to four industries and cover 505,469 employed individuals. From other sources we know that this figure might be an underestimate of actual employment, but for purposes of illustration the incompleteness of the data is of secondary importance. It is important to keep in mind that the figure for employment in the four categories represents about 36 percent of total employment, as reported by the census, of the Jews (linguistically defined) inhabiting the Pale of Settlement. For purposes of additional insight, the figures are broken down for three major regions of the Pale with a separate column provided for nine major cities[21] (not necessarily the largest Jewish communities), the population of which constituted 15 percent of the total Jewish population in the Pale (see also Appendix, table A5).

The results (table 4) for the four industry groups can be summarized in a number of ways. For our purposes it is significant that, on the average for all four industry branches and for diverse economic regions of the Pale, 82 percent of employment was in the area of production and 18 percent in the area of distribution. This raises an interesting point in connection with the problem of "vertical integration"—one of actual and "optimal" proportions of employment at the various stages of production and distribution. The actual distribution indicates that for our selected group one person employed in distribution sold the output of 4.6 individuals engaged in production. Let us, for example, calculate the proportion of types of employment which would have existed on a national scale in a free market situation under quite realistic assumptions. We could assume that in the industry branch X a factory worker (or artisan) produced goods at a factory price of 1,000 rubles for a year's wage of 300 rubles. Omitting the industrial entrepreneur from our example, we will assume that the wholesaler operating on a 5 percent margin and expecting a yearly income of 900 rubles would have to sell the product of labor of eighteen workers. The retailer in order to earn 600 rubles yearly and operating on a margin of 10 percent would have to sell the output of 5.7 workers. Thus, in our example, the vertical integration would require for the sale of 1,155 rubles' worth of the final product the labor of one worker plus one-eighteenth of a wholesaler plus about one-sixth of the retailer. If we are going to express the labor inputs in percentage terms, we would receive 82 percent for the worker and the remaining 18 percent for the retailer and wholesaler. Since we have omitted capital entirely, we cannot estimate the return to capital, and the assumed 455 rubles as the labor share of value added is divided

Table 4   Employment in Selected Industry Branches (1897 Census Data)

Branch of Industry and Types of Employment	Northwest	Southwest and South	Polish Districts	Total Pale	Nine Cities
I. Production of textiles, hides, and leather	18,301	16,169	19,285	53,755	13,702
Production of clothing and footwear	74,658	97,833	63,502	235,993	38,158
Trade in textiles, clothing and footwear	10,439	29,584	11,635	51,658	10,680
Total	103,398	143,586	94,422	341,406	62,540
II. Employment in production and processing of wood and furniture	16,156	20,571	6,876	43,603	7,622
Trade in wood products	1,190	3,157	1,204	5,551	1,202
Total	17,346	23,728	8,080	49,154	8,824
III. Employment in ceramics, construction, and repair	18,250	16,095	7,741	42,086	8,153
Trade in construction materials	9,142	12,903	3,986	26,031	3,581
Total	27,392	28,998	11,727	68,117	11,734
IV. Production of metals and metal products	14,944	18,563	6,797	40,304	6,869
Trade in metals and metal wares	1,381	3,339	1,768	6,488	1,275
Total	16,325	21,902	8,565	46,792	8,144
Employment in manufacturing	142,309	169,231	104,201	415,741	74,504
Employment in trade	22,152	48,983	18,593	89,728	16,738
Total employment	164,461	218,214	122,794	505,469	91,242

13

between 300 rubles for the worker, 50 rubles for the wholesalers and 105 rubles for the retailer in accordance with our original assumptions. Still another crude way of viewing the assumed proportions of employment in the example above is to say that the economic activity of a wholesale merchant created employment for eighteen industrial workers and a demand for services of more than three retail traders. One should be very careful, however, not to draw conclusions from the approximate proportions of production workers to those employed in distribution, as reflected in our example, with the actual results from the selected census data. The example only points out that the existence of data, either on the incomes of particular employment categories (available for workers and artisans) or for the volume of trade turnover for particular categories of merchants (such can be estimated for the purpose of empirical study), allows the estimation of a hypothetical distribution of employment categories for a certain population under conditions of free mobility of labor and capital and in the absence of discrimination, given the level of income and technology in Russia around the turn of the century. For the Jews, a national minority suffering from discrimination, we would expect the actual proportions of the different categories of employment to differ from the "optimal." It ought to be the task of economic historians to address themselves to the deviations of the actual from the expected distribution in order to find out more about the conditions that, historically and institutionally determined, have brought about the "deviations."

Let us take two branches of industry, the production of clothing and construction materials, and hypothesize about the likely existence of "deviations" from an optimal pattern. As far as the production of clothing is concerned, we could probably assume, taking some of the indicators from table 4 into consideration, that the output of Jewish-owned textile factories was smaller (and the output of Jewish workers engaged in textile production certainly smaller) than the value of raw materials used in production of clothing by Jewish tailors and dressmakers, while the value of trade of Jewish clothing merchants was approximately equal to the clothing production of the Jewish artisans and clothing manufacturers. Thus, within the "vertical integration" in the clothing industry, the production of clothing and the clothing trade were approximately in equilibrium, while within the conditions of vertical integration there was room for the expansion of textile production by Jewish entrepreneurs and for the expanded employment of Jewish workers in the textile industry. In fact, this relationship helps to explain the subsequent growth of Jewish entrepreneurship in the textile industry, at least in the territory of the Polish districts. In the case of construction materials, we find a distribution between production and distribution that is quite different from the pattern of the other industry groups. With many of the brick factories located in the rural areas, relying upon cheap rural labor, one would expect a lower proportion of Jewish artisans and workers employed there, while Jewish merchants were engaged in the sale of construction materials in the regional and the national market, thus purchasing and selling the products of non-Jewish labor in addition to the absorption of products manufactured by Jewish workers and entrepreneurs. Thus, the vertical integration in this branch of production had a potential for further development, provided other economic and noneconomic constraints were removed or inoperative (e.g., introduction of new technology which would help raise the wage level and abolition of the decrees prohibiting Jews to reside in rural areas).

In cases when vertical integration was impossible, the solution was often found in the export of goods in which Jewish traders were engaged. The most extreme case was trade in agricultural products, in particular, grain. Jewish farmers hardly produced any grain for the market; nevertheless, within the Pale of Settlement, most of the grain trade (measured in terms of actively employed individuals engaged in the trade) was heavily concentrated in the hands of the Jewish merchants. The only vertical integration possible would have been of grain purchases, flour milling, and utilization in the food industry. For a number of reasons which are described in the chapter on discrimination, the employment of Jews in the above-mentioned tasks (milling is a case in point) was relatively small; the significance of the Jewish participation in the grain trade was, apart from its effects upon the agricultural commodity markets,[22] reflected in the growth of grain exports. A similar case can be observed in the area of forestry, in which the largely seasonal nature of lumbering and the fact that it was traditionally an auxiliary activity of the peasant population explains the relatively small number of Jews among the lumberjacks, although Jewish employment in sawmills and in the transportation of wood was already noticeable in parts of the Jewish Pale. As in the grain trade, the participation of Jews in the lumber trade was very substantial, and as in the case of the former, most of the output was exported. In the areas of woodworking we find a heavy concentration of Jewish carpenters, cabinetmakers, and other artisans, their output sold in regional and interregional trade by Jewish merchants (see table 4).

Although some of the examples cited above had to explain the more spectacular deviations from a proportionate distribution of employment in a system of vertical integration, their shortcomings are obvious. Since capital endowment was left out of our considerations, the comparisons of branches of industry with different capital/labor ratios is a serious omission. Another serious omission is the lack of distinction between producers of new goods destined for the market and employment in the repair of goods, a service provided by artisans and important given the level of income and consumption in Russia. Moreover, it is not certain whether the trade in second-hand goods was of the same relative magnitude as the share of repair in the labor input by artisans (which might have led some observers to talk about the "hypertrophy" of Jewish artisans in some areas of production). In addition, I presented the process of vertical integration as taking place primarily according to the laws of the market, but it is clear that to disregard kinship relations, traditional attitudes, preferences, and tastes historically developed within the Jewish community would have meant to ignore an important part of the reality.

Vertical integration was neither a system invented nor an idea consciously implemented by council or consensus of deliberating bodies. It was a result of the opening up of new opportunities resulting from the process of industrialization, from capital widening but primarily deepening, of which the Jewish population availed itself and which required a degree of cooperation in an otherwise very competitive situation. It enabled its participants to take the maximum advantage during times of expansion of demand and provided a cushion at times of contraction, since the nature of cooperation between various employment groups within the system of vertical integration came close to a "first hired, last fired" relationship. Thus, in spite of the fact that Jewish workers worked for low wages and Jewish merchants might have been operating on low profit margins, the effect of vertical integration was the creation of employment and the augmentation of income within the Jewish community. Many innovative qualities of Jewish merchants, in the broader utilization of the goods purchased and the marketing of by-products, stimulated the Jewish manufacturers to utilize the by-products and created greater product differentiation and specialization.[23] The Jewish artisans and industrial entrepreneurs produced for as wide a market as possible, with special emphasis on cheaper varieties of goods that could be absorbed by the limited purchasing power of the peasants, thus helping the Jewish traders to widen the scope of their clientele. Symbolically, the market orientation of the Jewish producers could be expressed by the fact that there were more Jewish blacksmiths than jewelers and that the total share in Jewish craft employment that produced high-price and quality ("luxury") goods was not more than 10–12 percent of the total.

I have used throughout the preceding pages the term "vertical integration" instead of "vertical cooperation" or "vertical organization." It was used advisedly, since integration, cooperation, and organization are by no means synonymous descriptions. I wanted to indicate a dynamism in the organization of production and distribution and the tendency toward integration through cooperative effort. The development of cottage-type industry, with its dependence on the wholesale merchant who purchased the output and subcontracting by industrial entrepreneurs to craftsmen of a part of their production, thus saving on expenditures for capital equipment, represent a degree of integration of artisans' labor in the operations of large-scale industrial enterprises; the long-term agreements between industrial entrepreneurs and large-scale commercial firms for the marketing of their products; the increased use by wholesale merchants of *maklers,* purchasing agents, and salesmen, or of commission trade in the process of distribution. All these activities taking place almost simultaneously created an increasing interdependence of various economic functions within the Jewish community, a higher degree of integration within the body of the economically active Jewish population.

The Occupational Structure and Its Socioeconomic Corollary

One of the purposes of analyzing the occupational distribution of the economically active Jewish population is to derive a broad income classification of the population and to illuminate further some of the functional roles of the various groups in the organization of economic activity.

Unfortunately, the census data are not of much help, since they do not distinguish, within the area of production, between capitalists, clerical employees and workers, master craftsmen, journeymen and apprentices, or between wholesale and retail merchants. The JCA data report only about agricultural and artisan and factory employment, omitting trade, an important sector for the Jewish community. It is unfortunate that the census classified the Jewish population only on the basis of language, particularly because the distortion was greatest at the highest end of income.

For a number of reasons it is difficult to establish with any degree of accuracy the size of the highest income group within the Jewish population. One reason is a "definitional" one and has to do with the identification of individuals and their classifications as Jews. The question can be reduced to the following: Does conversion eliminate the individual from the category of Jews at the date of baptism?[24] Apart from the definitional problems, the history of the Jewish bourgeoisie in Russia was never studied in any systematic fashion, most probably for emotional or ideological reasons. Preponderance of capital in the hands of Jews was almost universally considered by the indigenous population as an argument against the Jews, on the assumption that there was a fixed amount of capital and, therefore, capital held by the Jews was income expropriated or acquired from their neighbors. (It is interesting to note that at the same time Jewish poverty was also considered a major liability—a manifestation of unproductive parasitism.) Jewish spokesmen or scholars also avoided investigation of the problem of the Jewish bourgeoisie in order to maintain what might be called a "low profile," and they preferred to discuss the poverty of the Jews as being primarily caused by discrimination against Jews. Perhaps, on the part of some Jewish historians, the avoidance of the theme of the Jewish bourgeoisie was an attempt to counteract the popular, apologetic theme of praising the successful and was coupled with an ideological bias in favor of the working population. A nationalist bias on the part of some historians made perhaps less attractive the activity of individuals who, reaching the apex of their career, embraced another faith, or could be suspected of using conversion for opportunistic reasons in furthering their goals of personal aggrandizement. Thus, whatever the reasons, whether ideological, moralistic, or other, the Jewish bourgeoisie in Russia and especially in the Pale is still *terra incognita* for both the historian and the economist.

Table 5 lists the data of the census in terms of Jewish linguistic identity for the groups under consideration for the empire and the territory of the Pale. In order to estimate the size of the Jewish bourgeoisie in the Pale of Settlement we will make certain assumptions.[25] According to our assumptions, we ought to get the following membership of the Jewish bourgeoisie in the Pale: hereditary nobles—25; personal nobles—1,286; honorary citizens—1,030; merchants—6,224; a total of 8,665.

A useful category among the occupational groupings in the census is that of the rentiers, of which there are 55,214 listed for the Pale. In order to avoid double counting and to eliminate an uncertain number of rentiers supported by others, etc., we could perhaps assume that 15 percent of this total of 8,282 economically active people derived their income from real estate and other forms of investments, which would give us a total of 16,847 as an estimate for the bourgeoisie covered by the census. We will assume that the 4,349 Jewish industrial enterprises reported by various

Table 5   Jewish Membership in Upper-Status Groups (1897 Census)

	Empire	Pale	Pale as % of Empire
Hereditary nobility	196	125	64
Personal nobility	3,366	2,191	65
Honorary citizens	6,171	4,121	67
Merchants	71,848	62,242	87

sources, were owned by the members of the above-estimated groups. Since of all the subgroups that come under the general umbrella of the bourgeoisie we have most data on the industrial entrepreneurs, we will look at them more closely. The significance of the Jewish industrial entrepreneurs is not only that they augmented their own incomes but that they created jobs and helped to generate incomes for other members of the community, primarily for the labor force. The industrial entrepreneurs of the turn of the century continued a tradition of Jewish entrepreneurship in Russia which goes back to at least the first half of the nineteenth century. The Jewish bankers in Warsaw, the woolen cloth manufacturers of the Volynia District, the sugar mill owners of the Kiev District—all were examples of entrepreneurship prior to what might be considered Russia's industrial revolution, working in an economic environment in which development took place through minute accretions of capital, labor, and technological improvement. Entrepreneurship as a source of capital accumulation for the Jews during the first half of the nineteenth century was of primary importance in the areas of foreign trade and alcohol distilling, where a small number of large fortunes were made. The accumulated capital was subsequently transferred into other areas when railroad construction, sugar refining, and, later, manufacturing also provided new outlets for capital investments. It was no accident that Jewish entrepreneurial activity during this early period was concentrated in industries closely supervised, controlled, or even administered by the government. Because Russia had a relatively narrow market sector (while a large part of the population produced most of what it consumed within the household), and had monopoly-ridden pockets in the market structure, the state provided a stable demand for some industries, not as the ultimate consumer but as monopsonistic buyer of goods which it sold to the consumers after charging an excise tax. Thus, the fiscal interests of the state favoring an assured and predictable supply of goods coincided with the preferences of some producers for a "guaranteed" demand and market in such areas as alcohol distilling, beer brewing, tobacco and match production, sugar, salt, and oil. The advantage for Jewish entrepreneurs in the participation in this government controlled market was its size. The various local and regional markets in the Pale of Settlement could hardly support larger-scale industrial operations, and the size of a government-controlled market offered greater opportunities to both trade and industry. Although Jewish entrepreneurs probably had few illusions about the government's discriminatory attitude, their attitude was marked by a strange optimism that reasons of state would eventually determine the government's economic policies. That the belief in *raison d'état* as a rational principle of government policies toward Jewish entrepreneurs proved disappointing in the long run is obvious to anyone familiar with the subsequent developments. In fact, biases or prejudices apart, fiscal considerations alone dictated the de-controlling of a particular industry or the ''nationalization'' without compensation of another, and affected the situation of Jewish entrepreneurs.[26]

Among the branches of manufacturing industries, it was the textile industry, originally the woolen and later the cotton industry, that attracted much of the capital and entrepreneurial resources of the Jews. The textile industry was rapidly growing, and its traditional center, the Moscow-Vladimir region, could not meet the demand for goods without allowing other areas of concentration to arise. Within the Pale at least two such centers were discernible, the cities and environs of Lodz and Bialystok. In both, Jewish industrial entrepreneurs became prominent. There are a number of generalizations that can be made about the Jewish industrial entrepreneurs and the socioeconomic role they fulfilled on the basis of the data supplied by the JCA Study.[27] The first relevant information pertains to the geographic distributions of the Jewish enterprises. Geographically they can be divided into 1,402 for the Northwest (Byelorussia and Lithuania); 1,143 for the Southwest (Northern and Western Ukraine); 539 (if one accepts the estimate of 151 for Kherson district) for the South (Southern Ukraine and Bessarabia); and 1,416 for the Polish districts. Thus in percentage terms we have 31.2, 25.4, 12.0, and 31.4 percent. The Jewish-owned enterprises differ from the non-Jewish ones in a number of respects, one of them being size, or scale of production. If we divide the enterprises into two categories, one of industrial enterprises using mechanical power (steam engines, motors, etc.) and the other of those without mechanical power, we will get the average number of workers per enterprise, as shown in table 6.

Table 6   Average Number of Workers per Enterprise

	Jewish Enterprises		Non-Jewish Enterprises	
Region	With Mech. Power	Without Mech. Power	With Mech. Power	Without Mech. Power
Northwest	37.2	17.2	50	26.4
Southwest	40.7	17.0	229	17.7
South	21.2	11.0	314	48.0
Poland	71.5[1]	15.0	135	28.2

[1]If we deduct from the Jewish enterprises in Poland the districts of Warsaw and Piotrkov, the average workers per enterprise with mechanical power for the remaining eight districts would decline to 29.8 workers per enterprise. Thus, we have the textile and metal enterprises of the two districts as chiefly responsible for the relatively high number of workers per enterprise.

The table indicates that the Jewish-owned enterprises were smaller in size within the two categories and within the same region. But a regional distribution by itself is not conclusive if there are marked differences between the industrial composition of Jewish-owned and non-Jewish enterprises. The available data for the textile industry and the sugar industry, however, support the claim of fewer workers per enterprise in the Jewish-owned industrial establishments. They also point to a less-than-average capital intensity for Jewish-owned enterprises. If we assume the same capital-output ratio for Jewish-owned and non-Jewish enterprises, the difference in the average size of production between the two groups would indeed indicate and support the hypothesis of a lower capital endowment of the Jewish-owned enterprises. The data for the value of production per Jewish-owned and non-Jewish enterprises, which are available for three regions, indicate the relationship shown in table 7.

I have, in fact, no qualms about the hypothesis of a lower capital endowment of Jewish enterprises, because there existed a number of factors that either caused it or made such behavior rational at least in the short-run. Among the factors I would like to mention are (1) the general relative scarcity of capital within the Jewish community and the higher costs of borrowing from the outside under circumstances of difficulties of ready access to the domestic or foreign capital market; (2) the insufficient size of the necessary outlays for large-scale investments that forced the Jewish entrepreneurs to start with smaller-than-average-size enterprises and to follow a pattern of plowing back profits, thus relying on continuing accretions instead of large discontinuous investments; (3) since the relative wages in the industries in which Jewish entrepreneurs mostly employed their capital were low and the labor supply relatively abundant, operating with a labor-intensive technology made them still competitive in the market.

But even if one accepts these arguments, a lower capital intensity of Jewish-owned enterprises would not demonstrate that we are dealing with a permanent phenomenon; it is not clear that this pattern persisted for the

Table 7 Average Production per Enterprise (in 1,000 Rubles)

Region	Jewish Owned	Non-Jewish Owned
Northwest	21.37	24.46
Southwest	37.6	52.2
South	47.0	132.6[1]

[1]Metallurgy, mining, and machine building located in Ekaterinoslav district helped significantly to tilt the balance in favor of the non-Jewish enterprises.

21

duration of the period under investigation. If we calculate from the Appendix, table A9, the value of output per worker, we get curious results for the regions for which the data are available in the JCA Study (see table 8).[28] The table reveals a tendency reflected in the comparison of the output per worker in the Jewish-owned enterprises of the particular regions, namely, that the production per worker was increasing inversely with the "age" of the industrial plant. The Southern region was the "youngest" one of the three and the Northwestern the "oldest." So that apart from the fact that the Jewish enterprises represented in the JCA Study do not seem to be inferior to their non-Jewish competitors using the value of output per worker as an indicator, the figures suggest the tendency of the Jewish entrepreneurs to increase the efficiency of their operation of which the growth of capital per worker was at least one ingredient. At the turn of the century, Jewish industrial entrepreneurs provided employment for at least 110,000 industrial workers in the territory of the Pale; by the end of the period the number of entrepreneurs increased substantially and their enterprises employed close to 200,000 workers.[29] Thus, the process of industrialization put the industrialists in the forefront of economic activity, and the number of this group as well as its socioeconomic significance were very much enhanced. The importance of industrial entrepreneurs within the Jewish community and their economic role were not determined by the size of the wealth of each of the members of the group. It was not even determined by the volume of their contribution to Jewish philanthropies or to the other needs of the Jewish communities; for this activity they were repaid by various honors bestowed upon them. The real determinant was the volume of employment for Jewish workers and the credit given to Jewish merchants—in other words, the opportunities to earn income that they created. After all, it was this group that created jobs for over 93 percent of the Jewish industrial workers. And while acting in their own self-interest, they

Table 8   Value of Output per Worker Employed (in Rubles)

Jewish-Owned Enterprises			Non-Jewish-Owned Enterprises		
Output	Workers	Output per Worker	Output	Workers	Output per Worker
Northwest:					
29,962,900	30,105	995	32,955,600	21,554	1,529
Southwest:					
42,939,900	28,142	1,526	116,489,100	80,627	1,445
South:					
18,280,700	5,262	3,474	164,319,900	69,513	2,364

helped satisfy one of the greatest economic needs of the Jewish community—the need for gainful employment.

A part of the Jewish bourgeoisie was described as rentier, as deriving their income from money capital or from urban real estate. The high interest rates within the Jewish communities made moneylending an attractive outlet for holders of liquid capital, and urban real estate became as attractive and safe an investment for Jewish businessmen as land was for the Russian or Polish businessman. Given the rate of rapid urbanization and the increasing population density in the sections of the cities occupied by Jews, real estate values in such sections were constantly rising. The supply of housing lagged behind the demand for housing; real estate values rose. Although we do not have any direct data on the urban real estate holdings of the Jews, except for the Polish districts for 1909, it is possible to get a rough estimate for the total Pale of Settlement of the income to owners of real estate and an estimate of rent payments of the Jewish population. Urban real estate incomes were used for further investment in housing construction, which also attracted investments from other sectors of the economy, and the available evidence points to the expansion of this type of economic activity.[30] Owners of real estate were more conservative than the industrial entrepreneurs and more traditional in their cultural outlook; most of their activities were confined to contacts with members of the Jewish community where their key role of controlling the housing market made them influential.

Merchants compose the next lower group on the social ladder, consisting of a mass of individuals employed in trading activities, for our purposes requiring differentiation because a wealthy wholesale merchant obviously had a different social function than an itinerant village peddler. While the wholesale merchants resided in the cities, in the trading and shipping centers, much of the retail trade was located in the small cities and towns close to sources of supply of raw materials and close to consumers of manufactured goods. The wholesale merchants were more specialized and fulfilled two functions, the collection of many small shipments of raw materials for export, for further processing, or for contract delivery, and the distribution of manufactured goods among a number of retailers. In some cases, a wholesale merchant also could act as the organizer of domestic industrial production, in which case he was combining the functions of distribution with entrepreneurial functions in production. It is difficult to estimate the number of wholesale merchants out of the total of the trading population. The employment data indicate that about 5 percent of the category of "general wholesale and retail trade" were employed in wholesale trade; a similar but even lower figure is quoted for the wholesale trade employment in "commission trade." There is no breakdown available for the more specialized branches of trade. A proportion of about 5 percent of the trading population would yield approximately 20,000–25,000 wholesale merchants, which seems to be a reasonable figure.

In terms of his role within the Jewish community, the wholesale merchant was among the traditional leaders going back to the time when a much higher percentage of employment was generated by him and his resources provided a support to the community.

The retail trader engaged either in general, undifferentiated trade, whether sedentary or itinerant, was the traditional mainstay of the preindustrial Jewish community. Much of the trade was conducted either at the fairs regularly scheduled for the cities or towns to which the peasants, lower nobility, and local craftsmen would be drawn, or in small stores and market stalls at times that did not coincide with the intensive agricultural work season. The income of the small trader depended upon the size of his "permanent" clientele, which in turn depended upon his interpersonal relations with his clients, the ability to meet their regular and extraordinary consumption needs, and the amount of credit that the merchant was able to extend from one season to the other. Given the limit of the size of the market, which was growing but probably at a slower rate than the trading population, specialization in trade was still not the optimal solution. The trader in the local markets had to possess the flexibility to barter poultry for salt, grain for cotton goods, livestock for agricultural implements, and the ability to pay cash for flax or hemp, etc. He had to be a walking price list and an efficient and quick supplier for his clients. Thus the trade with clients was but one phase of his operations. Another was the clearing of accounts with his fellow traders who either specialized in particular lines of commodity trade or resold the goods acquired to a wholesaler via the wholesaler's agents, in order to restock his goods.

The advent of the industrial age, the growth of the cities, specialization, and economies of scale altered the position of the typical retail trader. The railroad network penetrating the hinterland, the competition of more efficient systems of trading, and the influx of merchant capital also taught the peasants the advantages of cash payments over barter or semi-barter trade, and, although old habits of bartering and bargaining did not disappear overnight, the old ways of carrying on trade were seriously challenged. More capital was required to carry on the functions of distribution, less labor and time were necessary, and competition became fierce, not only as a result of the increase of the number of Jewish traders but also because of the influx of non-Jewish traders. Industrialization created a demand for goods and for distribution services, and it created an indigenous middle class.

In addition, the various forms of the cooperative movement spread in the countryside. Producer and marketing cooperative societies were formed, cooperatives for the supply of agricultural machinery and implements were organized, and these institutions lessened the demand for the services of traders by assuming some of their previous functions. The government trade policy of protection provided incentives for industrial producers and thus raised the prices of industrial manufactured goods to the consumers and created difficulties for merchants. When this was coupled with a heavy fiscal burden upon the agricultural population, the growth of the internal market fell short of the traders' expectations, and profits in trade declined. The result was a greater income differentiation within the traders' milieu and the younger generation's shift into crafts and industry, while some of the older generation were impoverished and became public charges, dependent upon community charity. Thus, the inadequacy of income-earning opportunities forced some groups within the trading population to accept lower profits (and incomes); the increased costs of entry into trade activities resulted in a shift into other occupations; and some within the groups were socially and economically degraded to the role of paupers. Curiously enough, emigration was a safety valve for this population group only to a limited extent. Whether one could attribute this to lack of capital for transportation or lack of skills (which consisted primarily of the facility of communicating with their customers), applicable in new conditions, or the conservative outlook which made them fear life outside of the traditional society, the fact remains that among the migrants overseas the Jewish traders were underrepresented as a share of total emigrants. It was in internal interregional migration that they occupied a prominent place. In traditional Jewish society artisans were considered a socially inferior group. Although there was a whole system of stratification within the Jewish crafts, with printers, engravers, silversmiths, and others occupying the top, and tailors and cobblers occupying the bottom of the scale, nevertheless as a group they were considered the inferiors in status of merchants and traders. There is no need at this juncture to go into the historical and social reasons for this attitude. For our purpose, it is sufficient to point out that under the impact of industrialization the share of this group in the total Jewish population was rapidly increasing, and, as the occupational structure indicates, the subgroups of the lowest status, the clothing and footwear producers, occupied a commanding position within the artisan group. Differentiation grew between the craftsmen who worked directly for the ultimate consumers of their products and the artisans who worked for the market, for merchants or entrepreneurs, and who were deprived of any direct contacts with the ultimate users of their products (the latter worked for a distant mass market, often producing goods of lower quality and receiving lower wages). It was these artisans who absorbed much of the influx of additional labor and who were much more affected by the changes in general business conditions, more exposed to competition from the manufacturing industries and factory labor, than the craftsmen. The craftsmen could keep their positions as long as industrialization was not very advanced, some markets remained fragmented, the density of roads was relatively low, and factory production did not sufficiently penetrate the consumer goods market. The diffused Jewish craftsmen could hold out for a while until they could make the necessary adjustments. However, the pressures on the second group, the artisans, led to two observable tendencies. It converted some of the craftsmen into cottage industry producers, in which the craftsmen with the aid of family members worked for a merchant or for a jobber who provided the raw materials and collected the finished product; second, it stimulated the establishment and maintenance of relatively large craft shops, primarily using manual labor without mechanical motive power and employing both journeymen and apprentices. The available data indicate that while in small towns the single craftsman or the cottage-type industry prevailed, in large cities the number of larger-scale craft shops, working for distant markets, was on the increase, perhaps reflecting the existence of economies of scale in craft production. For cottage industry and for large-scale craft shops, the transition to factory labor was a logical step. While in the crafts working directly for the consumers, the aspiration on the part of the journeymen to become independent producers still prevailed, among the cottage industry artisans and for the employees in the large craft shops this aspiration was becoming increasingly ephemeral because of the increased costs of setting oneself up as an independent craftsman, and in view of the fact that it was often through increasing the hours of work and accepting cuts in their wages that employment was maintained. Thus, the wages of artisans and journeymen were insufficient to accumulate the necessary capital for economic advancement, and continuing proletarianization became the outlook for an increasing number of craftsmen employed in the urban areas.

The transportation group was low in income and even lower in status. It consisted of wagoners and coachmen who owned horses, wagons, and coaches; it also included thousands of porters and loaders who transported goods on their backs and in little carts for which the porter substituted for a beast of burden. It included a few thousand floaters who accompanied the floats of lumber down the rivers. At the bottom of the social status scale were the factory workers. By and large, social status was congruent with income differentiation, but in the case of the factory workers an admixture of a "coefficient of dependence" explains their low social status in the absence of income differentials. Intuitively or perhaps empirically derived, the status stratification scale recognized that there is more to the relationship between an artisan and journeyman than to the impersonal, market-determined relation between an industrialist and factory worker. And it was not the size of the respective enterprises alone that was crucial. Instinctively, the effects of alienation of the worker and job insecurity were taken into account, but somehow the rate of dependency of the factory worker affected his social standing in the community. A product of the industrialization process, radicalized by community attitudes and by socialist propaganda, the factory worker allied himself with the journeymen and apprentices in a struggle for recognition. And although less politically radical than the journeymen and apprentices, the factory workers, active more in the economic sphere than in the political, were gaining in self-esteem, probably deriving more psychic income than tangible benefits from the struggle, and slowly overcoming the sense of social inferiority within the Jewish community, forcing the "coefficient of dependence" to give way to at least the criteria of income and skill.

The above short review of social corollaries to the employment structure of the Jewish population suffers from a number of omissions. Agricultural employment was excluded (as it was from the discussion of the employment structure); the liberal professions were excluded; the very interesting role of the educational and religious service groups also was excluded; but in terms of numbers, the huge group of private services, of domestics, of white-collar employees, and of day-laborers constitutes the most notable omission. Perhaps in the future, in a more detailed study, these groups will be included.

The Process of Urbanization

The process of urbanization has been very much neglected by competent scholars. At this point the source materials are still scattered, and a number of valuable sources were left untapped for this inquiry. Of primary importance for our purpose is not the question of why the urban population in the Pale increased but what the effects of urbanization upon the social composition of the Jewish population were. Thus, the question of whether the urbanization process was always a voluntary one or whether it was forced upon the Jews by legislation and administrative measures is of minor interest here. There is no doubt that the exile of the Jews from the rural areas of the fifteen Western districts of Russia forced urbanization upon many Jews; there is no doubt also that the remnants of the old privileges of *de non tolerandis Judaei* given by the Polish crown to many cities, or the policies of various Polish and Russian aristocrats who were the legal proprietors of cities, influenced the pattern of urbanization of the Jews even as late as the second half of the nineteenth century. But all these factors have to be taken as a datum, and space does not permit a discussion of these problems. It is clear from the available data that during the period 1881–97 not only was the total Jewish population increasing, but the size of its urban sector grew at an even higher rate. In fact, the rate of growth of the urban Jewish population was higher than the rate of growth of the non-Jewish population.

Our point of departure being 1897, we have to conclude that according to the Population Census figures, 2,393,008 Jews out of 4,910,327 in the Pale of Settlement, or 48.7 percent, resided in what were officially designated as urban centers. Since the designation of a particular center as urban was neither according to standards of size nor according to economic characteristics, one ought not to wonder that urban industrial centers of 30,000–40,000 people, like the cities of Sosnowiec or Zhirardov in the Polish districts and many in the South or Southwest districts, were still designated as rural settlements in the Population Census, and data on their total population or ethnic composition were absent from the Census. It is therefore clear that the above-mentioned percentage of the Jewish population designated as urban represents a lower estimate of the urbanization of Jews in the Pale of Settlement. It would therefore not be an exaggeration to state that at the time of the Census over half of the total Jewish population in the Pale were already urban dwellers.[31]

The data clearly point to the conclusion that the growth of the urban Jewish population prior to 1897 cannot be accounted for by the natural increase of the urban population alone, and that a migration process from less densely populated areas to the more densely populated centers was taking place. The data on the origins of urban inhabitants suggest that this population movement was not restricted to each administrative or geographic district but that the process of migration exhibited interregional patterns. We could, for example, assume that emigration from small towns in the Northwest districts had a number of alternatives of which three appear to be the most plausible. First, movement from the small town to a larger city within the district or the region; second, a move to a city into another region within the Pale; third, emigration abroad.[32] A choice among these can in most cases be explained in terms of the availability of information, the expected income differentials, and by the costs of transportation as well as the availability of means to pay the costs. It would therefore appear that, apart from the means to defray the transportation costs for each employment group, there existed a set of expectations which each emigrant must have held. We can also assume that the decision to migrate to a larger city within the district or the same region was arrived at with better information about available opportunities and therefore involved less risk. The risks appear to increase more or less proportionate with the distance, and they would be compensated only by general knowledge about the relative abundance of employment opportunities in other regions or abroad when compared with the region of origin. It is realistic to assume that, under such circumstances, most of the migrants into other regions would direct themselves toward the larger cities, as centers in which the demand for labor of different categories and skills would be the strongest and opportunities to find employment the most auspicious. In addition, they could have reasonably assumed that in the larger cities control over the job market was much more impersonal and newcomers would not have to break into the existing set of interpersonal, kinship relationships, which often determined the opportunities for work and employment in the small towns. The large city was also preferable when immigrants expected to change occupation or type of employment, since there was less overlap between the status structure and the employment structure than in the small towns. Therefore, it seems logical to assume that for sociopsychological[33] as well as for economic reasons, the interregional migration benefited the larger cities. Thus, taking migration into account, one would expect the Jewish population of the larger towns to grow at a higher rate than the total urban Jewish population and to observe the process of population concentration.

The process of industrialization in Russia led to a growth of the urban areas and their population. Some cities emerged as major industrial centers; some grew as centers of small-scale industry and trade. Within the Pale of Settlement we find both types of cities, and for the period 1897–1910 for which more ample data are available one can see the growth of the city population, a growth of other ethnic groups—Russians, Ukrainians, and Poles—at a higher rate than of the Jewish population. We thus find, for most of the regions within the Pale, a relative decrease of the share of Jews in the urban population, partly the result of the massive migration of Jews abroad.

The growth of the Jewish urban population between 1897 and 1910 can be summed up in the following data. For the cities for which there is information available, Jewish population grew 985,874 (from 2,559,544 in 1897 to 3,545,418 in 1910), or 38.5 percent. The lowest rate of growth was achieved by the districts of the Northwest—24.6 percent; the highest by the Southwest districts—45.5 percent; the Polish districts and the Southern districts occupying a middle position with a 41.6 percent and 41.7 percent increase, respectively. While in 1897 Jews inhabited 156 cities with a population of over 10,000 in the Pale, in 1910 Jews inhabited 229 cities of over 10,000 inhabitants.

But even more important than the above indicators of the ongoing urbanization of the Jewish population in the Pale, as measured by the population of urban settlements of a particular size, was the size distribution of the Jewish communities as an indicator of the shifts in employment and social and cultural conditions of the Jews in the Pale. In my view, the most revealing indicator is the growth of the Jewish communities of over 5,000 Jews from 130 in 1897 to 180 in 1910, and the growth of communities of above 10,000 from 43 to 76. As mentioned above, the growth of the Jewish urban population and number of Jewish communities was not identical for the various regions of the Pale. Table 9 indicates the changes for the particular regions, from which one could infer that, while population growth in the Southwestern and Southern regions of the Pale occurred in communities of all sizes, most of the growth in the Polish districts took place in the number of small communities,[34] and the increase in the Northwestern region took place in larger communities (see table 10). As one would have expected, the regions with a high percentage of Jews in the urban population tend to show a very similar pattern for both indicators as witnessed by the development in the Northwest and Polish districts. In the South and in some districts of the Southwest (Poltava and Chernigov) where the percentage of Jews in the total urban population was relatively smaller in 1897, the subsequent rate of general urbanization was greater than that of the Jews and is crudely reflected in the table.

But apart from the regional pattern, the main reason for classifying the urban settlements in terms of size is to investigate the pattern of growth of the Jewish communities, on the assumption that particular sizes were needed for the functioning of various institutions that catered to the cultural (or religious) needs of the Jewish populations, facilitated the economic interactions within the communities, and made possible a broad division of labor and a complex dependence of varying degrees of one employment group upon the other.

If this basic assumption is historically correct, then the process of industrialization in Russia and its accompanying urbanization created conditions

Table 9   Number of Jewish Communities by Size and Region (1897 and 1910)

Region	Above 5,000		Above 10,000		Above 25,000		Above 50,000	
	1897	1910	1897	1910	1897	1910	1897	1910
Northwest	32	34	15	18	6	11	1	2
Polish districts	31	58	6	15	2	3	2	2
Southwest	57	63	15	33	4	5	. . .	2
South	19	25	7	11	2	4	2	3
Total	139	180	43	76	14	23	5	9

Table 10   Number of Cities and Jewish Communities of Specified Sizes by Regions

Region	No. Cities Above 10,000		No. Jewish Communities Above 5,000	
	1897	1910	1897	1910
Northwest	24	33	32	34
Polish districts	34	50	31	58
Southwest	55	92	57	63
South	43	54	19	25
Total	156	229	139	180

under which it was possible for the Jewish population to counteract the effects of competition and discrimination and to survive economically because of the benefits of concentration in the larger communities. It is therefore worthwhile to inquire into the pattern of population growth in the largest communities of the Pale. While in 1897 382,600 Jews lived in the fourteen communities of the size 25,000–49,999, in 1910 the number was 485,303, or an increase of 26.8 percent. The number of Jews in the largest nine communities in the Pale (all of which by 1910 had more than 50,000 inhabitants) grew from 728,897 in 1897 to 974,904, an increase of 33.8 percent. Thus the largest twenty-three communities in the Pale exhibited a population increase from 1897 to 1910 of 348,710 (from 1,111,497 to 1,460,207), or 31 percent.

Migration

The fascinating process of migration of the Jewish population in Russia from the 1880s to World War I had a lasting impact upon the population distribution of the Jews in the world and upon their subsequent fate. While the migration abroad has been carefully studied, interregional migration in Russia is still little known. Although the impact of industrialization upon migration abroad was substantial, other factors contributed to this development to a larger extent than to interregional migration. Table 11 provides some basic information for the largest segment of the Jewish migration from Russia that came to the United States.

It is clear from simple inspection that while the sudden upsurge of migration in 1891–92 could be attributed to the famine in Russia, the upsurge of 1903–4 and the following years have as much to do with the pogroms (Kishinev and Gomel in 1903, and over the whole Pale of Settlement in 1906) and the revolution of 1905 as with the general economic conditions. If we assume that the migration to the United States was about 80 percent

Table 11   Immigration of Russian Jews into the United States

Year	Total	Year	Total	Children under 14 Years of Age
1883–84	15,122	1898–99	24,275	6,797
1884–85	16,603	1899–1900	37,011	7,772
1885–86	17,309	1900–1	37,660	9,415
1886–87	28,944	1901–2	37,846	9,840
1887–88	31,256	1902–3	47,689	11,922
1888–89	31,889	1903–4	77,544	17,060
1889–90	33,147	1904–5	92,388	20,325
1890–91	42,145	1905–6	125,234	35,066
1891–92	76,417	1906–7	114,932	28,733
1892–93	35,626	1907–8	71,978	17,944
1893–94	36,725	1908–9	39,150	10,179
1894–95	33,232	1909–10	59,824	15,554
1895–96	45,137	1910–11	65,472	
1896–97	22,750	1911–12	58,389	
1897–98	27,221			

of the total migration of Russian Jews abroad, then it becomes clear that for the period 1897–1913 emigration absorbed almost the total natural increase of the Jewish population in the Pale. The fact that this was a family type of migration, including the childbearing age group, children, and relatively fewer old people, meant that the migration process contributed to the lowering of the natural population growth of the Jews in Russia. Another important characteristic of the emigrants has to be kept in mind. According to the data of the U.S. Immigration Office (started only in 1908), the percentage of Jewish immigrants who were either skilled or semi-skilled was very high by comparison with other national groups. This is an additional indication that at least during the first decade of the twentieth century the emigrants were not just casualties of the industrial revolution in Russia but also its product in terms of skill acquisition. Even if the emigrants from Russia did not bring much money with them (from $11 to $24 per adult, depending upon the year), still they brought in human capital which was a result of previous investments made while still in Russia. Unfortunately, the data at our disposal are insufficient to provide either a more detailed age profile of the migrants (to establish with a higher degree of accuracy the relation between the various age groups for purposes of demographic employment analysis), except for the category of children under the age of fourteen, as reflected in the table, or to provide a detailed breakdown in terms of the various regions of the Pale (e.g., the Polish districts, the Northwest, etc.). The scattered available data for emigration from the Polish districts indicate a migration rate not exceeding the share of the districts in the total Jewish population. Circumstantial evidence points to the North-west as the largest potential supplier of migrants abroad as well as the source for internal migration. The migration from any particular region, if available, would tell us something about the economic pressures upon some segments of the population of the region; it would also indicate the extent to which the region was attractive to immigrants from other regions or allowed a population transfer within the region. In the absence of such data, we can turn to the available figures that indicate the general scope of internal migration. The available data on the growth of the urban popula-tion in the various regions of the Pale (already discussed in the context of the urbanization process) point to the lowest population growth rate in the Northwestern region. At the same time, the rate of growth of the urban population in the other regions was relatively high, exceeding the rate of the natural urban population increase, even in the absence of the actual mass migration from Russia. A few tentative explanations are therefore offered: (1) The migration process was caused by the differences in the availability of employment opportunities between regions, with the South-western and Southern regions offering the best opportunities for expanding employment. (2) The interregional migration was influenced by wage dif-ferentials, which favored the Southern region and Polish districts. (3) The interregional migration was influenced also by the intensity of migration abroad, thus "leaving room" for the substitution by migrants for the posi-tions left by the migration of the indigenous population (out-migration from the Northwest to other regions was lower because the region had such a great number of migrants abroad).

It appears, on the basis of the available data on urbanization that the migration pattern within regions was one of movement from the smaller cities to the larger cities, but since the Jewish population in the smaller cities also rose one would expect a parallel movement from small towns to small cities. In the districts of Poland, in which the 1882 decree of exile of the Jews from the rural areas was not operative, one can follow the relative changes in the distribution of the population between cities, towns, and rural areas. While the percentage of Jews in the rural areas as a share of the total Jewish population, according to the estimates for 1909, was approx-imately the same as in 1897, the percentage of inhabitants of the towns declined relative to the urban Jews. Thus, according to the estimates for 1909, 60 percent of the Jews in the Polish district lived in cities and only 27 percent lived in towns.[35] Therefore, one can assume that the immigration continued during the period 1897–1913 very much along the traditional pattern—gradual migration from small town to a small-size city and from the small-size city to a larger city, lessening the costs of acculturation by spreading them out over a time span of perhaps two generations. In contradistinction to the migration abroad which was predominantly a family migration, the interregional and intraregional migration was to a larger extent a migration of individuals. Apparently, the migration within the Pale of settlement was not viewed as a move that might destroy existing family ties or community allegiance. In terms of cultural intercourse between regions and communities, the migration process had a number of positive effects, like the spread of education and cultural enrichment, the heightened sense of mutual interest among various regions in the Pale, the experience of the effect of mobility upon the life of individuals, and inculcation of an active attitude in the attempts to improve one's material and cultural conditions. It is true that historically the Jews were more mobile and migrated more frequently (even voluntarily) than other national groups. Mobility of some merchant groups, of scholars, and of wealthy individuals marrying in other regions were well-known forms of migration, alongside the intraregional migration between rural areas, towns and cities. However, by comparison with the first three-quarters of the nineteenth century, the period under consideration was exceptional, even if we exclude the massive migration abroad. The economic pressures, the shift from trade to crafts and industry, coupled with the acquisition of industrial skills, and the emergence of new opportunities provided a powerful stimulus to an interregional migration on a much larger scale than before. It would probably not be an exaggeration to assume that during the period from the 1880s to the outbreak of World War I, at least 2 million Jews were involved in one or another form of migration. This constituted a very high proportion of the population and bears witness to the fact that industrialization, if it did not single-handedly cause migration, at least coincided with a weakening of the traditional roots of the Jews within their local communities and a readiness to move and respond actively to available opportunities.

Discrimination and the Response

This is not a general discussion of the problem of discrimination against the Jews in Russia. The discussion is limited to two aspects of the discrimination problem: first, to the economic aspects of discrimination, and, second, to the question of whether or not the process of industrialization in its multifarious forms intensified economic discrimination against Jews in Russia.

The Jewish minority was not the only one in Russia that was discriminated against.[36] It was, however, probably the one toward which discrimination was applied most relentlessly and consistently. Although the reasons for discrimination were usually of a religious nature rather than racial or national, the discrimination was embodied in the law and in attitudes. There is no doubt that the more serious of the two in terms of its economic effects were the legal forms of discrimination. The most serious of these was the enforcement of the Pale of Settlement, a prohibition of residence outside of a prescribed territory on the Western fringe of the empire. Thus, the basic feature of economic discrimination was the limitation of mobility for most of the Jewish population. (Only merchants of the first guild and some categories of craftsmen as well as retired soldiers of the army of Nicholas I, who had served for twenty-five years, were allowed to reside outside the Pale.) The exile of most of the Jews from Moscow in 1881 made it clear that even the few who were exempt from the restriction to living in the Pale could not be secure in their privileges. Another set of residence limitations was enacted in 1882 prohibiting residence in villages in fifteen out of twenty-five districts of the Pale. Thus, the Pale which created a high density of the Jewish population and the forced exile of Jews from the rural areas to the cities and towns of the Pale had powerful economic effects upon the Jewish population. Jews were virtually excluded from employment in the government bureaucracy or in local government; policies of discrimination applied in education forced a high percentage of eligible students to continue their studies abroad or to abandon their education too soon. Another feature of government policies, contrary to popular beliefs or myths, called in more Jewish recruits to serve in the Russian army than the percentage of Jews in the total male population would have warranted,[37] thereby forcing an additional number of Jews to forego income during the period of their military service. Jews were prohibited from using or mining government-owned land. Such legislation not only excluded Jewish entrepreneurs from mining enterprises in some of the richest coal, iron, and oil regions, forcing them at best into processing and distributing these products, but when applied to the lumber and grain trade it deprived Jewish merchants of the right to maintain warehouses at the freight stations of government-owned or operated railroads and ports. Thus, it made it uneconomical for them to engage in the processing of forest products or flour milling for export, consequently imposing higher costs on their enterprises and reducing national income.

Without any doubt the government-sponsored discriminatory policies either deprived the Jewish population of opportunities to enter new regions, new markets, new areas of employment, or made it considerably more costly to overcome the barriers erected by the discriminatory practices. In addition, there was no dichotomy between the policies expressed in the legal and executive orders of the central authorities and the everyday practice on the part of local administrators. The existing state of corruption of the imperial local administration allowed various individuals and groups, for a price, to escape some of the consequences of literal implementation of the discriminatory laws, but it was the existence of such laws that enabled administrators to build up a system of extortion and bribery from the Jewish population, not only for transgressions of the law but as an additional payment for protection to which they were entitled under the law. Thus, on the whole, actual administrative practices increased the economic burden of the discriminatory policies probably beyond what was implied or intended by the legislators.

The problem of attitudes of private individuals as reflecting discrimination against Jews is difficult to discuss, especially after such traumatic experiences as the pogroms in the Ukraine of 1919–21, and the Holocaust of World War II during which major groups of the population on the territory of the former Pale of Settlement actively assisted the Nazis in their work of genocide. To single out the populations of Eastern Europe as anti-Semitic *par excellence* does little justice and does not illuminate the problem. That fertile ground for anti-Semitic attitudes existed in the Russian Empire can be explained neither by the character of the population nor by the failure of a cultural symbiosis one would expect to develop, using other societies as a yardstick, out of the age-old coexistence of Slavs and Jews. In my opinion, the major role in the formation and persistence of hostile and discriminatory attitudes toward the Jews until the nineteenth century has to be sought in the political and social structure of the larger society and in the nature of political authority and social stratification of the population. The fact that for hundreds of years, including the period under investigation and up to the present, the role of arbitrary rule was stronger than that of law, is primarily responsible for such attitudes on the part of members of the society.[38] Moreover, it is very important to note that Jews in the Pale lived surrounded not by ethnic Russians but by other ethnic or national groups—Poles, Ukrainians, Byelorussians, Lithuanians, minority groups within the Russian Empire at various levels of national consciousness. There is no doubt that all these groups were subjected to policies of Russification and reacted with different levels of national consciousness. To state that official government policies followed the principle of *divida et impera* does not, however, explain the extent of success or failure of such policies. What is nevertheless most important is the fact that at various points during the nineteenth century some of the minority groups, notably the Poles, tried to ally themselves with the Jews but never as equals, invariably appealing to the Jews to join their cause but without any sense of reciprocity. The explanation for such an attitude has to be sought in the social stratification of society and in the fact that the leaders of such nationalist movements as existed were either members of the upper class themselves or imbued with the attitudes of the upper classes, which looked down upon the vast majority of the Jews as social inferiors or as an alien enigmatic group to be used but not to be understood or studied. Even though the labor and socialist movement in the areas of the national minorities assumed that the Jews were their natural allies, because of their low status and oppression, they treated them as allies who had no bargaining power because of their lack of alternatives. While these were the attitudes of the upper classes and the intelligentsia among the minority groups amid which the majority of the Jews resided, there was at least one group that subscribed to a continuation, if not intensification, of the discriminatory practices toward the Jews—the nascent middle class.

While the impact of industrialization in Russia upon the employment distribution of the Jewish population or upon its social stratification was to increase the percentage employed in production versus distribution, the impact of industrialization upon the non-Jewish population was not only to shift labor from the agricultural into the industrial sector but also to develop a middle class employed in distribution and recruited from individuals previously belonging both to the upper and lower classes. When the members of the new middle class encountered competition from the Jews, previously entrenched in some areas of trade, they resented it. For the scions of the nobility were reminded how low they had fallen, and the sons of peasants discovered an obstacle to their further advancement. As a competitor, the Jewish middle class was formidable, relying upon inherited and acquired experience, knowledge, and adaptability. The outcome of such competition in the short run, based solely upon criteria of economic efficiency in a "free-market" situation, was by no means certain for the young Polish or Ukrainian middle class. Even after a few decades, the existing legislation and discriminatory practice was still insufficient to assure the new middle class of the security of its position in the struggle against its Jewish competitors. The infusion of ideological elements into the competition, the use of a narrow economic nationalism, of such measures as a boycott of Jewish-produced or Jewish-sold goods, escalated the intensity of discrimination, especially in the Polish districts and partly in the Southern regions. Politics was infused into economic competition and raised the price of goods to the consumers. What were the economic circumstances, as distinct from the political and psychological ones, underlying this upsurge of discrimination, at least on the part of the middle class? As was mentioned in the introductory part of the essay, industrial expansion in Russia occurred in spurts; therefore, it is possible to assume, for example, that the increase in demand for services of a middle class, which occurred during the 1890s and was interrupted by the relative stagnation of the 1900–1910 period, caused difficulties for the new entrants into the field of distribution during the period when production was not expanding, or the purchasing power of the population did not increase. It also may be worth noting that, while the emphasis of the industrialization policies was centered around the capital goods industries and the transportation network, a much slower rate of expansion was registered by the consumer goods industries which usually generate more employment and income for the trading population. If we keep in mind this kind of constraint upon the growth of the middle class, we could probably better understand the fierce competition that led to the growth of discriminatory attitudes. I believe that a higher rate of industrial development and a more even and continuous growth of production and consumption would have lessened competition in trade and perhaps also the intensity of discriminatory attitudes.

But it would be a mistake to assume that only the middle class harbored discriminatory attitudes. We have no direct data that would reflect the attitudes of "big business," and all we could do would be to turn to the corporate sector of Russian industry, trade, and finance and examine its publicly enunciated policies and not its everyday practice. One would assume that in such a case personal preferences were subordinated to the interests of the corporation and would reflect primarily a profit-maximizing tendency. Although there is no way to judge whether this would result in intensified discriminatory attitudes or in more subdued and controlled behavior, I believe that a corporation would be considerably lower on a discrimination scale than a privately owned firm. The data used are the reports of corporations operating in Russia that were published in 1914, on the eve of World War I. There were numerous corporations that imposed restrictions upon foreigners; we find 104 corporations that clearly prohibited Jews from ownership of shares and 129 other corporations that specified that individuals of Jewish faith could not serve on their board of directors (thus prohibiting them from participating in the policymaking of the companies). A closer examination of the corporations excluding Jews either from shareholding or from a voice in policymaking is quite revealing. In terms of discrimination against shareholding we find sugar mills and sugar refining leading the list, followed by textiles, trade in draperies and haberdashery, flour milling, and forestry and steamship lines. In terms of appointment to the board of directors, oil drilling, and coal and metal ore mining led, followed by sugar mills and refining, and forestry. I believe the differences between the industries in the first and second categories to be significant in the explanation of the various forms of discrimination. While in the first group (discrimination against shareholding) the most heavily represented were the areas in which Jewish entrepreneurs made significant inroads and discrimination was a form of retribution in a competitive struggle by Russian (or Polish or Ukrainian) industrialists or merchants, the second group represents discrimination based more upon social prejudices than upon business competition. With perhaps the notable exception of the oil companies, the boards of directors and a significant portion of actual controlling interest were in the hands of the nobility or aristocracy, who provided a link between the business community and the government, and to admit non-baptized Jews in their midst who would have to be treated as equals was too much to expect of a social class not exactly a paragon of egalitarian virtues at the beginning of the twentieth century. One could, therefore, conclude that the attitude of big business toward discrimination against Jews as reflected by the pronouncements of its corporate sector was, by and large, either not expressed or neutral, the cases of antidiscriminatory attitudes openly expressed were not numerous,[39] and the segment that openly practiced discrimination did it because of competition or social and cultural prejudices.

An interesting and yet little explored phenomenon was the attitude of industrial workers toward their Jewish co-workers. I have omitted the attitudes of the non-Jewish workers toward their Jewish employers because the costs to a worker of discriminating against employers were too high to be taken into account. I have also omitted the attitudes of non-Jewish industrial entrepreneurs toward Jewish workers because in the absence of governmental discriminatory policies and the animosity of non-Jewish workers there seemed to be little reason for an industrialist to discriminate against Jewish workers. If in fact the number of Jewish workers in non-Jewish factories was minimal, the responsibility ought not to be laid exclusively at the doors of the non-Jewish industrialists. The attitudes of the workers appear to be crucial in a number of ways. The non-Jewish workers in their relation to the Jewish workers had to choose between workers' solidarity and nationalist ideology and behavior. In this area of choice, and perhaps even dilemma for the non-Jewish workers, they opted most often against workers' solidarity. This helps to explain why Polish workers went on strike against the hiring of Jewish workers and why German foremen often refused to train Jewish workers. Apart from deep-rooted suspicions and cultural differences, augmented by difficulties in communication with one another, there ought to exist other more tangible, if not more rational, explanations. It may be that the phenomenon of Jewish factory workers was so new that the non-Jewish worker simply could not within a single generation replace the age-old images of the Jew as alien, stranger, or petty trader. Especially since the confrontation took place predominantly in Jewish-owned factories, the presence of Jewish workers was considered part of a "Jewish plot" which would ultimately replace the non-Jewish worker. Thus, the fear of competition, even when imaginary, acted as a catalyst to reawaken the old images, fears, and hostilities. The truth of the matter was that in factories with a mixed labor force the non-Jewish workers represented the higher skills, and it was the monopoly of higher skills they were trying to protect.[40] In this connection it may be worthwhile to recall an observation by Salomon Margolin[41]—that during the process of industrialization in Russia the labor supply in various regions or industries within regions had pronounced ethnic characteristics. The Russians, Poles, Ukrainians, or any other group that gained an early entrance into a particular industry or enterprise tried to solidify their position and also tried to exclude other ethnic groups. In this respect, Margolin argued that it was unfortunate for the Jewish working population that it did not have the necessary resources (in terms of numbers) in each particular locality or lacked the necessary skills to occupy a leading position in the large-scale enterprises. This contention by Margolin about the ethnicity of the labor force distribution in Russian industrialization is an interesting one, but it needs further study before it can be accepted. It is not clear whether the discrimination of, let us say, Russians against Ukrainians is equivalent to the discrimination against the Jews, even if one does not invoke Max Weber's notion of the "pariah."[42] If we assume that the working classes of Russia were still very much a product of the existing social order and the prevailing value structure, that they were not far enough removed from their village origins to develop a sense of superiority with respect to the peasants, that discriminatory practices against Jewish workers did not cost anything and, in fact, promised some benefits, like the protection of their status as skilled workers and the benefit of working within their own cultural milieu, the behavior of the industrial workers who came into contact with their actual or prospective Jewish co-workers becomes more intelligible.

Finally, a few observations about discrimination by Jews against non-Jews. If we define as discrimination such favoring of one group over another, and if there is a willingness to pay a price for exercising this preference, then the Jews were, according to our definition, engaged in discrimination. Being a minority within the population, a minority that consciously and sometimes jealously and vehemently defended its right to hold its own beliefs and its autonomous culture, probably rendered its discrimination not very effective. Discrimination against outsiders, nonmembers of the Jewish community, limited social contacts; some business or employment contacts were proscribed by the religious code to which the majority of the Jews adhered. The dietary laws prohibited Jews from eating in the home of non-Jews; some family laws prohibited the contact of unchaperoned women with non-Jews; the laws of the Sabbath prohibited work and business on a day considered a working day by the majority of the population. In other words, the traditional Jewish way of life imposed impediments to a number of forms of socialization with non-Jews, while encouraging internal contacts within the Jewish community.

There is no doubt whatsoever that when we are dealing with most of the handicraft or cottage-type industries we observe a definite bias in favor of employing Jewish apprentices and journeymen. The elements of cultural affinity, under conditions when apprentices lived at the home of the master craftsman or when the journeyman spent 12–15 hours daily in the shop which was scarcely distinguishable from the home of the artisan, became paramount, and an alternative arrangement, for example, employment of non-Jewish apprentices, even if legally possible would have entailed heavy psychological costs. For Jewish apprentices or their parents the same dilemma might have existed, and the idea of entrusting a youngster to a non-Jewish master craftsman aroused the fear of the youngster's conversion. The traumatic experience of the forced recruitment of children in the army of Nicholas I was still alive for decades after the event and imbued an exaggerated fear of conversion.[43]

The most controversial issue was that of hiring Jewish workers by Jewish industrial entrepreneurs. About 50,000 Jewish industrial workers were employed by Jewish industrialists out of a total in Jewish-owned industrial enterprises of about 110,000 workers. The Jewish workers accused the industrialists of discrimination in hiring and attributed it to the employer's preference for hiring a labor force that was less "class-conscious," less easily organized, less radical in demanding higher wages and more humane treatment. Some Jewish industrialists retorted by pointing out their unwillingness to force Jewish workers to transgress the laws of the Sabbath, since factories with a mixed labor force had to be closed on Sunday. But the real reasons might be (1) the relative abundance of unskilled labor at a price lower than Jewish workers would accept,[44] (2) the resistance of non-Jewish skilled workers to the admission of Jewish workers, (3) fear that the experience of handicrafts where some journeymen after learning the trade would become independent producers would be repeated by some Jewish workers and would thus increase the competition for existing enterprises and that the entrepreneurs might not recover the costs of training of a mobile segment of the labor force, and (4) the fear of infusing a radical ferment into the labor force. Our tentative conclusion would, therefore, be that the costs of hiring Jewish workers by Jewish industrial entrepreneurs were real, although it is very difficult to estimate their magnitude, and they might have differed from one industry to another. If we take as examples the tobacco and cigarette industry in the Pale, an industry that employed a high percentage of women under conditions harmful to their health, we would find that the vast majority of this labor force was Jewish; the match industry was similar. Attempts to set up machine-building plants with a predominantly Jewish labor force (e.g., the factory of Jacobson in Minsk) or the shoe factories in Warsaw were for the most part successful, but whether the same was true in the various branches of the textile industry, for example, remains an open question requiring additional research. Thus, in general, Jewish industrialists could not be accused of discriminating in favor of Jewish workers, and they were accused of discriminating against them. On purely economic grounds, I would claim, they probably behaved neutrally. For the whole problem to be resolved, for both Jewish industrialists and Jewish workers to adjust to the long-term conditions of the market, time was required. We know that Jewish workers began to work on the Sabbath; as a result of traumatic experiences like the massive emigration or the subsequent Russian revolution, Jewish industrialists gradually got rid of some of their fears with regard to Jewish workers. The time span of industrialization in Russia prior to the revolution was, however, too short for the process to take its course toward a satisfactory solution.

A few observations are in order to deal with the response to discrimination. The growing awareness of the close relationship between economic discrimination and the political regime was one of the factors determining the sympathy of the majority of the Jewish population with the aims of democratizing the regime, with the revolution of 1905, the elections to the State Duma (Parliament), etc. On the cultural scene, the development of the modern literatures in Yiddish and Hebrew, the growth of the press, and the attempts to set up a modern school system contained the element of a response to discrimination and assertion of dignity and pride in the Jewish cultural heritage. It is in the economic sphere where significant responses to discrimination could be noted. Already in the second half of the 1890s a network of mutual credit institutions scattered over the Pale of Settlement were being set up in the hundreds. By pooling the savings of merchants and artisans (in many cases such societies were set up separately for each of the two groups), loans were made available for relatively short-term borrowing of funds for working capital. In some cases loans were made to meet the needs of consumer credit. The success of such institutions of mutual credit can be measured not only by their rapid spread but also by the actual decline of the interest rate on private borrowing in the towns and cities of the Pale. Resources previously underutilized were made available at least for working capital purposes.[45]

Accompanying the development of the institutions of mutual credit was an enlarged network of societies of mutual assistance, established either by artisans of particular trades or by workers of some of the industry branches, ostensibly for assistance in case of disease, accident at work, etc., but in the case of the workers also as accumulation of strike funds, an embryonic form of trade unionism. This was followed by the establishment of clandestine trade unions and later, when trade union activity was legalized, of trade unions that not only addressed themselves to the routine problems of labor relations but became instrumental in the fight of Jewish workers to enter into the enterprises that discriminated against them.

It is true that the enumerated responses to discrimination were perhaps only peripheral to the solution of the causes and manifestations of discriminating practices or attitudes. They do, however, indicate the attempts to alleviate some of the results of discrimination and the understanding that discrimination had to be fought collectively if the particular group was to survive as a separate cultural entity and that economic discrimination would be separated from other aspects of discrimination.

The "Productivizatsia" Debate or a Postscript to the Inquiry

The debate on the problems of bringing more Jews into industrial and craft occupations is at least several hundred years old and probably goes back to the notion of the Physiocrats that farming is productive and trade is nonproductive. Certainly since the end of the eighteenth century non-Jews and Jews alike were intellectually and practically engaged in attempts to make Jews into a "productive" social element. Shelves of books and pamphlets were written on this subject, and ideological constructs were erected and applied in order to justify particular solutions or to propose new ones.[46]

The first precondition of an examination is to strip the debate of as much of its ideological garb, acquired over time, as possible. It will therefore be assumed that maximization of income of the members of the community in the long run was a reasonable goal for the community as a whole and that the aims of any policy of achieving a shift in employment had to be congruent or in agreement with this goal. Such an assumption also implies that neither the overall goal nor the aims of a specific policy can be neutral with respect to income distribution. Therefore, on the one hand, if a proletarian party desired to increase the number of Jewish workers at the expense of the middle class for ideological reasons and was thereby ready to decrease the income of the community, we would find such aims at variance with our assumptions; on the other hand, the appearance of a few "Rothschilds" without a clear benefit for the majority of the community is also in conflict with our assumption about the income distribution. We should ask the question: if the economic development of the country would have allowed the growth of the middle class (including merchants and liberal professions) and discrimination against the Jews would not have been a matter of governmental policy (let us say the Pale were abolished and access to all kinds of employment would have become a matter of merit), would there have been a need for proletarization or other employment shift of the Jews?

The answer would probably be in the negative, unless one subscribes to the early Marxian prediction that the middle class was on the verge of disappearing and the development of society would leave only two classes, proletarians and capitalists.[47]

When one moves from the area of ideology to that of social reality, however, the problems of occupational shifts become more complex. The first "complicating" factor was serious underemployment. Let us, therefore, restate some of the general conditions which brought this about. I would assume that as a result of the relatively low rate of growth of per capita disposable income and therefore slow growth of consumption expenditures of the total population, the problem of shift in employment for the Jews had its roots in two areas: the lack of capital, and the presence of discrimination. Lack of capital alone was, in the long run, not the crucial limiting factor, because the Jews were able to impose upon themselves a higher rate of savings. In the absence of ruinous, deliberate taxation a sizable proportion of Jews was able to invest either in physical assets or in education, although in the short run with difficult problems. The presence of discrimination, however, not only thwarted the process of capital accumulation but limited the opportunities to earn income, to invest, or to receive the market rate of return on past investments.

In this respect the history of the Jews in Western Europe and in the United States in the nineteenth and twentieth centuries differed radically from the experience of the Russian Jews. Neither being confined to any Pale of Settlement nor being victimized by other serious discriminatory practices, the Jews in the West did not become the objects of "employment structure" campaigns or debates. Depending upon their economic position as individuals, they suffered from, or benefited from, the consequences of industrialization just as did other non-Jewish members of their social or employment group. In Russia, discriminatory policies prevented a part of the Jewish population from benefiting from the fruits of industrialization. Since the process of industrialization causes shifts in employment and intensifies income differentiation, the number of the Jewish poor was probably not decreasing in Russia during the quarter century preceding World War I. If we are to judge by families receiving aid in various forms from the Jewish community and charitable organizations for the years 1894–98, the number was steadily increasing.[48] Whether the data reflect improved reporting, or a growing sensitivity of the community organizations to the problems of the poor, or that public aid became a more frequent substitute for private charity, or actually a response to increasing misery is difficult to establish. What is, however, important is the sheer size of the section of population that turned to the community's aid agencies for assistance. In 1898, according to the JCA Study, the number of families who received assistance was 132,855, or 19 percent of the number of Jewish families covered by the study.[49] It is, therefore, psychologically understandable why the debate was chiefly concerned with the problem of underemployment and poverty as its paramount issue. To relieve the misery of the poor, apart from temporary relief, skill training in craft and industry appeared to be the less expensive solution, at least in the short run. This coincided with the shift in employment from trade into crafts and industry.

The process of growth of the craft population was influenced by a few other factors, which although they do not contradict the basic assumption of transfer from trade (actual or expected) need to be taken into account because they bear upon the particular realities of the process. One of the sources of recruitment into crafts and industry was the Jewish population from the rural areas and small towns where either government policies or the limited purchasing power of the local peasantry made economic survival precarious. Such a recruitment into crafts and industry was made possible by the process of both internal migration and migration abroad of large numbers of artisans. The emigration to Western Europe, where Eastern European immigrants constituted the majority of Jewish industrial and craft employment, and later the migration to the United States made room for the influx of population into crafts and also enabled the migrants from the rural areas to settle in middle-sized towns, while the migration from middle-sized to large-sized towns continued. The interregional migration of craft population to the Southern regions of Russia or to the Polish districts from the densely populated cities and towns of the Northwest was also instrumental in enabling the transfer into crafts.

It was assumed that skill training absorbed some of the savings of individuals and even some of the community funds earmarked for preparing Jews for gainful employment in craft and industry. It is also correct to assume that for some types of skills education was a prerequisite. Given the available data, this assumption can be substantiated, and the magnitude of the investment in education indicates that a relatively high rate of return was expected. This seems to contradict a widespread myth about the Jewish community and merits some consideration. There exists a widespread myth about literacy among the Jews (at least among the male population). This myth is based upon the correct assumption that the majority of males received the traditional instruction in the religious schools and therefore could read the prayers and even the Bible. What is often forgotten, however, is that the instruction concentrated primarily on reading, not on writing, and that the reading of Hebrew characters in the prayer book did not guarantee the ability to read newspapers, books, etc. The typical product of such elementary traditional instruction, which was the entire education for the poorer classes, was a person semi-literate even in his own language. If we add to the semi-literacy of a large part of the male population the illiteracy of the majority of the female population, we will understand why the contemporary studies of education among the Jews deviate so much from the mythology. Skill training involved not only literacy in one's mother tongue but quite often also literacy in the language of the country. Thus, when one talks about investment in the human agent, in skill acquisition, one has also to assume as a prerequisite literacy, or the result of a secular education. Such investments were costly and were often made at an adult age out of one's own earnings rather than by the family or by the community. The progress during the 30–40 years prior to WWI was indeed amazing. Among the Jews it was started by the upper classes and followed by the lower classes. The acquisition of elementary education as the first in a series of consecutive steps was vigorously pursued, as witnessed by the growth in enrollment in all kinds of new, nontraditional schools, a process that continued with increasing intensity until WWI.

Thus, *prima facie* the response of individuals who invested in skill acquisition in crafts and industry and combined it with investment in education appeared to be congruent with the impact of industrialization in Russia upon the Jewish milieu. However, what was labeled as the "productivizatsia" debate was a quest for a long-term policy, not necessarily a short-term response.

A rational, collective policy on the optimal use of community funds would require some estimates of the amount of capital needed for the employment of an additional individual in each of the employment categories, or a measure of capital costs (perhaps including costs of training) per expected unit of income in each category (industry, craft, trade, services, etc.). It is my distinct impression that the debate on occupational shifts and related issues was conspicuously lacking in such estimates. I hope it is not presumptuous to suggest that a study of this kind might help us settle, in retrospect, the issues in a debate that absorbed so much energy in past generations.

Appendix

Table A1 Total Jewish Population in the Pale of Settlement, 1897 Census Data

District	Total Pale			Cities		
	Male	Female	Total	Male	Female	Total
Vitebsk	83,212	92,407	175,629	53,313	60,524	113,837
Minsk	166,753	178,262	345,015	68,853	69,764	133,617
Mogilev	97,408	106,538	203,946	37,160	40,233	77,393
Vilna	98,193	106,493	204,686	41,683	45,632	87,315
Kaunas	99,657	113,009	212,666	29,422	32,773	62,195
Grodno	135,473	145,016	280,489	71,546	76,924	148,470
Total Northwest	680,696	741,735	1,422,431	296,977	325,850	622,827
Chernigov	55,053	59,399	114,452	25,954	28,835	54,789
Kiev	209,782	223,946	433,728	70,829	74,079	144,908
Poltava	54,073	56,871	110,944	39,525	41,474	80,999
Volynia	191,928	203,854	395,782	57,587	61,659	119,246
Podolia	79,612	191,000	370,612	49,539	53,349	102,882
Total Southwest	690,779	735,070	1,425,518	243,434	259,396	502,824
Ekaterinoslav	51,679	49,409	101,088	32,671	31,353	64,024
Crimea	31,499	29,253	60,752	20,559	18,774	39,333
Kherson	168,425	171,485	339,910	119,516	121,452	240,968
Bessarabia	112,662	115,866	228,528	53,932	55,723	109,655
Total South	364,265	366,013	730,278	226,678	227,302	453,980

Suwalki	28,489	30,706	59,195	14,197	15,281	29,478
Siedlce	58,850	62,285	121,135	30,576	32,669	63,245
Lublin	75,147	81,074	156,221	35,033	38,676	73,709
Lomza	44,760	46,634	91,394	17,144	17,940	35,084
Plock	24,668	26,786	51,454	14,690	16,172	30,862
Warsaw	70,974	180,968	351,942	138,351	148,446	286,791
Piotrkow	09,533	113,025	222,558	80,541	83,130	163,671
Kalisz	34,563	37,094	71,657	20,971	22,693	43,664
Radom	54,633	57,690	112,323	24,455	26,297	50,752
Kielce	40,595	42,626	83,221	17,538	18,580	36,118
Total Polish districts	642,212	678,888	1,312,100	393,496	419,879	813,375
Total Pale of Settlement	2,577,621	2,521,706	4,910,327	1,160,579	1,232,427	2,393,006

Table A2   Age Distribution of the Jewish Population (1897)

Years	Russian Empire				European Russia (except Polish Districts)				European Russia, Urban Population (except Polish Districts)			
	Males	Females	Total	% Dist.	Males	Females	Total	% Dist.	Males	Females	Total	% Dist.
Below 1	84,537	80,749	165,286	3.17	58,283	55,890	114,173	3.01	26,304	25,432	51,736	2.95
1–9	657,364	656,914	1,314,278	25.20	471,037	471,979	943,016	24.89	203,523	203,909	407,432	23.26
10–19	582,449	666,160	1,248,609	23.94	422,070	488,725	910,795	24.035	197,086	229,511	426,597	24.35
20–29	427,372	445,220	872,592	16.73	311,549	327,379	638,928	16.86	160,716	159,370	320,086	18.27
30–39	293,209	304,046	597,255	11.45	209,763	217,794	427,557	11.28	98,995	101,631	200,626	11.45
40–49	203,511	219,627	423,133	8.11	152,277	165,019	317,296	8.37	70,796	75,343	146,139	8.34
50–59	152,207	164,073	316,280	6.06	112,975	119,788	232,763	6.14	51,028	54,228	105,256	6.01
60–69	96,260	89,397	185,657	3.56	71,824	65,499	137,323	3.62	32,836	30,243	63,079	3.60
70–79	40,093	32,627	72,720	1.39	30,111	23,483	53,594	1.41	13,227	11,121	24,348	1.39
80–89	8,112	7,522	15,634	.30	5,877	5,239	11,116	.29	2,434	2,517	4,951	.28
90–99	986	1,322	2,308	.04	677	829	1,506	.04	273	371	644	.037
Over 100	72	146	218		48	68	116		14	35	49	
Unknown	972	858	1,830	.035	684	581	1,265	.033	342	312	654	.037
Total	2,547,144	2,668,661	5,215,805		1,847,175	1,942,273	3,789,448		857,574	894,023	1,751,597	

**Table A3   Regional Distribution of the Economically Active Jewish Population
in the Pale (1897)**

District	Males	Females	Total	% of Females	Armed Services
Vitebsk	40,692	14,112	54,804	25.75	1,158
Minsk	77,749	23,390	101,139	23.13	1,147
Mogilev	43,353	12,685	56,038	22.64	608
Vilna	48,141	18,244	66,385	27.48	1,307
Kaunas	47,285	18,847	66,132	28.50	1,934
Grodno	67,717	22,128	89,845	24.63	3,341
Total Northwest	324,937	109,406	434,343	25.19	9,495
Chernigov	25,241	7,672	32,913	23.31	266
Kiev	100,168	24,440	124,608	19.61	1,758
Poltava	26,878	7,363	34,241	21.50	648
Volynia	88,239	21,207	109,446	19.38	2,714
Podolia	81,904	17,712	99,616	17.78	1,906
Total Southwest	322,430	78,394	400,824	19.56	7,292
Ekaterinoslav	27,314	5,592	32,906	16.99	510
Crimea	16,074	2,893	18,967	15.25	1,280
Kherson	85,649	21,042	106,691	19.72	2,995
Bessarabia	55,153	12,202	67,355	18.12	1,007
Total South	184,190	41,729	225,919	18.47	5,792
Suwalki	13,289	3,342	16,631	20.10	827
Siedlce	24,980	5,117	30,097	17.00	885
Lublin	33,940	8,967	42,907	20.90	2,439
Lomza	20,464	4,549	25,013	18.19	1,967
Plock	6,761	2,073	8,834	23.47	608
Warsaw	77,954	25,884	103,838	24.93	3,647
Piotrkow	51,828	14,221	66,049	21.53	824
Kalisz	14,213	3,803	18,016	21.11	96
Radom	24,086	5,480	29,566	18.53	624
Kielce	17,516	4,073	21,589	18.87	253
Total Polish districts	285,031	77,509	362,540	21.38	12,170
Total Pale of Settlement	1,116,588	307,038	1,423,626	21.57	34,749

Table A4 Jewish Urban Population

District	Census 1897 by Religion	Census 1897 by Language	Comparable Coverage 1897	Comparable Coverage 1910	% Increase 1897–1910
Vitebsk	113,837	112,480	113,882	138,632	121.73
Minsk	133,617	132,278	133,278	147,515	110.40
Mogilev	77,393	77,082	77,402	131,982	170.51
Vilna	87,315	85,250	94,936	109,736	115.59
Kaunas	62,195	61,694	62,265	80,611	129.46
Grodno	148,470	146,907	143,395	171,118	119.33
Total Northwest	622,827	615,691	625,499	779,594	124.64
Chernigov	54,789	54,401	60,506	89,436	147.81
Kiev	144,908	142,222	225,670	343,202	152.08
Poltava	80,999	80,491	82,019	107,307	130.83
Volynia	119,246	118,727	145,429	207,244	142.51
Podolia	102,844	102,204	143,025	208,541	145.81
Total Southwest	502,826	498,045	656,649	955,730	145.55

Ekaterinoslav	64,024	62,602	73,759	138,322	187.55
Crimea	39,333	34,248	44,466	53,714	120.80
Kherson	240,968	223,769	249,066	338,201	135.79
Bessarabia	109,655	109,065	114,623	152,951	133.44
Total South	453,980	429,684	481,914	683,188	141.77
Suwalki	29,479	29,463	29,480	44,729	151.73
Siedlce	63,245	63,290	61,097	90,933	148.83
Lublin	73,709	72,926	69,640	95,591	137.26
Lomza	35,084	35,013	33,159	46,951	141.59
Plock	30,862	30,685	30,862	44,664	144.72
Warsaw	286,791	252,236	286,793	411,921	143.63
Piotrkow	163,671	156,256	163,678	203,675	124.44
Kalisz	43,664	36,897	43,664	70,106	160.56
Radom	50,752	50,671	48,682	75,503	155.09
Kielce	36,118	35,962	28,427	42,833	150.68
Total Polish districts	813,375	763,399	795,482	1,126,906	141.66
Total Pale of Settlement	2,393,008	2,306,819	2,559,544	3,545,418	138.52

Table A5   Selected Census Data on Employment of the Jewish Population, 1897, by Region

Crafts & Industry	I Northwest	II Southwest & South	III Polish Districts	Total Pale	Outside the Pale	Total Empire	Total 9 Cities	Cities as % of Pale
Textiles	11,399	8,223	13,687	33,309	1,303	34,612	10,458	31.4
Hides, leather	6,902	7,946	5,598	20,446	1,030	21,476	3,244	15.9
Clothing & footwear	74,658	97,833	63,502	235,993	18,931	254,384	38,158	16.2
Wood, furniture	14,334	19,690	6,379	40,403	2,122	42,525	7,385	18.3
Ceramics	2,329	2,083	765	5,177	181	5,358	625	12.1
Construction & repair	15,921	14,012	6,976	36,909	2,110	39,019	7,528	20.4
Tobacco	3,301	3,881	620	7,802	54	7,856	2,430	31.1
Food	15,827	17,213	11,757	44,797	1,359	46,156	5,465	12.2
Beverages	2,283	2,698	991	5,972	610	6,582	1,077	18.0
Metals	14,944	18,563	6,797	40,304	4,603	44,907	6,869	17.0
Printing	7,268	11,384	5,631	24,283	5,153	29,436	8,020	33.0
Total Craft & Industry	69,166	203,526	122,703	495,395	36,916	532,311	91,259	18.4
Trade								
Agricultural products	9,321	43,263	10,553	63,137	1,743	64,880	4,124	6.5
Incl. grain	5,473	34,664	7,164	47,301	1,662	48,963	3,595	7.6
Textiles & clothing	7,779	23,401	8,648	39,828	4,355	44,183	9,045	22.7

Hides, furs	2,660	6,183	2,987	11,830	721	12,551	1,635	13.8
Construction materials	9,142	12,903	3,986	26,031	1,682	27,713	3,581	13.7
Domestic wares & furniture	1,190	3,157	1,204	5,551	302	5,853	1,202	21.6
Food	42,398	67,033	29,389	138,820	6,239	145,059	17,699	12.7
Beverages	4,971	2,135	4,893	11,999	137	12,136	1,965	16.4
Metal products	1,381	3,339	1,768	6,438	361	6,849	1,275	19.6
Luxury products	883	1,150	803	2,836	229	3,065	1,034	36.4
Commission trade	2,457	8,602	4,190	15,249	726	15,975	4,626	30.3
General wholesale & retail	18,504	39,592	32,703	90,799	5,416	96,215	14,152	15.6
Total Trade	100,686	210,758	101,124	412,568	21,911	434,479	63,933	15.5
Services								
Transportation	16,494	17,577	9,905	43,976	1,642	45,618	7,388	16.8
Domestic service, day labor	45,321	69,242	55,087	169,650	6,082	175,732	38,838	22.9
Central & local admin.	682	1,062	554	2,298	289	2,587	307	13.3
Religious services	5,631	9,472	4,024	19,127	1,008	20,135	1,868	9.7
Teaching & education	12,058	15,817	6,390	34,265	1,008	35,273	4,428	12.9
Law & medicine	2,850	4,330	1,955	9,135	1,672	10,807	1,674	18.3
Hygiene	2,617	3,966	1,958	8,541	456	8,997	1,717	20.1
Art, literature, sciences	751	925	544	2,220	650	2,870	624	28.1
Agriculture	13,895	14,391	5,664	33,950	1,311	35,261	430	1.2
Forestry	1,822	881	497	3,200	180	3,380	237	7.4

Table A6   Number of Employed and Their Dependents within the Jewish Population, Russian Empire, 1897 (Census Data)

Crafts & Industry	No. of Employed	No. of Family Members	Proportion of Family Members to Employed
Textiles	34,612	58,686	1.70
Hides, leather	21,476	50,744	2.36
Clothing & footwear	254,384	528,070	2.08
Wood, furniture	42,525	96,951	2.28
Ceramics	5,358	15,333	2.86
Construction & repair	39,019	113,659	2.91
Tobacco	7,856	9,690	1.23
Food	46,156	137,160	2.97
Beverages	6,582	19,395	2.95
Metals	44,867	108,845	2.43
Printing	29,436	52,075	1.77
Total crafts & industry	532,311	1,190,608	2.24
Trade			
Agricultural products	64,880	235,293	3.63
Including grain	48,963	172,624	3.53
Textiles & clothing	44,183	114,700	2.60
Hides, furs	12,551	42,153	3.36
Construction materials	27,713	94,094	3.40
Domestic wares & furniture	5,853	15,967	2.73
Food	145,054	442,048	3.05
Beverages	12,136	44,440	3.66
Metal products	6,849	20,899	3.05
Luxury products	3,065	7,695	2.51
Commission trade	15,975	53,511	3.35
General wholesale & retail	96,215	302,722	3.15
Total trade	434,479	1,373,522	3.16
Services			
Transportation	45,618	154,546	3.39
Domestic service & day labor	175,732	159,105	.91
Central & local administration	2,587	8,453	3.27
Religious	20,135	67,776	3.37
Teaching & education	35,273	90,241	2.56
Law & medicine	10,807	16,415	1.52
Hygiene	8,997	18,237	2.03
Art, literature, sciences	2,870	5,252	1.83
Agriculture	35,261	136,075	3.86
Forestry	3,380	9,496	2.81
Welfare work	197	432	2.19

Table A7 Jewish Artisans, 1898–99 (according to reports by correspondents)

District	Males				Females			
	Total	Craftsmen	Workers	Apprentices	Total	Craftsmen	Workers	Apprentices
Vitebsk	23,473	10,671	7,077	5,725	5,163	1,629	1,366	2,168
Minsk	35,587	18,429	10,451	6,707	5,881	2,307	2,238	1,336
Mogilev	25,849	12,821	7,649	5,379	4,002	1,752	1,222	1,028
Vilna	26,240	18,404	3,241	4,595	5,342	2,969	963	1,410
Kaunas	23,525	14,313	3,591	5,621	4,748	2,394	651	1,703
Grodno	44,829	23,263	11,561	10,005	6,664	2,557	1,942	2,165
Total Northwest	179,503	97,901	43,570	38,032	31,800	13,608	8,382	9,810
Chernigov	11,063	5,196	3,666	2,201	2,062	828	756	478
Kiev	43,386	21,744	14,511	7,131	5,647	2,158	2,346	1,143
Poltava	8,815	4,924	2,097	1,794	1,971	838	629	504
Volynia	36,964	18,146	12,729	6,089	4,799	1,926	1,805	1,068
Podolia	40,621	19,573	13,392	7,656	6,754	2,405	2,429	1,920
Total Southwest	140,849	69,583	46,395	24,871	21,233	8,155	7,965	5,113

(continued)

Table A7 (Continued)

District	Males				Females			
	Total	Craftsmen	Workers	Apprentices	Total	Craftsmen	Workers	Apprentices
Ekaterinoslav	8,039	4,910	2,220	909	1,092	459	423	210
Crimea	7,466	3,732	2,237	1,497	1,017	419	341	257
Kherson	24,782	11,036	8,530	5,216	2,609	957	925	727
Bessarabia	20,976	8,580	7,075	5,321	3,863	1,120	1,366	1,377
Total South	61,263	28,258	20,062	12,943	8,581	2,955	3,055	2,571
Suwalki	5,321	3,318	840	1,163	820	390	167	263
Siedlce	11,467	4,817	3,977	2,673	1,538	534	524	480
Lublin	16,631	8,910	4,879	2,842	2,716	774	1,398	544
Lomza	10,303	5,466	2,490	2,347	1,429	763	234	432
Plock	5,826	2,909	1,194	1,723	760	304	171	285
Warsaw	23,287	16,149	3,540	3,598	1,673	600	575	498
Piotrkow	16,349	7,800	5,680	2,869	1,884	468	938	478
Kalisz	7,795	3,635	1,476	2,684	1,220	503	214	503
Radom	15,938	7,253	5,205	3,840	2,262	573	956	733
Kielce	6,454	3,397	1,220	1,837	632	284	165	183
Total Polish districts	119,371	63,654	30,501	25,216	14,934	5,193	5,342	4,399
Total Pale of Settlement	500,896	259,396	140,528	101,062	76,548	29,911	24,744	21,893

Table A8   Jewish Artisans by Major Occupations according to the JCA Study

Employment Category	Northwest	Southwest	South	Polish Districts	Total Pale
Tailors and dressmakers	39,441	36,014	17,703	35,306	128,464
Cobblers and shoemakers	27,288	17,737	8,100	18,731	71,856
Joiners and carpenters	11,503	10,258	3,555	4,805	30,121
Bakers and pastry cooks	9,562	4,493	1,722	7,165	22,942
Butchers and fishmongers	8,162	6,232	1,870	5,919	22,183
Linen drapers and seamstresses	5,927	6,106	1,682	5,256	18,971
Hatters and capmakers	4,329	5,815	2,860	3,250	16,254
Blacksmiths	6,604	5,629	2,101	1,335	15,669
Coppersmiths and tinsmiths	3,768	3,509	2,072	2,452	11,801
Furniture & cabinetmakers	6,291	2,778	737	1,697	11,503
Stovemakers	6,431	2,905	433	1,438	11,207
Weavers	3,138	660	14	4,425	8,237
Housepainters	2,962	1,777	1,686	1,768	8,193
Knitters	4,106	1,501	483	1,152	7,242
Bookbinders	2,118	2,399	1,112	1,596	7,225
Tanners	3,122	2,293	131	1,517	7,063
Glaziers	2,123	2,231	716	1,623	6,693
Bleachers, dyers	2,630	1,571	928	983	6,112
Barbers, hairdressers	1,873	1,659	700	1,822	6,054
Tobacco cutters, cigarette makers	2,489	1,900	982	625	5,996
Locksmiths	1,974	1,265	1,422	1,040	5,701
Musicians & musical instrument makers	1,472	2,242	759	1,011	5,484
Watchmakers	1,455	1,316	1,053	1,248	5,066

Table A9 Jewish-owned Industrial Enterprises

District	Official Data for 1897			Data of the Jewish Colonization Association Investigation, 1898/99		
	No. of Enterprises	Value of Output (in 1000 rubles)	No. of Workers Employed	No. of Enterprises	Jewish Workers Employed in Jewish Enterprises	Total Jewish Industrial Workers
Vitebsk	120	1,936	2,200	97	2,402	2,525
Minsk	209	4,448	5,119	232	4,308	4,409
Mogilev	186	2,787	5,364	197	1,340	1,417
Vilna	178	6,901	4,281	165	2,322	2,407
Kaunas	134	2,731	1,543	180	1,328	1,402
Grodno	575	11,160	11,598	530	9,304	10,119
Total Northwest	1,402	29,963	30,105	1,401	21,004	22,279
Tchernigov	78	1,173	1,672	39	189	416
Kiev	347	21,335	15,935	168	2,230	2,430
Poltava	152	10,060	2,499	121	977	1,275
Volynia	409	7,316	6,544	288	3,517	3,947
Podolia	157	3,055	1,492	170	1,218	1,528
Total Southwest	1,143	42,940	28,142	786	8,231	9,596

Ekaterinoslav	626		78	3,045	10,713	201
Crimea	387		42	1,147	3,321	81
Kherson	n.a.		n.a.	n.a.	n.a.	n.a.
Bessarabia	1,045		102	1,070	4,247	106
Total South	2,058	2,058	222	5,262	18,281	388
Suwalki	1,196	1,191	109			109
Siedlce	571	537	72			72
Lublin	1,389	1,329	179			179
Lomza	439	428	61			61
Plock	246	246	121			121
Warsaw	4,181	4,047	194			194
Piotrkow	3,119	2,964	287			287
Kalisz	670	662	179			179
Radom	405	387	136			136
Kielce	164	163	78			78
Polish districts[1]	12,380	11,947	1,416			1,416
Total Pale	46,313	43,240	3,825			4,349

[1] Data of the JCA study.

Table A10 Participation of Women in the Industrial Labor Force (Data of the Jewish Colonization Association)

District	Total Jewish Workers	Accounted For	Adults		Children		Percent of		
			Males	Females	Boys	Girls	Women	Girls	Total Females
Vitebsk	2,525	2,518	1,524	661	145	188	26.2	7.4	33.6
Minsk	4,409	4,409	2,162	1,535	286	426	34.8	9.7	44.5
Mogilev	1,417	1,409	958	226	160	65	16.0	4.7	20.7
Vilna	2,407	2,346	1,977	146	66	157	6.2	6.6	12.8
Kaunas	1,402	1,292	673	252	136	231	19.5	17.8	37.3
Grodno	10,119	8,349	4,399	2,672	596	682	32.0	8.2	40.2
Total Northwest	22,279	20,323	11,693	5,492	1,389	1,749	27.0	8.6	35.6
Chernigov	416	406	186	124	12	84	30.5	20.7	51.2
Kiev	2,430	2,430	1,743	128	247	312	5.3	12.8	18.1
Poltava	1,275	1,275	772	431	37	35	33.8	2.8	36.6
Volynia	3,947	3,947	2,966	259	358	364	6.6	9.2	15.8
Podolia	1,528	1,476	1,079	46	206	145	3.1	9.8	12.9
Total Southwest	9,596	9,534	6,746	988	860	940	10.3	9.9	20.2
Ekaterinoslav	626	626	438	27	38	123	4.3	19.6	23.9
Crimea	387	387	225	49	84	29	12.6	7.5	20.1
Bessarabia	1,045	1,045	979	30	36	—	2.8	—	2.8
Total South	2,058	2,058	1,642	106	158	152	5.1	7.4	12.5
Total 14 Districts	33,933	31,915	20,081	6,586	2,407	2,841	20.6	8.9	29.5

Table A11   Transportation Employment, 1898/99 (Data of the Jewish Colonization Association)

District	Coachmen	Carters	Raftsmen	Street Porters, Day Laborers	Total
Vitebsk	693	698	185	851	2,427
Minsk	1,391	1,710	491	1,240	4,832
Mogilev[1]	760	640	96	1,207	2,703
Vilna	807	1,106	430	1,651	3,994
Kaunas[1]	469	885	335	791	2,480
Grodno	861	877	438	1,609	3,785
Total Northwest	4,981	5,916	1,975	7,349	20,221
Chernigov	235	267	11	260	773
Kiev[1]	1,064	772	2	2,009	3,847
Poltava	474	449	—	667	1,590
Volynia	705	665	65	1,890	3,325
Podolia	1,042	766	63	3,218	5,089
Total Southwest	3,520	2,919	141	8,044	14,624
Ekaterinoslav	296	173	7	548	1,024
Crimea	52	86	—	1,206	1,344
Kherson[1]	915	5,689	813	5,758	13,175
Bessarabia	612	709	16	1,953	3,290
Total South	1,875	6,657	836	9,465	18,833
Suwalki	199	172	56	234	661
Siedlce	218	126	16	692	1,052
Lublin	321	345	47	796	1,509
Lomza	358	247	8	224	837
Plock	99	105	—	430	634
Warsaw	667	1,348	9	3,109	5,133
Piotrkow[1]	500	382	6	637	1,525
Kalisz	175	198	1	606	980
Radom	242	302	11	424	979
Kielce	105	102	7	518	732
Total Polish districts	2,884	3,327	161	7,670	14,042
Total Pale	13,260	18,819	3,113	32,528	67,720

[1]Data were either incomplete or lacking for the cities of Mogilev, Kaunas, Kiev, Odessa, and Lodz.

Notes

1. *Recueil de materiaux sur la situation economique des Israelites de Russie, d'apres l'enquete de la Jewish Colonization Association,* vols. 1 and 2 (Paris: Felix Alcan, Editeur, Librairies Felix Alcan et Guillaume Réunies, 1906); referred to here as JCA Study.

2. It might be of interest to note that the Austro-Hungarian Census considered Yiddish a German dialect and reported the Yiddish-speaking Jews as German speaking. Thus, for Austria-Hungary, we have only one figure for Jewish identity—that of religion.

3. The foreign languages reported by Jews as their mother tongue in the Pale were: Polish (46,783), Russian (43,129), German (4,302), Tartar (3,542, by the so-called Krimchaki in Crimea), Lithuanian (533), and other (1,541).

4. One might mention as a "compensating factor" among the Yiddish-speaking population in the Pale, 5,364 members of non-Jewish religious denominations, a certain number of hereditary nobles, priests of the Christian churches, Cossacks, etc.

5. This procedure of the Census might help to explain the inexplicably low census figure of Jews in the liberal professions and the small number listed as bourgeois.

6. See Jacob Lestschinsky, "Evreiskoe Naselenie Rossii," in *Soiuz Russkikh Evreiev: Kniga or Russkom Evreistve* (New York, 1960), pp. 187–88.

7. The cities of European Russia and the Polish Districts also exhibited a higher percentage of the male population in the working-age groups than the average for the regions in general. An analysis of the data for each of the ten Polish districts reveals that the percentage of males of working age is closely correlated with the degree of industrialization and urbanization of the respective districts. So, for example, the districts of Warsaw and Piotrkov had 42 percent and 41 percent of males of working age, while the Suwalke and Lomza districts had 38 percent males in these age groups; the average of males in those age groups in the Polish districts was 41 percent. While the Warsaw and Piotrkov districts were the most industrialized, Suwalke and Lomza were the least industrialized districts. Most of the adjustment took place through internal migration.

8. The JCA Study finds 101,062 apprentices among artisans, and 5,248 children employed in large scale industry in fourteen districts of the Pale. It is clear that the above figures, which account for 18 percent of the 10–19-year age group of the European Russian and Polish districts are not exhaustive, and an estimate of 25–30 percent for the gainfully employed in this age group would probably not be an exaggeration.

9. Probably for cultural reasons the reported total of employed women falls short of actual gainful employment, although another source of the underreporting might be the employment of women in cottage-type industries, which typically utilized much of family labor and in which the tools or machinery (whether a weaving machine or sewing machine) were intensively used almost around the clock, exhibiting a low capital-labor ratio.

10. The data of the JCA Study as reported in the Appendix, table A7, indicate for craft employment a percentage of women of 29.5. It is true that the percentage of females in factory employment as reported in the JCA Study is only 20 percent, but the omissions pertaining to the textile industry and some deficiencies in the reporting of large cities result in an underestimation of the share of women in factory employment. Since within the category of child employment girls make up a higher percentage than boys, we would have, therefore, to assume that at a relatively early age the majority of women disappeared from the labor force. Two explanations are possible: one, that this was the traditional pattern, that marriage signaled the withdrawal of women from the labor force; another would be that the data indicate the emergence of a new pattern of women's employment under conditions of indus-

trialization, of a higher percentage of women's participation in the labor force and of a return of women into the labor force after some time interval. Given the economic conditions of the Jews in Russia, and also taking into account the declining birth rate, etc., I am inclined to accept the second explanation as a plausible one. Unfortunately, we do not have sufficient data to establish the hypothesis, but the occupational structure of Jewish crafts and industrial employment suggests a possibility of substitution of women's employment for male labor in some areas.

11. The first group supposedly includes both employers and employed in the production of goods which would include industrialists, craftsmen, and factory workers. Other data from the JCA Study indicate the existence of over 500,000 employed in crafts and about 46,000 factory workers. Thus, this category is clearly underestimated. Employment in transportation includes coachmen, wagoners, porters, floaters, etc. Employment in private services is a very heterogeneous group, including domestic servants, day laborers, and some private white-collar workers, but also employment in barbershops, baths, and the category of medicine and law (9,135). Employment in trade includes wholesale as well as retail trade. The category of communal services includes teaching, religious services, and community administration.

12. Abraham Menes, "On the Industrial Population among Jews in Russia, 1897" (The JCA and the Census), *Shriften für Wirtschaft and Statistik,* vol. 1 (Berlin, 1928), pp. 255–56.

13. He suggested that to avoid the most glaring deficiencies of both the Census and the JCA Study, the number employed in craft and industry in Warsaw and Lodz (primarily in the textile and metal working industries) ought to be increased by 18,000–20,000, and the industrial employment in Odessa, Bialystok, Ekaterinoslav, and Vilna by at least an additional 15,000. This would increase craft and industrial employment for the territory covered by the JCA Study to about 580,000. For the territory not covered by the JCA Study, Menes assumed an industrial and craft employment of only about 80,000–90,000, since the 22.2 percent of the population omitted in the JCA Study inhabited predominantly small towns and rural areas with a low percentage of industrial and craft employment. Menes is arguing in favor of an estimate of craft and factory employment in the range of 650,000–670,000.

14. One is that the data of the factory inspection (which covered only large-scale factory enterprises) provide higher estimates of employment in a number of industries in which Jewish factory workers were prominently represented (e.g., tobacco and matches); the other is that women's employment in the garment crafts according to the JCA Study is almost four times as high as in the Census. With respect to the latter deficiency, it is possible that the exaggerated figure of personal services and domestics hides at least a part of the employment in the garment industry crafts. I would, however, be inclined to assume that the deficiency of the Census, if compensated for, ought to add at least about 100,000 women to the labor force, with perhaps as high as 60–70 percent adding to craft and industry and the balance to trade. This would perhaps represent an approximation to the employment of full-time equivalent workers in the craft and domestic industries as well as in the small-scale businesses.

15. While the Census data do not distinguish between craft and factory employment, the JCA Study makes such a distinction and provides a somewhat more detailed classification of the occupational distribution within craft employment. The results of both sources are presented in the Appendix tables, which provide the territorial as well as the occupational distributions, and in case of the major crafts provide a ranking of the specific groups in terms of their size. Since the data in the tables are largely self-explanatory, there is no special need to comment on their significance.

16. Ministerstvo Torgovli i Promyshlennosti, Otdel Torgovli, *Remeslenniki i Remeslennee Upravlenie v Rossii* (Petrograd, 1916), pp. 50–54. The reports include data from nineteen out of the twenty-five districts of the Pale.

17. Total Urban Employment in Crafts for Selected Years

	Vitebsk District				Minsk District		
Year	Master Craftsmen	Journey-men	Apprentices	Year	Master Craftsmen	Journey-men	Apprentices
1900	7,760	5,129	2,637	1912	8,511	7,150	4,279
1906	6,970	5,782	4,537	1913	9,127	8,003	5,132
1907	6,649	5,791	4,059	1914	10,121	7,645	3,944
1910	10,206	7,400	4,273				

Source: Akademia Nauk Belorussko, SSR, *Dokumenty i Materialy po Istorii Belorossii (1900–17 gg.)*, vol. 3 (Minsk, 1953), pp. 119, 122, 124–28.

Unfortunately, the evidence cited above is for all craftsmen, without specifying the participation of Jewish artisans. Since the sources do not indicate any radical change in the ethnic composition of the craftsmen, we would assume that the Jewish artisans participated in the growth of craft employment.

18. See section on "The Process of Urbanization" for a discussion of problems of urbanization.

19. The bias in underreporting the cities of Warsaw, Odessa, and Kiev is probably balanced by the underreporting of the rural areas and very small towns. Therefore, I am inclined to accept the distribution between craftsmen, workers, and apprentices as being a close approximation to the existing reality in the Pale.

20. Since the Jewish artisans represented also a higher share in urban crafts than in the total artisan population of the districts, it is difficult at this point (without more detailed information at hand) to separate the occupational characteristics of particular crafts from the effect of the size of the cities. It appears that both effects reinforced each other and produced a higher concentration of Jewish artisans and journeymen in larger shops than for the non-Jewish artisans.

21. The cities are Warsaw, Lodz, Odessa, Vilna, Minsk, Kishinev, Dvinsk, Bialystok, and Gomel.

22. The relatively large number of individuals engaged in the grain trade tended to increase the degree of competition and led to the penetration of the hinterland, higher prices for the producers, breaking down some of the institutionalized patterns of the grain trade in the countryside established previously either by the village "kulaks" or by the wholesale merchants, and contributed to the increase of the marketable share of grain production.

23. Good examples are the utilization of varieties of fish previously outside the purview of the fishing trade, the utilization of grain mixtures, the utilization of inferior qualities of wool for carpeting, the mixture of varieties of cotton for particular industrial purposes.

24. This was more than rhetorical in view of the fact that a substantial number of the owners of capital in the Polish districts, many sugarmill owners, railroad builders, bankers, etc., were converts or descendants of converts, who, although still involved in specific Jewish charities, considered themselves Poles. A similar process took place in St. Petersburg and Moscow. A curious insight in the psychology of the times can be gained from the anecdote ascribed to the famous railroad builder, Jan Bogumil Bloch, who, in reply to a complaint from Jewish merchants who were being forced to advertise using their Jewish rather than polonized first names, said: "What difference does it make if you advertise Stanislaw instead of Samuel? Take me as an example; I am baptized but the Tsar in St. Petersburg, the count Zamoyski in Warsaw, the Jews and I myself know that Bloch is a Jew."

25. (1) We should assume a size of five members per family for families of the hereditary nobility. (2) We will include only male members for the personal nobility (a total of 1,286).

(3) We will assume a family size of four for honorary citizens. The status was awarded at an advanced age when perhaps some of the children were already married and not included in the family membership. (4) For the merchants we will assume that only 50 percent fall in the category of bourgeoisie and that five was the average family size.

26. Abolition of the salt monopoly and étatization of the alcohol industry serve as examples.

27. The JCA Study provided data for twenty-four out of the twenty-five districts of the Jewish Pale, the Kherson District being the exception. Therefore, I have raised the number of Jewish enterprises from 4,349 reported in the JCA Study to a total of 4,500.

28. Sampling is just one of the problems of the data reported by the JCA Study. Since the study relied on the population and not on a representative sample, the fact of major omissions makes the results less reliable.

29. Aleksander Woycicki, in his *Dzieje Robotnikow Przemyslowych w Polsce* (Warsaw, 1929), claims that in the districts of Poland in 1909, a total of 2,450 Jewish-owned enterprises existed employing 107,000 workers with an output of 200 million rubles (p. 207). He does not provide any source for his data, which might or might not compare with the data of the JCA for 1898:1,416 Jewish-owned enterprises and 43,011 workers for the districts of Poland. The growth would be impressive even if the JCA Study was deficient in its coverage in 1898.

30. At a yearly return of about 10 percent on the capital in real estate, excluding capital appreciation and taxes, it was possible to obtain mortgage loans at a relatively low rate of interest in special mortgage banks with the existing real estate as collateral.

31. For purposes of comparison with the number of Jews residing in cities during 1910, the figure of 2,559,549 was used for 1897, but even this figure underestimates the real number of Jews residing in cities. I would not be surprised to find that a more complete canvass of available sources would bring the number of Jews living during the Census in urban areas of the Pale to at least 2.6 million.

32. The alternative of moving beyond the Pale into central Russia was excluded in view of the existing discriminatory regulations.

33. Citing our previous example of migration from the Northwest to the South or to the Polish districts, one can illustrate the cultural problems entailed by calling attention to the fact that a *misnaged* would hardly be socially accepted in a small town dominated by typical Hasidic attitudes, while the likelihood of his being accepted in a larger city with a less culturally homogeneous community was much greater.

34. This ought not to be interpreted as saying that most of the actual absolute population increase took place in the smaller communities. In fact, Warsaw alone accounted for a population increase of 86,933.

35. Wladyslaw Grabski, ed., *Rocznik Statystyczny Krolestwa Polskiego* (Rok, 1913; Warsaw, 1914), pp. 19–35. Even the data in this source underestimate the percentage of Jews living in cities owing to the classification of some relatively large population centers as towns.

36. One could cite as an example the "encouragement" of the exodus of almost 200,000 Tartars from Crimea and Southern Ukrania to Turkey in the late 1850s. The double rate of taxation of the "old believers" is an example of discriminatory policies in a list that includes other groups as well.

37. According to the data of the 1897 Population Census, the Jewish male population of military conscription age in the Pale constituted 11 percent of the total age group. During the subsequent years of mass emigration the actual percentage declined further. The table below reflects the number of Jewish recruits from the Pale and the share of the Jewish recruits in the total inducted into the army from the Pale.

Jewish Army Recruits from the Pale, 1890–1909

Year	Number	Percent of Total	Year	Number	Percent of Total
1890	14,707	12.9	1900	16,083	13.7
1891	15,823	15.0	1901	16,969	13.8
1892	15,429	14.8	1902	17,255	14.0
1893	15,292	14.7	1903	17,281	13.3
1894	14,162	13.3	1904	15,963	9.0
1895	15,154	13.7	1905	16,091	9.7
1896	15,811	14.0	1906	18,291	10.4
1897	15,113	14.0	1907	17,257	10.0
1898	16,362	14.0	1908	17,635	10.0
1899	16,881	14.4	1909	14,419	10.2

It may be of interest to note that the government collected 300 rubles per recruit failing to respond (even if the recruit was dead or abroad) only from Jews and their families, and they inducted other Jews into the army who were legally exempt from military service. Thus Jews were treated not as individuals, but as a group mutually responsible for military service.

38. By analogy, I would like to use the celebrated case of the low level of business ethics on the part of Russian merchants (a point often stressed by Professor Alexander Gerschenkron). How could one expect standards of honesty on the part of Russian merchants when the norms of honesty did not apply in other areas of social interaction, when the body of commercial law was observed in the breach and inviolability of contract was alien to the Russian government, and when there was no recourse to the courts as bodies independent of government administration?

39. Most anti-administration declarations or petitions on the part of groups of Russian businessmen concerned themselves with particular blatant cases of discrimination against individuals of the Jewish faith and invariably invoked the argument of utility rather than right.

40. The classical example is of the textile industry in which the majority of the Jews worked as hand-loom weavers, while the power looms were operated predominantly by non-Jewish workers. The strikes and hostile attitudes of the non-Jewish power-loom weavers delayed the transition of the Jewish textile workers to power-loom employment, causing mass unemployment and reduction of income to thousands of Jewish weavers, many of whom as a result ended up manning the power looms of Paterson and Passaic in New Jersey instead of Lodz and Bialystok.

41. See Salomon Margolin, *Zeitschrift für Demographie and Statistik der Juden* (Berlin, 1908).

42. As a digression, I might mention that Karl Kautsky in a letter written in 1902 called the Jewish workers of Russia "pariahs among the proletarians."

43. It is interesting to note that the conversion of a certain number of people to the Greek-Orthodox faith carried with it the award of the Order of St. Anne. Thus, proselytizing was not only welcomed by the church in Russia but actively encouraged by the government as well.

44. Especially recent migrants from the rural areas, whose families remained in the villages, had lower expenses for housing and food than dwellers in what is now called the "inner city"; they would also accept a lower wage.

45. We do not know the impact of the mutual credit institutions upon the age-old system of interest-free loans provided within the Jewish communities by neighbors and friends, usually for a few days in order to meet an emergency. We know, however, that in the localities where institutions of mutual credit were established, the interest rate on small loans by private

money lenders decreased. The same phenomenon could be observed after 1900 also in Galicia (part of the Hapsburg empire).

46. The particular policies to settle Jews on land, started by Alexander I and continued by Nicholas I, are outside the purview of the problem and will not be discussed here.

47. It is true that the early development of capitalism, which through the competition of large-scale industry caused the pauperization of many small-scale producers, pointed toward such a tendency, but by the end of the nineteenth century it became clear even to socialists (e.g., Eduard Bernstein) that both the growth of the service sector and the survival of a middle class invalidated the early Marxian predictions.

48. The JCA Study provides the following figures for the number of families on a comparable territory receiving assistance from the organized charities: 1894—85,183; 1895—88,459; 1896—93,126; 1897—100,106; 1898—108,922 (JCA Study, vol 2, table 59). We must remember that these years were the heyday of industrialization in Russia, when industrial employment and urban incomes for the country as a whole were growing rapidly.

49. See JCA Study, vol. 2, table 58.

TWO

The Urbanization Process of the Jews in Nineteenth-Century Europe

The purpose of this essay is to consider some aspects of the urbanization process of European Jewish communities in the second half of the nineteenth century. They were selected according to their relevance to the experience of the Jewish communities in the United States. In other words, an attempt is made to inquire into those aspects of the problem that suggest a similarity of experience between European and American Jewish communities. The body of evidence consists primarily of data pertaining to Germany, with some addition, for illustrative purposes only, of data from Galicia.[1] The data pertain to the "later" phase of the urbanization process in Central Europe rather than to the initial period of the massive influx into the cities from the rural areas. The period under consideration, 1880–1914, was one of general urbanization; the share of the Jewish population within the overall urban sector did not increase.

The selected aspects of the urbanization discussed in this essay can be subsumed under the following headings: (1) the record of urbanization and the differential growth rates of various types of cities, (2) the pattern of spatial mobility and migration into the large cities, (3) the employment characteristics of recent migrants from abroad compared with those of the local population, (4) the movement toward the suburbs and the fate of the old "Jewish neighborhoods," (5) the problems of social services for the indigent part of the Jewish population. The process of urbanization of a particular population represents the growth of those members of the group who move from the rural or semi-rural areas to the cities. The urbanization process, in most cases, leads also to changes in the employment distribution of the population and creates adjustment problems of a varied nature for the migrants.

Although it is often assumed that the Jews were a predominantly urban element, this characteristic is only partially true for the first half of the nineteenth century in Central and Eastern Europe.[2] Institutional constraints such as general settlement laws (in Germany on the books until 1848), special discriminatory legislation against Jewish migration or settlement, and lack of civil rights, etc., were still operative during the first half of the nineteenth century.

Therefore, the Jewish migration to the cities, which took place during the 1850s and 1860s, should be considered as the effect of removal of discriminatory legislation and institutional constraints of the earlier period. In addition, the massive stream of overseas migration during the second half of the nineteenth century, which was directed primarily toward the United States but also greatly affected the Jewish communities of England and France, overshadowed in the eyes of historians, demographers, and students of migration the intra- and interregional migrations which contributed to urbanization.

In a number of cases reflecting the migration patterns within a particular country one is confronted with regional migrations of which the urbanization process is an accompanying phenomenon. Within Germany the most conspicuous case is the outmigration from the northeastern region, which included East and West Prussia, Pomerania, and Posen—a migration that started already in the first half of the nineteenth century when the share of this region in the total Jewish population of Germany declined from about 22.7 percent to 13.4 percent (60 percent of the decline came from the province of Posen). Berlin became the chief attraction, intensifying this migration stream. Interregional migrations diminished the share in particular regions, including those of Silesia and Alsace-Lorraine.[3] While the population of Silesia gravitated either toward Berlin or neighboring Saxony, the Jews from Alsace-Lorraine apparently moved to the cities of the Rhineland.

The Jewish population of the larger cities grew at the expense of the smaller cities, while the Jewish population of the middle-sized cities remained stable. The examples of such population concentration, apart from the spectacular growth of Berlin, the capital, were the growth patterns of such cities as Leipzig and Dresden in Saxony, Munich and Nuremberg in Bavaria, Stuttgart in Württemberg, Mannheim in Baden, Cologne in the Rhineland, or Frankfurt am Main and Hanover in Prussia.[4] That the Jewish population of those cities grew as a result of immigration rather than natural growth is abundantly clear from the evidence pertaining to Berlin, Leipzig, and Munich and could be substantiated by the available evidence from other cities.

In conjunction with the role of migration in the Jewish population growth of the large cities one should note the contribution of immigration from abroad. The various data pertaining to the large cities register the arrival and presence of immigrants from Austro-Hungary and Russia.[5]

Such immigrants had problems adjusting, which were different in kind from the problems of the German Jews. The linguistic and social problems of such immigrants, their attitudes toward the traditional culture and toward the demands of their new environment, and their employment problems obviously differed from those of the majority of German Jews involved in interregional migration.

Curiously enough, the descriptions of the East European Jewish immigrants in Germany and their problems bear a great deal of similarity to the contemporary and later descriptions of the Eastern European immigrants into the United States.

One of the results of the urbanization process of the Jewish population in Germany was the decline of the birthrate for the period 1880–1910. The decline can be surmised from the general population data if we take under consideration that the migration out of Germany of the Jewish population did not exceed the immigration from other countries.

However, we also have data that indicate that population growth was declining. For example, the census of 1910 for Prussia indicated that, while the share of the Jews in the total population was 1.04 percent, the share of Jews in the population obliged to attend elementary schools was only 0.70 percent. The data for the city of Hamburg appear to be typical for the Jewish urban population (table 1). Another example of the decline of births is provided by the data for Bavaria where the crude birthrate declined from 32.5 per thousand in 1876–80 to 16.75 per thousand in 1906–9.

The decline of the rate of natural growth of the Jewish population as exemplified by the Hamburg data represented an adjustment of the birthrate to the decline in mortality throughout the century. The precipitous decline in the birthrate was also caused by the increase in income, and perhaps by the substantial increase in mixed marriages and a rising number of conversions to other religions. The increase in the percentage of mixed marriages, although differing among cities and regions, was quite substan-

Table 1 Deaths and Births of the Jewish Population in Hamburg (1881–1910) (per 1,000)

	Births	Deaths	Natural Increase
1881–95	29.5	17.5	12.0
1886–90	23.2	13.9	9.3
1891–95	23.6	14.0	9.6
1896–1900	19.1	11.6	7.5
1901–5	18.4	10.7	7.4
1906–10	15.2	11.4	3.8

Source: *Zeitschrift fur Demographie und Statistik der Juden*, vol. 15, #5–7, pp. 82–88 (hereafter *ZDSJ*).

tial, rising from about 10 percent of the total marriages of Jews around 1880 to as high as 25 percent in some cities on the eve of World War I.[6] The doubts that one harbors about the effects of mixed marriages upon the rate of population growth are mostly due to our ignorance about the identity of the children of such marriages.

During the urbanization period of 1880–1910 in Germany, the Jewish population shifted from trade into industry and the professions, and Jewish women increased their participation in the labor force. In the absence of data for the employment census of 1882, a comparison can be made only for the shorter period between the census of 1895 and that of 1907 (table 2). The increased participation of women in the labor force took place in industry as well as in trade and in the professions, especially in teaching. It is also of considerable interest that within each of the major categories of industry and trade the share of women among the employees and workers was much higher than among the entrepreneurs and managers. This clearly reflected to some extent the late entrance of women into the labor force and the limitations of their skills.

The problem of occupational shifts the Jewish population in Germany experienced and the economic pressure to which it was subjected by the process of urbanization and industrialization was one that not only individuals had to resolve but that had to be faced by the Jewish community as a collective. In order to facilitate the process of skill acquisition in the transition from trade to industrial and craft employment, we find already in 1813 the ''Gesellschaft zur Beforderung der Industrie'' operating in Berlin, its objective to help in training craftsmen. During 1812–25 the society facilitated the training of 107 trainees, and during 1825–98, 1,125 trainees acquired a craft in the school maintained by this society. The 1880s witnessed the setting up of craft training schools in other areas of

Table 2 Distribution of Employed Jewish Population in Germany (1895 and 1907)

	1895		1907	
	Male	Female	Male	Female
Agriculture	2,163	1,208	2,175	1,571
Industry	35,630	10,363	48,089	14,906
Trade	114,328	19,123	117,760	27,846
Public service and professions	12,888	1,753	15,792	2,056
Laborers	207	682	357	993
Domestic servants	73	6,298	26	4,771
Total employed	165,289	39,427	185,978	51,359
Total population	577,356		566,999	

Germany such as Düsseldorf, Cologne, Marburg, Strassburg, and Pankov near Berlin, which combined schooling with craft training and social welfare (maintenance of orphanages).[7] As much as such schools were clearly of importance and served as models for other Jewish communities in helping to resolve the problems of occupational shifts, the majority of individuals who acquired industrial skills apparently used either the existing apprenticeship system or the general technical schooling system rather than the special institutions set up by the Jewish communities or Jewish philanthropies.

A special labor exchange in Berlin placed a total of 34,719 persons in jobs between 1898–1913. The total figure consisted of 12,749 Berlin Jews, 15,272 from other places in Prussia, 911 from other German areas, and 5,821 foreign Jews of which 3,587 were from Austria-Hungary and 1,734 from Russia.[8] Other shifts in the employment structure of the Jewish population, such as expansion into the professions, public service, etc., took place primarily as a result of investments in education and training which were more costly to the individuals and took a longer time but probably yielded a higher return than the skill acquisitions in the craft employment mentioned above.

The quest for education was undoubtedly one of the stimulants of migration and a contributing factor to the urbanization process. At the same time, the urbanization of the Jewish population provided a stimulus of education to the extent that secondary and higher education provided the means for upward social mobility and entrance into the professions. Since institutions of secondary and higher education existed for the most part in the urban center, the solution for the inhabitants of rural areas or of small towns was to send their children there, or to resettle the whole family. Thus, the acquisition of secondary and higher education on the part of the Jewish population could serve as an additional indicator of urbanization, both as a cause and effect. The relative importance of education in the Jewish milieu can be illustrated by the data that we have for Prussia for 1913–14, which indicate that the enrollment of Jews in institutions of secondary education exceeded their share in the total population for males by 5.7 times and for females seven times (see table 7). Data for Jewish enrollment (German Jews only) at Prussian universities indicate the following percentage share in the student body:

1899–1900	8.1 percent
1902–1903	7.4
1905–1906	7.0
1908–1909	6.8

Although the relative share was declining, the absolute numbers were still increasing and represented a very high share by comparison with the 1 percent share of Jews in the total population of Prussia. Similar data are available for the Jewish population of Austria and even Galicia. In the latter, the number of Jewish students in the secondary schools rose from 3,870 in 1900 to 7,897 in 1910, and the number of students at the institutions of higher education (universities and engineering colleges) located in Lvov and Cracow rose from 164 in 1880 to 2,028 in 1910 (see table 7). During the academic year 1909–10 in seven out of nine universities in Austria, all in major cities and growing Jewish communities, the enrollment of Jewish students reached 6,259 (see table 8).

The above data at least suggest that the relationship between educational aspirations and urbanization is one that ought to be taken into account.

However, the existence of secondary schools and universities in major urban areas was attractive to more than Germany's Jews. Discrimination policies limited the access of Jewish students to the universities of Russia, prompting migration of Jewish students from Russia to Germany. Russian Jewish students constituted one of the major groups among the foreign student population at the German universities for the academic year 1913–14: 1,833 students (including 1,393 in medical schools) and 423 in engineering schools. The highest enrollments were in Berlin, Leipzig, Munich, Königsberg, and Breslau—all large cities and most with a growing Jewish population (see tables 3–12).[9]

The movement of a part of the Jewish population from the core of the cities to the suburbs is well documented for Berlin, Hamburg, Frankfurt, and other communities (see table 12, for Berlin). The movement to the suburbs created a number of problems such as the dispersion of the institutions serving the cultural and religious needs of the Jewish population, the maintenance of community cohesion, new forms of assimilation, etc. But while the movement toward the suburbs was taking place, the old tradi-

Table 3   Jewish Population of Munich by Birthplace (1880–1910)

	1880	1885	1890	1895	1900	1905	1910
Born in:							
Munich	1,483	1,729	1,989	2,308	2,573	2,882	3,161
Bavaria	1,552	1,736	2,024	2,186	2,433	2,507	2,568
Other Germany	742	918	1,301	1,602	1,828	2,079	2,324
Total Germany	3,777	4,383	5,314	6,096	6,834	7,468	8,053
Abroad	367	471	794	1,076	1,905	2,588	3,030[1]
Total	4,144	4,854	6,108	7,172	8,739	10,056	11,083

[1]Of the 3,030 born abroad, 1,605 were born in Austria, 861 in Russia, and 329 in Hungary.

Table 4 Jewish Population of Hamburg by Birthplace (1910)

Born in:	
Hamburg (city)	9,190
Prussia	5,956
Rest of Germany	1,655
Outside Germany	1,819
Total Population	18,620

Source: *ZDSJ*, vol. 15, #5–7, p. 80.

Table 5 Jewish Immigration to Berlin from Eastern Europe by Country of Origin

	Galicia	Rumania	Russia	Eastern Europe		
				Male	Female	Total
Before 1881	152	10	389	323	226	549
1881–85	145	17	105	136	131	267
1886–90	390	32	223	366	279	645
1891–95	427	49	253	404	325	729
1896–1900	698	78	357	683	450	1,133
1901–5	1,180	147	772	1,177	922	2,099
1906–10	3,090	233	1,501	2,946	1,878	4,824

tional "Jewish" neighborhoods were not necessarily taken over by non-Jewish groups. A number of the larger cities experienced the influx of Jewish immigrants from abroad, expecially from the East European regions, who moved into the old "Jewish" neighborhoods and shared them with the less prosperous members of the local Jewish communities. Thus, the phenomenon of the "Ostjuden" or Eastern European Jewish immigrants emerged as a series of socioeconomic and cultural problems which both the local communities and the immigrants had to face. The East European immigrants who settled in Germany had a great deal in common with the immigrants who went to the United States. They were young (the majority were 15–30 years old and male), willing to work, with a high savings rate out of their current income. Because learning German was easier

Table 6 Enrollment of Jewish Students in Higher Education in Galicia (1880–1910)

	1880	1890	1900	1910
University of Cracow	45	191	209	481
University of Lvov	88	209	405	1,350
Polytechnic at Lvov	31	17	97	197

Table 7   Jews Enrolled in Secondary Schools in Prussia (1913–1914)

	Number	% School Population
Males:		
Gymnazium and progrimnarium	7,266	6.2
Realgymnazium	4,274	6.0
Ober real schools	2,003	3.8
Real schools	2,324	6.5
Total	15,868	5.7 (average)
Females:		
Lyceums	10,509	7.2
Oberlyceums	223	2.4
Other	526	11.9
Total	11,258	7.0 (average)

Table 8   Enrollment in Austrian Higher Education (1909–1910)

	University	Technical
Vienna	2,281	794
Prague (German)	355	278
Prague (Bohemian)	67	87
Lvov	1,281	205
Cracow	422	. . .
Chernovets	414	. . .
Brno	. . .	132
Graz	50	38
Innsbruck	5	. . .
Total	4,875	1,534

Table 9   Jewish Population of Leipzig by Birthplace

	1885	1890	1900	1905	1910
Leipzig (Saxony)	945	1,109	1,674	1,214	1,180
Other Germany	1,763	1,730	1,849	1,619	1,878
Austria Hungary	526	793	1,774	3,127	4,029
Other	406	503	874	1,716	2,397
Total	3,640	4,135	6,176	7,676	9,484

Table 10   Birthplace of the Jewish Population in Selected Cities (1880)

	Berlin	Breslau	Frankfurt	Posen	Königsberg
Local origin	18,949	4,273	5,681	4,314	2,670
Province	4,148	8,495	2,003	2,103	
Prussia	25,520	3,616	1,085	322	831
Other Germany	1,711	115	4,345	10	24
Russia	2,014	483	139	250	1,529
Austria Hungary	940	446	216	13	12
Total	53,916	17,543	13,856	7,063	5,082

for them than English, they could seek employment in all areas of the cities and could also settle near their workplaces. Nevertheless, many immigrants settled in Berlin's old Jewish quarter (Grenadierstrasse, Dragonerstrasse, Schendelgasse), near the old Jewish communal institutions and orthodox houses of worship, where they, in the eyes of the German Jews, tried to perpetuate their Eastern European life-style. "Women sat in front of the houses"; "In the evening the streets are teaming"; "Bookstores and libraries abound;" "Yiddish newspapers are read here"; and similar statements appeared in studies of the immigrant community. They have a familiar ring; they can be substituted easily in the descriptions of the "pletzel" in Paris, the East End of London, and New York's East Side. To the extent that the system of "Jewish organization" of the clothing trades was developed in Germany prior to the arrival of this wave of immigrants, they didn't fit into the managerial or entrepreneurial roles and were employed as workers. Perhaps a new, typically Jewish immigrant industry

Table 11   Jewish Population in Selected German Cities (1880–1910)

	1880	1885	1890	1895	1900	1905	1910
Berlin	53,916	65,611	80,761	94,391	106,656	103,487	142,289
Frankfurt	13,856	15,554	17,426	19,488	21,974	23,476	26,228
Breslau	17,543	17,655	17,754	18,449	19,743	20,356	20,212
Hamburg	16,014	16,848	17,877	17,308	17,949	18,798	18,932
Cologne	4,523	6,719	6,859	7,932	9,745	11,035	12,156
Munich	4,144	4,845	6,108	7,172	8,739	10,056	11,083
Mannheim	. . .	4,672	4,873	4,768	5,478	5,998	6,627
Posen	7,063	5,309	6,126	5,810	5,988	5,761	5,605
Hanover	3,450	3,627	3,933	4,151	4,540	4,923	5,155
Stuttgart	2,864	2,985	3,196	3,125	3,505	3,896	4,291
Leipzig	3,179	3,640	4,136	4,872	6,176	7,676	9,434
Total	. . .	147,474	169,049	187,466	210,493	242,462	262,012

Table 12 Jewish Populaton of Greater Berlin

	1840	1852	1861	1871	1875	1880	1885	1890	1895	1900	1905	1910	1915	1925
Greater Berlin	6,456	11,840	18,953	36,326	45,464	53,916	65,611	80,761	95,391	106,656	130,487	142,289		172,672
Berlin City				36,015			64,383	79,286	86,152	92,206	98,893	90,013		87,242
Charlottenburg				142			478	1,475	4,687	9,701	15,604	22,508	30,557	
Shöneberg				8			14		354	989	4,297	9,698	20,924	
Wilmersdorf				35			159		1,399	2,994	6,929	11,641	16,115	
Neukölln							82		220	450	1,176	2,980	2,742	
Lichtenberg				6			41		185	316	471	685	1,458	

was cigarette making; initially produced in the home by the family, it was expanded into a major local industry employing Jewish immigrant women. In terms of poor relief, the immigrant community did not become a special burden to the locals, although their share of support received, for example in Berlin, slightly exceeded their share in the total Jewish population.[10]

Some of the existing studies[11] provide the characteristics of urban poverty as we know them from the studies of urban life elsewhere. Thus, the condition of overcrowding in substandard housing (lack of toilets or water), the inadequacy of furniture (of 1,560 people observed in the Frankfurt study, 767 had their own beds, 772 slept two in a bed, and 21 slept three in a bed), the presence of boarders in more than half of the apartments, many of which were not separated from the family's sleeping quarters, were familiar features. The high share of rent in the incomes of the poor, the concentration of poverty in the categories of low skills, the presence of either small and numerous children on the one hand, or old people on the other hand, sometimes combined with poor health (high incidence of tuberculosis, heart illness or mental disorders) and undernourishment, are some of the additional characteristics of poverty among the Jews in the large cities.

The brief and sketchy discussion of some of the problems of the urbanized Jewish communities in Europe, using the case of Germany as an illustration, was intended primarily to demonstrate the usefulness of studying the history of European Jewish communities in order to gain a better understanding of the urbanization problems of Jews in the United states. Anyone studying the United States who ignores the wealth of documentation about European Jewry in the urban context will have "to discover America after Columbus."

Notes

1. The data for England, France, Vienna, Budapest, and the Russian Empire are left out, all for what I consider valid reasons.

2. The term "urban" would also depend upon one's definition, whether the term is applied to settlements according to a particular administrative convention, or whether one would define a city in terms of size larger than 1,000, 2,000 or 5,000 inhabitants.

3. The share of Silesia declined from 9.1 percent to 8.1 percent and Alsace-Lorraine from 8 to 5.5 percent.

4. See table 11.

5. We have in mind the immigrants who arrived there primarily for economic reasons with the resolve to settle in Germany rather than the numerous students who came from Russia for the completion of their education and acquisition of specialized skills. We will deal with the

problem of foreign students later while considering the relationship between urbanization and education.

6. The data for Hamburg indicate a rise of mixed marriages from 13.1 percent in 1886–90 to 24.3 percent in 1906–10. See *ZDSJ* 15, #5–7:85.

7. See *ZDSJ* 4, #1–2 (1927): 16–19, for the activities of such societies and the number of trainees.

8. See *ZDSJ* 11, #2–3: 29.

9. *ZDSJ* 10, #4: 61–62.

10. See, for materials on the above topics, the article by Dr. Klara Eschenbacher, "Die Ostjudische Einwanderunsbevölkerung der Stadt Berlin," *ZDSJ* 16, #1–6: 1–24.

11. See especially the article by Dr. Gustav Löffler, "Die Wohnverhältnisse der minder-bemittelten jüdischen Bevölkerung in Frankfurt am Main vor dem Kriege," *ZDSJ* 12, #7–9: 91–104.

THREE

Notes on Jewish Entrepreneurship in Tsarist Russia

It is incumbent upon an economic historian dealing with a particular area of economic activity to put the activity and the participants of the economic process not only in a historical context but also within categories of a body of economic theory.

Thus, by focusing upon the phenomenon of entrepreneurship of individuals who shared a common religious, cultural, or national heritage, in this case a Jewish one, it is still necessary to explain, or argue, in which sense their activities can be considered entrepreneurial.

Economists and economic historians have variously described the entrepreneurial function emphasizing different aspects of those functions as risk taking, innovation, etc. Entrepreneurial activity is described as one that grows out of the ability of certain individuals to deal with disequilibria in the market.[1] Such disequilibria are not necessarily limited to short-term discrepancies between two sets of prices, nor do they consist of unanticipated profit opportunities arising out of the difficulties in discounting the effects of market situations. Entrepreneurial activity arises often as a by-product of change, out of changes in factor prices, etc., and concerns the reallocation of resources, the reorganization of production or distribution, based upon the entrepreneur's perception of change and foresight about its direction. It is, therefore, convenient to focus upon the element of economic change as both the cause and the effect of entrepreneurial activity. Economic change can often be quantified and its effects attributed to changes of particular factors. Therefore, it is possible to study entrepreneurship within the context of economic change using some of the tools provided by economic growth theory. Jews constituted a minority of the

Occasional Paper no. 57, Wilson Center, Kennan Institute for Advanced Russian Studies, 1978. Published in G. Guroff and F. Carstensen, eds., *Entrepreneurship in Imperial Russia and the Soviet Union* (Princeton, N.J.: Princeton University Press, 1983).

population and were therefore acting according to behavioral norms or patterns characteristic of a minority. Jewish entrepreneurship might have had different effects upon the Jewish community—the "economy of the Jews"—than upon the community at large.[2] The difference owes to the minority position of the Jews and to discrimination. The vast majority of the Jewish population and also the chief areas of their entrepreneurial activities were located in the so-called Pale of Settlement, a territory outside of which Jews could not settle in Russia. A detailed knowledge of the economy of this region is needed for an evaluation of Jewish entrepreneurial activities and for the economic structure of the Jewish community. But while largely confined to the Pale of Settlement, Jewish entrepreneurs, with increasing success, attempted to break out of the discrimination they met with in the Pale. Thus, during the latter part of the period entrepreneurial activity undertaken by individual Jews outside the Jewish Pale of Settlement became more frequent and their effect upon the Jewish community weakened.

A special problem for the study of entrepreneurial activity by Jewish businessmen is the paucity of data that could throw sufficient light on the family and social backgrounds, education, source of capital, and scope of activities of a large number of entrepreneurs which would permit the construction of representative samples for the different categories of Jewish entrepreneurs.[3] In the absence of such data a student of Jewish entrepreneurship runs into the danger of generalizing from a very small and often unrepresentative sample and using anecdotes instead as a substitute for evidence. The availability of biographical material would certainly enhance our ability to categorize Jewish entrepreneurs in terms of observed patterns of entrepreneurial activity whose origins may be either in commerce or banking, in technical expertise pertaining to industry, or in the accumulation of experience and capital leading from craft to larger-scale industrial enterprise. Such data could presumably explain their ability to adapt foreign models for their activity and help us to understand the complex motives as well as their attitudes to the different economic and cultural environments within which they operated. The absence of detailed data on most of the entrepreneurs puts severe limitations upon the analysis of their role and activity.

Since discussion of the historical background for Jewish entrepreneurship in Russia is outside the scope of this essay, it is perhaps necessary to point out a few of the changes in the legal and social status of the Jews which had a direct bearing upon the activities of actual or potential entrepreneurs. While the Pale of Settlement for Jews in Russia was to a large extent a *de jure* recognition of the *de facto* settlement which the Russian Empire inherited as a result of the partitions of Poland, the only exception for Jewish settlement of the "Russian" territories was made with respect to the provinces adjacent to the Black Sea. Those provinces, an object of Russian colonization policies of the eighteenth and nineteenth centuries, were opened for Jewish agricultural and urban settlement, while the rest of the empire remained closed for the resettlement of Jews.[4] However, until 1850 not all provinces within the Pale of Settlement were treated alike, since until that year the territory of Congress Poland had its own tariff, and until about 1860 the legal status of the Jews in the Polish provinces was based upon the legislation of Congress Poland, while in the Lithuanian, Byelorussian, and Ukrainian provinces Imperial legislation prevailed. Given the limited autonomy of the Polish provinces and their attempts to industrialize during the early decades of the nineteenth century, Jewish businessmen were treated perhaps more favorably than in the rest of the Pale, although this treatment did not reflect a recognition of their rights as much as a more lenient extension of individual privileges granted by the authorities. Within the other provinces of the Pale, the Jewish entrepreneurs suffered the most from disabilities imposed upon the whole Jewish population until about the beginning of the reign of Alexander II (1855). The general liberalization of government policies during the late 1850s and the 1860s also affected the Jewish entrepreneurial group, providing the merchants of the first and second guilds permission to conduct their business outside the Pale, at least for part of the year, or for Jews with higher secular education or especially "useful" skills to practice within or outside the Pale. While there existed a certain inconsistency between the granting of rights and the enforcement of such rights, left to the local administration, the general liberalization trend made possible an increase in the acquisition of higher quality skills. However, given the enthusiastic response to the opening up of new economic and educational opportunities, during the 1880s the trend of governmental policies toward the Jews was reversed and caused a number of economic dislocations in the employment structure of the Jewish community. While new economic opportunities during the previous period had a favorable economic effect and even contributed to a rapid rate of population increase of the Jewish population, the growth of the market in the Pale of Settlement was insufficient to provide employment and incomes for the growing Jewish population. The restrictions on rural settlement and rural trade imposed by the government legislation of the 1880s further aggravated the high intensity of competition in the trade sector and hastened the shift from trade into crafts and industrial employment for the Jewish population within the Pale. It also intensified the process of spatial migration within the Pale and the urbanization process. Last, it provided additional momentum to a migration, the latter presumably depriving Russian Jewry of a mobile, enterprising element within the population. Thus, both the changes in governmental policies toward the Jews during its more "liberal" and more restrictive periods contributed to processes of employment shifts, changes in regional and demographic distribution of the population, income differentiation, and the formation of a Jewish bourgeoisie and a Jewish industrial proletariat. It is important to keep this background in mind while discussing the problems of Jewish entrepreneurship.

The Origin of Capital of the Jewish Entrepreneurs

One of the "classical" theses about the origin of capital at the disposal of Jewish entrepreneurs follows closely the analogy with non-Jewish entrepreneurs in economically backward countries, or at the early stages of industrial entrepreneurship, preceding the development of a banking system. This is the thesis of government contracts and tax farming: government or army supply contractors as well as alcohol tax-farmers, invested in textile mills, tanneries, or distilleries in order to assure a portion of their supplies or to derive an additional profit. Beginning at the end of the eighteenth century Jewish army contractors in Poland, and, during the first half of the nineteenth century, Jewish alcohol tax-farmers in Russia, followed this practice.[5] However, it would be mistaken to generalize from a very small population. A much more plausible case for the origins of capital is presented, at best, for the first half of the nineteenth century, by the profits derived from foreign trade. The participation of Jewish merchants in foreign trade, especially along the Western borders was significant. However, there were limitations to this growth imposed by the slowly growing demand of Russia's Western neighbors. At the same time it was observed that a number of merchants engaged in foreign trade were investing in textile factories and tanneries, and some of their output was among their exports.[6] If we assume that only half the profits in foreign trade (assumed as 10 percent of the trade turnover) were invested in industry, this would clearly exceed any estimate of growth of capital in Jewish industrial enterprises.[7] Thus, both the direct evidence of capital transfers from foreign trade to industrial entrepreneurship, the profits from foreign trade, the locational proximity of capital accumulation in foreign trade, and establishment of industrial enterprises during the first half of the nineteenth century make foreign trade activity a plausible source for capital used by Jewish entrepreneurs.

Entrepreneurial activity, spread out over a large territory, originally perhaps with a low density and often outside the reach of a capital-market, derived its largest source of capital from those engaged in internal trade. Certainly a pattern of entrance into industrial entrepreneurship from the commercial or financial side of industrial activity points to the importance of domestic trade as a major source of capital. The data on about 350 industrial establishments owned by Jews in the textile centers of Bialystok and Lodz for the period of 1861–1900 seem to confirm this pattern in the textile industry. The data on growth of output and of capital in a large portion of those textile enterprises imply a rate of return that exceeded the profit rate in trade achieved by Jewish merchants in a number of gubernias as reported in the works by Jan Bloch and Subbotin for the 1880s. If we also assume that intense competition in trade tended subsequently to lower the profit margins, it would follow that during the later period the rate of return to capital in industry exceeded that in trade and made a transfer of capital not only plausible but economically advantageous where such opportunities existed.

Large-scale industrial entrepreneurship, however, required credits of substantial size, not only for the initial capital outlays but also as operating capital for the purchase of raw material, for wages, storage, transportation, and credit to customers. Such credits, both long and short term, could be provided only by banking institutions. During the first half of the nineteenth century industrial entrepreneurs would typically obtain bank financing by taking in the private bankers as partners in their enterprises. Since most of the private banks owned by Jews were located originally in trade centers rather than in industrial areas, and the banks were apparently engaged in lending to landowners and to the government, etc., extending loans to low-risk customers, the instances of financing of industrial entrepreneurs were not numerous. By the mid-century the situation began to change in two directions. First, Jewish bankers in some financial centers became more amenable to the idea of extending at least short-term credit to industrial entrepreneurs, and, second, industrialists began to support the establishment of commercial banks in the industrial centers to serve growing industries. The new banks, established in the 1870s with active participation of Jewish businessmen, found their task facilitated by the growing vertical integration of Jewish enterprises and thus served both producers and distributors of manufactured goods. Vertical integration enabled the new banks greatly to increase the scope of their lending operations without having to expand their capital proportionately. Drawing both upon the balances of the merchants and the industrialists, the banks were able to increase the velocity of their assets.

Jewish banks made a special effort to attract savings from non-Jews and to borrow from Jewish banks abroad. In both endeavors, they appeared to be quite successful. The record of Jewish participation in private banking in Russia indicates that the banks were capable of paying high interest and dividends and their connections with the Jewish banks in Germany and later in France resulted in capital imports to Russia.[8]

Our discussion on the origin of capital of the Jewish industrial entrepreneurs would be incomplete without mentioning the gradual, incremental self-financing by industrialists themselves. The plowing back of profits, typical of small-scale enterprises, took place on a massive scale among Jewish entrepreneurs.[9] Given the relative scarcity of capital, the limitations upon investment opportunities, a high saving ratio and the plowing back of profits appeared to have been rational.

The Attitudes and Characteristics of Jewish Entrepreneurs

The prevailing view of the character of entrepreneurship suggests a type of deviant personality, risk prone, and rebellious against the established order. We might better stress their heightened perception of new opportunities and of regularities in organization and activities where others perceived none. They can better be thought to restore equilibrium and promote their own economic and social status than to destroy an order. Within the Jewish milieu, entrepreneurs were judged as individuals in relation to the benefits their activities conferred on the Jewish community. Thus, there was no reason to assume a *prima facie* conflict between the Jewish community and the Jewish entrepreneurs.

There was hardly an area of entrepreneurial activity from which Jewish entrepreneurs were successfully excluded. Apart from the manufacturing industries in the Pale, they were at the oil wells of Baku, in the gold mines of Siberia, on the fisheries of the Volga or Amur, in the shipping lines on the Dnieper, in the forests of Briansk, on railroad construction sites anywhere in European or Asiatic Russia, on cotton plantations in Central Asia, etc. Their mass was concentrated in the Pale, with a much lower density outside. Thus, the ones in the Pale were the most typical, and they differed from the ones operating outside of the Pale by degree only. They came mostly from the so-called middle strata, from a merchant rather than craftsmen background, and possessed above-average education. The ones who came from a poorer background must have possessed even more talent, discipline, drive, and perseverance to overcome initial disabilities. The acquisitive instinct of some was proverbial. Some of them would seek publicity, some anonymity. Only a minority, the ones who rose from the ranks of craftsmen mostly, gained a reputation within the Jewish milieu as ruthless exploiters. Status within the Jewish community followed the rise of wealth with a substantial time lag. The traditional leadership within the community was not eager to share power and influence with the newcomers; the plebeian masses had a traditional distrust of the rich.

Some historians writing about eighteenth- and nineteenth-century Jewish history assumed that entrepreneurial activity, or, for that matter, an intensive business contact between Jews and Gentiles involving people at a higher level of secular culture, created a dilemma for those Jews who they perceived had a choice between assimilation and the traditional Jewish culture. The relatively high percentage of religious conversions and strong assimilationist tendencies among German Jews or Warsaw Jews involved in high finance colored the views of such historians. Broadening of the informational base about Jewish entrepreneurs sheds considerable doubt upon this traditional view. For the majority of first-generation Jewish entrepreneurs such a dilemma did not seem to exist. It is true that some of them operated in two distinct worlds, one of intensive business contact with the outside and the other of the organized Jewish communities. But very few of them considered those two worlds incompatible for the following reasons. First, the typical large urban Jewish community with its concerns for education, training, welfare, and religious needs was a modern and not medieval institution. Second, the religious and cultural values of their heritage were not considered insignificant to be exchanged for an approving nod of the Gentile world, but a rich spiritual heritage. Third, the experience of the 1880s taught Jewish entrepreneurs that the acquisition of a Russian cultural veneer was insufficient to protect them against persecution and discrimination and that the language assimilation alone would not earn them the status in Russian society to which they felt entitled by the criteria of wealth and cultural sophistication. Thus, they opted for a combination of the indigenous Jewish culture and elements of modern European culture.

The disapproval of the larger environment was discounted by the satisfaction derived from philanthropic or cultural activity within the Jewish milieu, and the disapproval of the ultraconservative elements within the Jewish community was countered by activity in modernizing certain features of Jewish life. Therefore, Jewish entrepreneurs appeared occasionally impervious to slurs and slights suffered from Russian bureaucrats and their competitors but cherished an inner pride in their own accomplishments. Over and above, it was a group of rational men, knowledgeable of the realities of the world, of the marketplace, and of their own worth and calling.

Certain behavioral traits common in the traditional society from which they hailed were discernable in their business and personal relations. The reliance upon kinship ties in their business, the arrangement of the proper marriages which would maximize their business opportunities were a part of the behavior of business-oriented groups in many cultures, and we find it also among Jewish entrepreneurs.[10] The sense of ''noblesse oblige'' among owners of inherited wealth toward the Jewish community did not weaken with social advancement.[11] However, generational change produced some conflict between the first generation of Jewish entrepreneurs and their children: some of their children remained in the businesses and followed successful business careers, some opted for the professions, the arts, and some became leading personalities in the revolutionary movements,[12] but most of them moved away from the Jewish milieu.

The Role of Jewish Entrepreneurs in the Transition from Serf to Free Labor in Industry

The existence of industrial production based upon the use of serf labor in eighteenth and first-half nineteenth century Russia is well known to students of economic history. Not only in metallurgy but also in textiles and food-processing industries a large proportion of the employed labor force consisted of serfs. Most of the industrial enterprises used raw materials produced on estates and the available labor with little capital expenditures. Even enterprises established by non-noblemen tried to receive an allotment of serf-labor resources at a relatively low price from the state.

It is therefore of considerable interest to find Jewish entrepreneurs already during the first decades of the nineteenth century in a number of regions acting as administrators of industrial establishments of the gentry or leasing such establishments for various periods of time. It might not be an exaggeration to state that gentry-owned industrial establishments were among "the first schools of industrial management" for Jewish entrepreneurs. It is in such regions as Volynia, Grodno, and Podolia that we find a heavy concentration of Jewish entrepreneurs engaged in industrial activities in the woolen industry. The data for 1828–32 show that among non-nobility industrial enterprises in Volynia, 93.3 percent belonged to Jewish entrepreneurs and in Podolia 32 percent. Most of the enterprises belonged to Jewish merchants of the first guild, while among the burgher entrepreneurs the participation was relatively smaller, 75 percent for Volynia and 43.8 percent for Podolia.[13]

As leasees of the landlords' establishments the Jewish entrepreneurs surpassed the often absentee owners by increased concentration on the financial aspects of the enterprises, by their ability not to rely exclusively on the state's demand for military woolen cloth, by seeking new markets either in the Ukraine or abroad (even in the Chinese trade), and by utilizing some of the skills of Jewish weavers acquired in the Grodno region at the end of the eighteenth century, and by the establishment of a training factory in Kremenchug in 1809. Thus, we find migration patterns for skilled workers from Grodno and Kremenchug to Jewish-leased or Jewish-owned woolen enterprises already in the first decades of the nineteenth century. Both Jewish- and Ukrainian-owned enterprises had the advantage of greater flexibility of location,[14] the access to a free labor force and more advanced technology which, using more capital, economized on the costs of labor and decreased the costs of production.[15]

The competition between the two types of woolen industry, the serf-based enterprises and the one based upon free labor took place at two levels: within the same region and between regions. In both types of competition Jewish enterprises were pitted against the serf-based enterprises. The Jewish woolen mills of Volynia and Podolia undersold the serf-based enterprises of those regions, and Jewish firms of the Bialystok region (of Grodno gubernia) successfully competed in the Ukraine with the local serf-based enterprises. As a result of this competition, by the late 1850s, even before the emancipation of the serfs, there were no serf-based woolen establishments left in operation.

Jewish entrepreneurship in the sugar industry, beginning in the first half of the nineteenth century, followed a similar pattern. The Russian sugar industry based on sugar beets started in the early years of the nineteenth century on the estates of the large landowners in Poland and the Ukraine, where it grew the fastest. As in the case of the woolen cloth, Jewish entrepreneurs entered the sugar industry as lenders to the noble owners of sugar mills, or as leasees and partners with the owners. This was the ''apprenticeship'' period for Jewish entrepreneurs to learn the intricacies of the industry in question. Later they would establish their own sugar mills, and succeed by adopting technological improvements and expanding the supply of raw materials by entering forward contracts with estates and peasants. The system of forward contracts permitted both the improvements of the quality of the raw material as well as the quality of the products.

While some of the Jewish entrepreneurs had prior experience, many entered alcohol distilling from trade or finance and therefore concentrated on improving distribution more than production. This type of activity coincided with the expansion phase of the sugar industry, and the search for markets and marketing techniques was timely. Jewish sugar entrepreneurs, contrary to the customs prevailing among the noble producers, would sell their output either at the mills, or at the nearby railroad stations; Jewish manufacturers introduced a system of forward contracts, negotiated at the exchange in Kiev, and the larger producers began to develop separate sales networks, based upon established warehouses located in the major urban and mercantile centers of Russia, and employing itinerant salesmen working on a commission basis for the particular sugar companies.[16]

Not only did free labor replace serf labor in the sugar industry of the Ukraine, but the various forms of corvee-type labor which existed during the first decades after the serf emancipation quickly disappeared following the example of the Jewish enterpreneurs in sugar production. Technological improvements and higher skill requirements both dictated a free mobile labor force which could adapt itself to the demands of the industry.

The relative success of Jewish entrepreneurs in the sugar industries could be. illustrated by the available data for the Ukraine on the eve of World War I. About one-third of the sugar mills belonged to Jewish owners and produced about 52 percent of the refined sugar. In the corporate sector of the industry, Jews constituted 42.7 percent of the board members and 36.5 percent of the board chairmen.[17]

The employment opportunities for Jews created by Jewish entrepreneurs in the sugar industry were substantial, although the exact figures are not available. Given the existing severe limitations on Jewish settlement in the rural areas, especially after the legislation of 1882, and the availability of cheap rural labor for most of the menial occupations in sugar production, one would not expect a high participation rate of Jewish workers in the sugar mills. Except for a few cases earlier in the century where Jewish entrepreneurs acquired land and settled on it, Jewish families who worked in these sugar mills[18] were more likely to be employed in jobs requiring higher technical skills and in the offices of the mill administration.[19]

There were a number of industries in which the distinction between serf and free labor was less significant than the existence of a dual economy. Alongside many small craftlike enterprises, operating with primitive techniques, there existed highly specialized large-scale enterprises, in flour milling, leather tanning, tobacco, and also in fisheries and wood processing.

The entrepreneurs had to collect goods which were produced in small quantities over an extensive territory relying on the existing network of trading peasants often labelled as kulaks, with monopoly positions in the different localities, and who paid prices to the producers which often reflected the market conditions, and failed as a sufficient incentive to increase production.

The Jewish entrepreneurs, with long-term goals in mind, had to break up the local monopolies, and through agents they entered into competition with the local kulaks. As a rule the primary producers benefited from this new competition between the old and new intermediaries and often responded with an increase of their marketed output. Alongside of the organization of the raw materials supply, the use of by-products in the processing of the raw materials often became an important concern of the entrepreneurs. The case of the Azov Sea and Volga fisheries provides a good example of this type of activity of the Jewish entrepreneurs.[20] Until they entered the fisheries industry, only the high-priced fish varieties were processed, while a large part of the fish catch would simply be thrown out or used for fish oil. It was their use of the less expensive varieties of fish that increased the value of the catch very substantially. The use of the raw materials for the production of new goods, such as modern ties for the railroads, the broadening of the assortment, the finding of substitutes for previous uses, and the decrease of the waste of raw materials created new sources of incomes and profits. The standardization of the products and its preparation to suit the taste of the clients was another area of entrepreneurship. The examples of hundreds of skilled Jewish fish processors and packers (called *uborschiki*) employed in Astrakhan to suit the tastes of Western Russia and foreign consumers, the employment of thousands of Jewish overseers (brackers) skilled in the production of railroad ties and construction materials for the tastes of German and British importers were examples of the significance attributed to the product improvements. Last, the opening up of Western European markets for frozen fish from the Amur River in far eastern Siberia illustrates the ability of entrepreneurs to utilize the latest developments in refrigeration technology, to increase production, and to broaden the market for their products.

The Entrepreneur in Service of Governmental Policies

The subordination of economic interests to the interests of the state was an old standing tradition in Russia, and the use of various social groups for the achievement of government objectives continues there up to this day. Whether the state tried various combinations of incentives, persuasion, and force, depended to a large extent upon the degree to which the interests of the state were congruent with the interests of a particular group and upon the urgency behind particular policies or services demanded by the state.

The important role of the contractor, serving the military, the central, or local government is well known in the historical literature and does not require special elaboration. Jewish contractors were not given priority in any kind of contracts but had to compete in price and quality. If the various government institutions would have followed the practice of the marketplace, their decisions, even with discrimination, would have followed a middle course in awarding the contracts, but as quasi-monopolists, in fact, institutional decision makers probably practiced strong discrimination. This forced the entrepreneurs among the Jewish contractors to devise means to reduce their costs by comparison with non-Jewish competitors. They organized a network of subcontractors, and sped up their operations, diminishing the cost of capital.

The real test of the ability of contracting took place not at the stage of commodity supply contracts to the military, in which cases contractors were even forced to organize their own manufacturing facilities for goods in which no reliable supply could be obtained, but at the level of large construction projects involving railroad and port facilities. Such projects involved not only hiring large quantities of labor and procurement of new types of producer goods but also very substantial capital outlays and organization of credit flows.

The first experience for Jewish entrepreneurs in this kind of contracting was the construction of the Warsaw-Vienna railroad[21] and involved a consortium of Jewish contractors and financiers of Warsaw. Jewish contractors gained additional experience in the construction of the Moscow-Smolensk and Moscow–Brest Litovsk railroads. This accumulated experience was utilized by Samuel Poliakov, who built the Kozlov-Voronezh-Rostov line, the Kursk-Kharkov-Azov line, the Oriol-Griazi, the Bender-Galatz lines, and participated in the construction of others. The "secret" of Poliakov's success was his ability to obtain credits from Russian and foreign banks, to organize the system of subcontracting, and the speed, if not necessarily the quality, of construction and exploitation.[22] In a situation of scarce capital and relatively low wages, this was probably an optimal strategy for an entrepreneur.

The participation of Jewish entrepreneurs in large-scale construction projects had a number of effects both upon the employment of Jews in the Pale, from among whom the subcontractors were drawn, creating a kind of backward linkage, and for the Russian economy for which the participation of foreign capital not only in the sale of railroad bonds, but also in lending operations for construction was important.

The Entrepreneur's Role as Promoter of Integration and Efficiency

During the early stages of industrial development, the chief function of the industrial entrepreneur, in the Schumpeterian sense, was the creation of new productive factors in order to increase output of old and new industrial goods. Simultaneously, the entrepreneurs operating in the commodity and financial markets facilitated the growth of the market for goods and factors of production.

At a more advanced stage of industrial development, a new field of entrepreneurial activity opened up: the integration of existing industrial and productive capacities with the existing social overhead and the distribution system, thereby achieving higher levels of efficiency out of these combinations. With a railroad system the analogy would be to create out of various existing unplanned railroad lines an efficient, unified network.

This field of entrepreneurial activity opened up in Russia in the years

1908–17.[23] As in other European countries, this process of integration of industrial firms, elements of overhead capital and business services in Russia, took place with the assistance of banks. The case of Jewish entrepreneurship in the area of water transportation provides an interesting example of this new field of entrepreneurial activity.

The mass participation of Jewish entrepreneurs and Jewish employees in the fields of land and water transportation on the territory of the Pale of Settlement was long-standing and could be explained by their participation in the commodity trade. Thus, already by the middle of the nineteenth century one could find well-organized enterprises in river transportation on the Vistula, Neman, and Dnieper.[24] But the interests of the Jewish entrepreneurs were not limited to the area of the Pale with its meager resources and expansion potential. By 1876, the banking firm of E. Ginzburg founded the "Shipping Company for the Sheksna River" which provided an opening to the Volga River waterway. By the end of the 1870s the entrepreneur Grigorii A. Poliak established his transportation firm in Nizhniy-Novgorod for shipping on the Volga, and in the 1880s entered the field of water transportation of oil and oil products on the Volga and the Caspian Sea. The field of oil tankers and the transfer of oil from the tankers to the railroads attracted the activities of the successful entrepreneurs Dembot and Kagan, who further expanded Jewish participation in the production, transportation, and trade of oil.[25]

The entrepreneurial activity of interest to us was not the founding of shipping companies, construction of docks and warehouses, or even shipbuilding in which Jewish firms were engaged but the attempts to bring order into water transportation. This later activity coincided with the government's vision of increasing the Russian share in goods transportation at the expense of foreign shipping companies in both internal and foreign trade. However, for the entrepreneurs there were two areas of immediate concern. First, to gain control over a sufficiently large number of ships in order to modernize carrying capacity and to redistribute them over the waterways to conform to the demand. Second, to improve the structure of insurance rates for the goods in transit. The expectations of the entrepreneurs were that because of the economies achieved in both areas which would, at least in part, be passed on to the users of these services, the total volume of shipments would increase and thus justify the investments. Two Jewish entrepreneurs, the Hessen brothers, with the help of the banks gained additional control over the shipping on the waterways that connected the Caspian and Baltic seas as well as control of some major insurance companies.[26]

The practical operation of the Hessen scheme was begun during the war, then interrupted by the revolution and ultimately carried out according to the original blueprint during the NEP, not anymore as a voluntary but as a government-sponsored scheme.

Another attempt, albeit unsuccessful, to create an integrated structure of industrial companies, railroad construction, insurance and foreign trade enterprises, using federated banks and interlocking directorates, was one by the Poliakovs. The Poliakovs, heirs of the railroad builder and banking entrepreneur S. Poliakov, were probably the first in Russia to attempt the creation of a conglomerate out of their diverse investments and operating firms to be controlled by their banks. Their scheme, undertaken at the downswing of the business cycle, failed. Although the State Bank helped to prevent the ruin of the Poliakovs' business empire, they were forced to divest themselves of some of their enterprises.[27] A more modest but successful attempt at integration of diverse companies was carried out later by the Russian entrepreneur Vtorov.

Still another attempt to improve efficiency within an entrepreneurial context was provided by a "Jewish" bank, namely, the Azov-Don Bank. In the early 1890s this bank began to petition the Ministry of Finance for permission to move its headquarters from Taganrog to St. Petersburg. The chief argument in favor of the move was the correct observation that, as a bank heavily involved in grain export financing, its business suffered from violent seasonal fluctuations. The sharply fluctuating demand and supply of money in the region of its operation and the inefficiencies involved in its corresponding relation with the St. Petersburg banks in its foreign exchange dealings threatened its position. The Azov-Don Bank argued that proximity to the St. Petersburg exchange could provide an outlet for its idle funds and closer connection with foreign bank representatives who could provide short-term credits needed for its seasonal loan operations and would improve the efficiency of banking operations. The petitions of the Azov-Don Bank made it clear that costs of the provincial banks were higher than for the St. Petersburg banks, and subsequent discussions related to liquid assets, discounts of commercial paper, and transfer of funds by the provincial banks point to shortcomings in the operation of the banking system. The Azov-Don Bank was able to preserve its degree of specialization and also to move its headquarters to St. Petersburg. A number of other provincial banks could not survive the competition of the branches of the St. Petersburg and Moscow banks in the process of concentration of banking in the capitals. The lack of data prevents judging the extent to which the subsequent improved access to the St. Petersburg money market alleviated fluctuations in the volume of credits extended by the Azov-Don Bank to the grain producers in the area of its operation. For the country as a whole, the seasonal fluctuation in the money supply provided by the State Bank in response to the grain harvest, persisted until at least the late 1920s.

Entrepreneurs in the Corporate Sector and Their Responses to Discrimination Policies

Given the existence of discriminatory legislation against Jewish business, as a component of general anti-Jewish legislation, Jewish entrepreneurs had to behave in a manner that would have provided them with alliances that could counteract the strict enforcement of the legislation. Toward the end of the nineteenth century the only group that could enter into an alliance with the Jewish entrepreneurs was the Russian business community. Beginning in the 1880s Jewish entrepreneurs increasingly organized in defense of their interests. Jewish entrepreneurs had to act in such a way that Russian businessmen would overcome their own prejudices and take the side of the Jews when the Tsarist bureaucracy strengthened discrimination policies. Of all places, it was in Siberia that Jewish entrepreneurs as individuals and a "Jewish" bank, the Siberian Bank, gained a great deal of support from the local Russian business community. The Siberian Bank gained its notoriety by being different than the Russian banks operating there.[28] While most of the banks operating in Siberia concentrated on financing the mining industry, the Siberian (Commercial) Bank branched out into the areas of commodity trade, and in turn also served the interests of Siberian agriculture. Given the large distances in Siberia and the low population density, the Siberian Bank nevertheless greatly expanded its branch network, serving communities of different sizes and thereby contributing to a more even growth of the Siberian economy. Instead of specializing in a few areas of the economy, the Siberian Bank acted as a development bank, responding to the needs of various sectors. Although adversaries accused the Siberian Bank of attempts to achieve monopoly power in various regions and branches of the Siberian economy, there is evidence that points to its effort to foster the growth of the Siberian economy and to purchase good will from a broad spectrum of the business community. Jewish entrepreneurs also benefited from the Bank's policies and during the early twentieth century engaged in feverish activity in different branches, starting with the primary industries and finishing with housing construction.

A somewhat different response to discrimination was the ready acceptance of the corporate status and structures by the Jewish entrepreneurs. There were three basic reasons for the acceptance of the corporate form by Jewish entrepreneurs. The first was capital scarcity and the hope to attract more capital for their ventures. The second was to avoid some of the more blatant forms of discrimination which operated against individual or family firms but not against corporations. The third was the opportunity to cooperate within corporate firms with non-Jewish associates. While corporations were permitted to discriminate against any "undesirable" group, whether by specifying the exclusion of such groups in share ownership or in the administrative bodies of the corporations, one could discern a trend among non-Jewish corporations to lower the discriminatory barriers. Prior to World War I, there remained very few corporations indeed that prohibited Jews from owning shares. Most of the corporations trading their shares on the stock exchange eliminated this provision.

The developing interlocking directorates between the banks and the industrial enterprises, along the lines of the German model, increased the incidence of participation of Jewish experts in the management of non-Jewish corporations and representatives of these firms and institutions in the predominantly Jewish—owned corporations. Thus, the corporate form of business organization was less suitable for the exercise of discrimination than the family—owned firm, an additional reason for the Jewish entrepreneurs to prefer to deal with, and within, the corporate sector of the Russian economy.

Conclusions

Jewish industrial entrepreneurs made a significant contribution to the industrial development of Russia primarily in the early stages of industrialization in the Jewish Pale of Settlement. They contributed to the transition of industry from the stage of reliance upon serf labor to freely hired labor. By concentration in areas of processing raw agriculture materials they not only contributed to the growth of commercial agriculture but also to the consumers goods industries. The growth of the consumer goods industries created a demand for capital goods (machinery and equipment) and led to the rapid growth of certain branches of machine building. It was to some extent due to the efforts of Jewish entrepreneurs that the provinces of the Pale became industrialized sooner than other provinces of the Russian empire. Jewish entrepreneurs helped some of the industry in the Pale (particularly textiles) to withstand competition with other regions of the empire. Inside and outside the Pale Jewish entrepreneurs engaged not only in the development of primary production but participated actively in the construction of substantial overhead capital in Russia. Through their links with the trading and banking sectors, Jewish entrepreneurs were able to introduce a higher degree of efficiency in their operations and to build an effective network of business relations which economized on scarce resources. Like other industrial entrepreneurs, they provided employment and contributed to raising the skill levels of the labor force, while creating a demand for capital and providing high returns to capital.

Within the Jewish milieu the role of the Jewish industrial entrepreneurs was even more significant than for the economy at large. On the one hand, they were instrumental in mobilizing the savings of the community and providing a high rate of return, but the capital resources of the community became insufficient when entrepreneurship developed on a large scale. Borrowing from the outside became necessary, and this "import" of capital helped to raise the output of the community. On the other hand, and most important, Jewish entrepreneurs provided the bulk of employment opportunities for Jewish workers. The spread of industrial employment within the Jewish community took place under conditions of declining wages and incomes of skilled labor in the "Jewish economy." Because of a general decline of income in other branches of employment Jewish wage earners and the self-employed turned to factory work. There was also a less than enthusiastic response on the part of the Jewish entrepreneurs to employ Jewish factory labor. However, the net result was the growth of Jewish factory labor in the Pale of Settlement, an opportunity provided primarily by the Jewish entrepreneurs at a time when employment shifts and discrimination threatened large segments of the Jewish population with outright pauperization, an opportunity that affected the social structure and the mobility of the Jewish population.

Last, the activities of Jewish entrepreneurs tended to raise the costs of anti-Jewish economic discrimination and perhaps, even to a limited extent, tended to improve the economic structure of the Jews in the Russian empire prior to World War I.

Notes

1. See Theodore W. Schultz, "The Value of the Ability to Deal with Disequilibria," *Journal of Economic Literature* 13, no. 3 (September 1975).

2. On the conceptual and analytical problems of such treatment see Arcadius Kahan, "A Note on Methods of Research on the Economic History of the Jews," *For Max Weinreich on his Seventieth Birthday: Studies in Jewish Language, Literature and Society* (The Hague: Mouton & Co, 1964); and Salo Baron, Arcadius Kahan, and others, *Economic History of the Jews* (New York, 1976).

3. Published sources and biobibliographical dictionaries were biased in their emphasis on Jewish scholars rather than on businessmen.

4. At one point the Russian government considered opening up Siberia to Jewish colonization but quickly changed its mind.

5. The famous Shmul Zbytkover in Poland, the ancestor of the Bergson family and the famous Ginzberg in Russia, entered their industrial careers from this background.

6. The evidence is available from a comparison of the lists of merchants whose foreign trade turnover exceeded 50,000 rubles. Such lists were published yearly by the Ministry of Finance under the title *Vid na Vneshneiu Torgovliu za . . . god.* The names of Jewish mer-

chants on these lists correspond to lists of Jewish industrialists in Volynia and Grodno gubernias.

7. The estimated 5 percent of the turnover in foreign trade by Jewish merchants gives us the yearly average over five-year periods in silver rubles: 1830–34—430,000; 1835–39— 400,000; 1840–44—430,000; 1845–49—502,000; 1850–54—650,000, and 1855–59— 1,150,000. The above-mentioned estimates were derived from the yearly reports on foreign trade by separating the names of Jewish merchants. Although the above data were not deflated by the price index, and the growth during the last five-year period might be less in terms of the purchasing power of money, there is no doubt that the above sums exceed the volume of possible investments in industry.

8. The participation of Jewish private banks in Prussia in lending operations on the territory of the Polish provinces annexed by Russia goes back to the 1790s. The establishment of Jewish banks in the Polish provinces was also greatly influenced by the immigration of Jewish bankers or their agents from Prussia. Kinship relations between Jewish bankers in Warsaw with bankers in Berlin and Frankfurt, which were mentioned before, facilitated transfers of loans across national boundaries.

9. In a large number of cases, especially among the small-scale industrialists, the available data permit us to follow this process.

10. The family and kinship ties within the Warsaw Jewish business elite in the nineteenth century are documented and would make a fascinating study. The same is true about their connection with German-Jewish banking families.

11. Examples of subscriptions by second-generation Christianized grandchildren to Jewish philanthropies started by their grandparents were not unusual.

12. The Wissotsky family of tea merchants and entrepreneurs provided the brothers Gots; other families supplied their share of revolutionaries.

13. See Alexander P. Ogloblin, *Ocherki Istorii Ukrainskoi Fabriki, Predkapitaisticheskaia Fabrika* (Gosizdat Ukrainy, 1925), pp. 47–49.

14. They could be established not necessarily in the rural areas on estates but near commercial centers.

15. As an example of competitiveness of Jewish-produced woolen cloth, we find already in 1817 three partnerships of Jewish suppliers who received government contracts for the output of their enterprises in the sum of 1,280,750 rubles. See A Yuditski, *Yiddishe Burzhuazie un Yiddisher Proletariat, in der Ershter Helft xix Jh* (Kiev, 1930), p. 23.

16. This system was later copied in a number of other industries, such as oil, agricultural implements, and sewing machines. It was first developed for the sugar industry by I. Brodskii and Sons.

17. H. Landau, "Der Onteil fun Yidn in Der Rusish-Ukrainisher Tsuker-Industrie," in *Shriftn for Ekonomik un Statistik,* vol. 1 (Berlin, 1929), pp. 103–4.

18. The reference is to the settlement of Morgunovka, a sugar mill village acquired in 1848 by the Jewish owner of the sugar mill.

19. Shortly before World War I, there were in the sugar mills of the Ukraine 79 Jewish chemists out of 283, 62 out of 240 overseers of beet plantations, 71 out of 302 bookkeepers, 68 out of 423 deputy directors, and 53 out of 341 mill directors. (See Landau, n. 17.)

20. For achievements of Jewish entrepreneurs in the Russian fisheries see I. M. Bikerman, "Rol' Evreev v Rybnom Delie," in *Ocherki po Voprosam Ekonomicheskoi Deiatelnosti Evreev v Rossii,* vol. 1 (St. Petersburg, 1913), pp. 127–230.

21. The first two railroads in Russia, the St. Petersburg-Tsarshoselsk R.R. and the Nikolaev R.R. connecting Moscow with St. Petersburg were built directly by the government, supported by *ad hoc* and chaotic arrangements with contractors. The construction of the 609 verst of the Nikolaev R.R. lasted for almost nine years (1842–51).

22. Poliakov's Kursk-Karkov-Azov line of 763 verst was built within twenty-two months, and he was able to receive the government subsidy upon completion and to begin receiving revenues from operation; adjustments and repairs were made on a line that was already yielding revenue.

23. In a certain sense, this process was revived during the period of the NEP and provided some of the increases in efficiency that marked the NEP period in comparison with the pre-revolutionary period.

24. By the middle of the nineteenth century, E. Fajans established his transportation firm on the Vistula, followed by the firms of Rogozik and Friedman. Margolin reorganized the water transportation of the Dnieper during the 1880s and 1890s.

25. Such activities resulted in the expansion of Jewish employment in the trade and production of oil at various levels of their mercantile and technical skills.

26. Their scheme was supported by the Russian-French Bank of Commerce, the Odessa Merchant Bank, and the Union Bank. They gained control over the "Eastern Company," "Caucasus & Mercury" shipping companies, and over the insurance firm "Volga," having earlier secured the cooperation of the first and Second Insurance Companies.

27. It is interesting to note how the majority of the banking community in Russia viewed the Poliakovs' attempt: "The selfish interest of a business dynasty came into conflict with the proper criteria for banking operations and was therefore an object lesson of how not to abandon traditional criteria of sound banking." See I Levin, *Aktsionernye Banki* (Petrograd, 1917), p. 281.

28. The Siberian Bank was the brainchild of A. Soloveichik, who founded it in 1872 and was succeeded in the directorship by his son, M. A. Soloveichik, who died in 1916. The bank had its headquarters first in Ekaterinburg and later in St. Petersburg.

FOUR

Economic Opportunities and Some Pilgrims' Progress

Jewish Immigrants from Eastern Europe in the United States, 1890–1914

The purpose of the following essay is to evaluate the existing economic opportunities for Jewish immigrants from Eastern Europe and to indicate the pace of their economic progress during the period 1890–1914.[1] This purpose can best be achieved by viewing the mass migration of these European Jews in the proper perspective, that is, in terms of the dynamics of their situation at the places of original habitat; second, by differentiating successive cohorts of immigrants in terms of their skill composition, literacy, and degree of experienced urbanization, all elements important for the adaptability to and utilization of existing economic opportunities; third, by analyzing the structure of the U.S. industries that provided employment opportunities to the East European Jewish immigrants; fourth, by assuming the income level and standard of living of the native-born labor force as the yardstick for measuring the economic progress of the immigrants. Such an approach may broaden our understanding of the mechanism of adjustment that enabled the Jewish immigrants from Eastern Europe both to take advantage of existing economic opportunities and to create new ones.

Because I focus on economic opportunities and relative progress, I do not deal explicitly with the issue of discrimination against the immigrants. On the one hand, the degree of discrimination did not change much during the period under investigation; on the other hand, the difference between private discrimination in the U.S. marketplace and the legislated, institutionalized governmental discrimination in Eastern Europe constituted a great deal of psychic income to the immigrants. This psychic income out-

Originally published in *Journal of Economic History* 38, no. 1 (March 1978). Copyright © The Economic History Association. Reprinted with permission.

To the memory of Joel Seidman, scholar and friend, labor economist, and historian of the labor movement.

My colleagues Stanley Lebergott, Arthur Mann, and Roger Weiss read an earlier version of this essay and offered valuable suggestions. The responsibility for errors of judgment rests solely with the author.

weighed some of the effects of the actual discrimination to which they were subjected in the United States.

The history of the mass migration of Eastern European Jews to the United States is a well-documented topic.[2] The origin of the mass migration which started in the 1880s and lasted until 1914 has to be sought in the demographic, economic, and political conditions of the Jewish communities in Eastern Europe. Within the framework of early industrialization, a growing population was pressing against the existing economic resources; this development and increasingly discriminatory governmental policies set in motion a process of occupational shifts within the Jewish communities. The essence of the shift was the movement away from trade and personal services, toward crafts and industrial factory employment. One of the most visible features of the process of shifting employment was the accompanying intensification of spatial mobility. This mobility was characterized by a rapidly growing urbanization and by three migration streams: one, intraregional, flowed from the rural to the urban areas; another was interregional, from the relatively depressed areas to industrializing areas; a third involved migration abroad, of which the most important component became the move to the United States. The relative magnitude of the spatial mobility was very considerable. The total population of Eastern European Jews at the turn of the century was about 6–7 million, and about one half of this population was involved in one or another form of spatial mobility.[3]

In order to understand the economic problems of the Eastern European Jewish immigrants, we can draw upon our knowledge of the employment structure of the population at their places of original habitat.[4] Immigration involved a process of self-selection which can only be fully appreciated when we understand the differences between the economic structure of the population and the socioeconomic profile of the immigrants. One cannot treat the immigrants of the 1890–1914 period as a homogeneous group. It is, therefore, proposed to treat them as three successive cohorts, differing in industrial skills, size of commercial element, degree of literacy, and urban background.[5]

While the Jewish immigrants from Eastern Europe brought along little money[6] or physical assets, their value for the U.S. economy and the source of their expected incomes consisted of their skill endowment and their ability to employ their skills gainfully. We have available for the period 1899–1914 the distribution of Jewish immigrants by various categories of gainful employment, as they were reported to the U.S. immigration authorities. With some reservations, the distribution below represents an occupational profile of the immigration (see table 1):[7]

The occupational distribution in table 1 is characterized by a high par-

Table 1 Percentage Shares in Total of Gainfully Occupied Jewish Immigrants Prior to Their Arrival in the U.S.

	1899–1902	1903–1907	1908–1914	1899–1914
Agricultural pursuits	1.6	1.3	3.5	2.3
Manufacturing:	62.7	64.2	64.0	64.0
Clothing	28.5	33.1	34.9	33.4
Animal products	6.9	5.5	4.9	5.4
Wood and construction	11.1	11.5	8.3	9.7
Food	2.8	4.0	3.8	3.9
Metal	2.8	3.7	2.4	2.9
Other	10.6	6.7	9.6	8.5
Commerce	7.2	5.0	5.4	5.5
Laborers and servants	23.3	23.4	18.2	21.0
Professionals	1.0	1.3	1.5	1.3
Residual	4.2	4.8	7.4	5.9

ticipation in manufacturing, the highest among the ethnic immigrant groups for this period. In addition, the Jewish immigrants were concentrated in the clothing industry—a special feature of the Jewish occupational structure in Eastern Europe. Only in textiles and clothing did more than half of the immigrant workers have previous working experience. The textile and clothing industries were fortunate to have access to new workers with previous experience; they thus saved the costs of on-the-job training. From the immigrants' point of view, it was important that this industry was expanding. The census data pertaining to the clothing industry suggest that this was a growing industry, with relatively high rates of growth of output and an expanding labor force. The major indicators for the clothing industry can be summarized as shown in table 2.

The salient features of the growth of the clothing industry were on the one hand the completion of the shift from custom-made clothing to factory-made clothing for men, a process that started in the 1860s–1870s; and what is more important, the very rapid growth of ready-made clothing produc-

Table 2 Major Indicators of the Clothing Industry as Reported by the U.S. Census of Manufactures[1]

	1889	1899	1904	1909	1914
No. of establishments	8,235	10,449	10,071	13,191	13,477
Value of product ($1,000)	415,623	567,875	764,030	1,129,733	1,207,515
No. of wage earners	253,935	291,665	342,038	461,412	466,357
Amount of wages ($1,000)	88,761	106,288	139,055	214,190	230,070

[1]The following branches were included: men's, youths', and boys' clothing; women's and children's apparel; men's furnishing goods; shirts, corsets, and allied garments; fur goods.

tion for women, the fastest growing sector in the clothing industry during the period under consideration. This latter division of the industry accounted for almost two-thirds of the growth of the factory labor force in the total clothing industry during 1899–1914. We can calculate the absorption capacity of the clothing industry with respect to the period for which we have data on the arrival of immigrants who possessed relevant skills. For the years 1899–1914 a total of 458,476 tailors, dressmakers, and seamstresses was admitted to the United States.[8] The percentage of Jewish immigrants among them was 60.3 percent,[9] or a total of 276,517. The census data suggest for the period of 1899–1914 a net increase in clothing-industry employment of about 175,000. If we assume a labor turnover of five percent yearly due to retirement and transfers to other occupations (a very low estimate for this period) and allow on the average for each year 15,000 new entrants[10] over and above the net increase, the industry would absorb 225,000 entrants during the fifteen years 1899–1914. On balance, the clothing industry is thus estimated to have absorbed 400,000, which comes close to the total number of immigrants who declared the possession of such skills. Of course in many cases the immigrant women possessing such skills chose not to enter the labor force, which enabled other categories of immigrants to enter the industry. But basically the official data for the clothing industry point to the fact that the skilled immigrants had the opportunity to find employment (table 3).

My contention is, however, that the official census data underestimated the absorption capacity of the clothing industry by a substantial margin. The source of the bias is revealed in the structure of the industry itself and is contained mostly in the census category of "contract labor," as distinguished from "factory labor." The clothing industry consisted of a labor force employed in factories or large-scale shops, and of a putting-out system, or home industry, which performed a number of production pro-

Table 3   Value of Retail Sales for Selected Branches of Trade (in Millions)

	1889	1899	1909
Grocery, independent stores	1,668	2,027	2,934
Dry goods stores	487	436	638
Apparel stores	551	781	1,315
Furniture, independent stores	346	395	670
Candy stores	115	161	288
Total retail	7,551	9,840	17,807
Total above	3,167	3,800	5,845

Source: Harold Barger, *Distribution's Place in the American Economy since 1869* (Princeton, 1955), pp. 148–49.

cesses under contract for the industrial or commercial entrepreneurs. It was this latter sector, known as home industry, often referred to as the sweat-shops, that was the segment of the labor market through which the immigrants, Jewish included, were passing on the way to the garment factories.

For the Jewish immigrants, employment in the putting-out system or home industry sector of clothing production was the result of a number of factors. Insufficient information about the full range of opportunities in the labor market, combined with lack of ability in English, made the home industry sector more accessible to new arrivals. Employment in this sector permitted the immigrants to remain within their own cultural milieu with little separation between family dwelling and workplace. It also provided a means by which family members who subsidized the passage of immigrants could recover their subsidy or even make a profit on the new arrivals. Although the immigrants knew that their labor in the home industry sector was marshaling a lower wage than in the factory, they could also see that they had an opportunity to use more of the labor resources of the household members than would have been possible within the framework of factory employment. This compensated for the wage differential between the industry sectors. In addition, given the seasonal nature of employment in the clothing industry, the ability to mobilize maximum labor resources during the peak of the seasons was most probably another advantage in their view.[11] The size and volatility of employment in the home industry sector of the clothing industry are poorly reflected in the census data, and one must conclude that the official figures understate the degree to which Jewish immigrant labor was absorbed by this particular industry.

There is another important issue which ought to be mentioned in connection with the clothing industry. Most industrial employment for Jewish immigrants was provided during this period by Jewish industrial entrepreneurs. Thus, employment of Jewish immigrants depended upon the relative success of Jewish entrepreneurship in the clothing and related industries. This symbiosis of Jewish employees and Jewish employers created a curious interdependence which was marked by low wages, very low search costs,[12] and low barriers of entrance into entrepreneurial activity. It made for a growing, highly competitive industry, one in which the supply of labor fed by immigration kept the wages consistently below the level of average wages in manufacturing.[13] But since relative wages in the clothing industry did not decline secularly, there was no marked exodus of Jewish immigrant workers from this industry. As long as the industry was absorbing new immigrants, with older cohorts moving from the home industry sector, from the sweatshops into the factories, into clerical positions, management, and entrepreneurship, there existed a special dynamic pattern of economic adjustment for this group, the largest single occupational group in the Jewish immigration.

A notable feature of the relationship between skills in the clothing industry and the pattern of economic adjustment of the Jewish immigrants involved the location of industry and the residence pattern of the immigrants. Due to the growing production of women's clothing, the initial high concentration of the clothing industry in the large urban centers of New York, Pennsylvania, Massachusetts, Maryland, and New Jersey was maintained and even strengthened during the period under investigation. In Illinois most of the growth of employment was accounted for by the expansion of men's clothing. The major ports of entrance for the immigrants were New York, Boston, and Baltimore; Philadelphia and Newark were close by, and Chicago had special opportunities to offer. These cities were thus the places of "natural" habitat for the Jewish immigrants and were also the preferred locations for the clothing industry. They had an available labor supply and were attractive markets in view of the patterns of urban growth.[14]

The above described pattern of entrance of Jewish immigrants into the clothing industry held also for another branch, one with lower absorption capacity, namely, the cap and millinery trades. The analogy with the other branches of the clothing industry is so close that it really does not require separate documentation.

There was, however, one case of almost automatic transfer and utilization of skills acquired in Eastern Europe which is worth mentioning. This was the case of the silk weavers in Paterson, New Jersey.[15] The silk industry in Paterson was not founded by Jewish entrepreneurs; in fact Jewish businessmen and Jewish workers were the latecomers in Paterson. But with the setting up of factories by Jewish entrepreneurs, a stream of Jewish silk weavers from the Pale of Settlement in Russia began to arrive. The Jewish immigrants entered and remained at the very bottom of the industrial pyramid, with wages considerably below most of the other immigrant groups.[16] To the extent that wages were not only a result of skills from the old country but were highly correlated with the length of residence in the United States, the Jewish silk weavers were at a relative disadvantage as latecomers to the United States. By 1909, 46 percent of the Jewish male labor force had been in this country less than five years and 38.4 percent between five and nine years.

The Jewish silk weavers from Paterson possessed two characteristics, however, which set them apart from the "typical" Jewish immigrants and indicate the change in the characteristics of successive immigrant cohorts: 91.4 percent of the males had worked as factory hands in textile mills prior to their arrival in the United States, and 16.7 percent of the females had previously been textile factory operatives. Also, 100 percent of the males could read and 99.8 percent could write, while among females the comparable figures were 95.1 percent and 92.7 percent. These were clear indicators of their urban, industrial background in Russia.

During the period under consideration the employment pattern in the large centers of the clothing industry was one of utilization of existing skills, acquisition of higher skills, mobility from the home industry sector into the factories, and, for a minority, a move to management and entrepreneurship. Other, accompanying, processes related to the clothing industry were meanwhile taking place. One pertained to those immigrant tailors who, for a number of reasons, settled outside the centers of clothing production in one of the twelve hundred American urban communities with a small number of Jewish immigrants. The tailors in such environments continued to work as independent, self-employed craftsmen, as custom tailors, as repair and cleaning men: skills and a minimum of capital brought about dispersion instead of the concentration that took place as a result of industrial employment.

The participation of Jews in the clothing industry also created a vertical structure extending into the area of distribution, a development that in part accounts for the special role of Jewish immigrants in the clothing trade. To be certain, the Jewish immigrants could not and did not compete with the mail-order houses or with the established large-scale firms in the clothing business, but both in the larger cities and in the dispersed smaller towns they entered the clothing retail trade. Whether the road led from the jobber, from the participant and entrepreneur in the putting out system, or from a clerical position in the factories, a knowledge of the industry and the market was helpful in getting established, provided credit could be obtained from the manufacturers. Thus, the relatively large proportion of clothing shops, men's furnishing stores, etc., established during the early phases of penetration by Jewish immigrants into commerce should be considered as a by-product of their experience in the clothing industry,

With respect to the clothing industry one can describe the mechanism of adjustment on the part of the Jewish immigrants, but with regard to other areas of their economic activity one can only conjecture. In specific areas of the food industry, such as baking and meat production, one would expect the Jewish immigrants to be represented both as small entrepreneurs, and traders and workers. To the extent that certain religious requirements were involved in the preparation of food, it was necessary to employ Jews who possessed the knowledge and skills to produce at least for the consumption of the Jewish immigrant population. The sheer growth of this population assured employment in those branches of the industry. In addition, in some centers of those industries a small number of Jewish workers were employed by the large American firms (Chicago meat packing is a case in point).

Numerous skilled Jewish immigrants were also employed in the building trades. According to the information furnished by the immigrants during 1899–1914, 9.7 percent of all previously gainfully employed belonged to the category of woodworking and building trades, with joiners and carpenters, painters, and glaziers making up the majority. Given the nature of the labor market—where union policies could be important but were overshadowed by the preferences of entrenched ethnic groups—one would expect certain barriers to the entrance of skilled Jewish immigrants into those trades.[17] It is clear that their initial entrance was into the areas of repairs and maintenance of existing housing; involvement in new housing construction came as a second step.[18] Since, however, the period of Jewish mass immigration coincided with several building booms in major urban areas where large tenement buildings were constructed, the demand for labor during these periods absorbed skilled craftsmen as well as some unskilled laborers among the Jewish immigrants. During years of depression in the construction industries, however, some of the skilled immigrants were forced to seek employment in other trades. Since Jewish entrepreneurship in real estate development was very limited during these years, Jewish craftsmen lacked the support the Jewish immigrants received in the clothing industry.

The employment of Jewish immigrants in the metal and machinery industries presents an interesting panorama of diversification. Of the imported skilled workers, the most numerous were locksmiths, blacksmiths, and tinsmiths. But it was only in the last of the three that the Jewish immigrants could gain and maintain a permanent foothold. Although some locksmiths and blacksmiths were employed in small shops or became self-employed, a certain number of immigrants apparently had to acquire additional skills to gain employment in other branches of the metal and machine-building industries, such as foundry and machine shops, locomotive building, cutlery and tool manufacturing, car building and repairs, and sewing machine manufacturing. As late as 1909, the majority of these immigrants had been in the United States less than five years. They were arrivals of an immigration cohort that not only possessed skills but was ready to invest in additional skills in order to enter large-scale machine-building manufacturing plants. Their previous experience had been in the crafts, but in some cases they had been factory operatives and thus had previous acquaintance with factory discipline, division of labor, and cooperation in the production process.

It would be possible to elaborate on a number of crafts in which the

Jewish immigrants were prominently represented. An interesting example is cigar and cigarette making, in which Jewish workers, primarily women, were heavily represented in the Pale of Settlement; the Jewish immigrants in England, prior to the mass migration to the United States, had also gone into this branch of production, either as a home industry or in shops. Other crafts could be cited, but they did not absorb much employment during the period of the mass migration.

The least data is available for the trading sector of the Jewish immigrants. The pieces of evidence we do have are not sufficient to enable me to present a documented pattern; what follows are observations which might prepare the agenda for a thorough discussion of the problem. My basic assumptions are the following:

1. There was scarcity of capital within the immigrant milieu, and although the capital requirements for entering into commerce might have been relatively low, there was a significant time factor involved in accumulating savings or in obtaining credit in order to enter into commercial activity.

2. There was an abundance of commercial skills among the Jewish immigrants, either from past experience in commerce or from general familiarity with the activities and attitudes of businessmen. Such skills and attitudes were latent until the opportunities presented themselves, or were sought, and the means of communicating with potential customers were developed.

3. Because of the time element involved, one would expect commercial activity on the part of the immigrants to be developed first within the confines of the concentrated Jewish immigrant settlements and only later with those outside the immigrant communities.

4. The decision to engage in trade would depend in part upon the existence of opportunities to engage in production activities. Thus, one might expect greater pressure to engage in commerce in smaller Jewish immigrant communities, where there might be difficulty in utilizing industrial skills. This is not to say that the Jewish immigrants considered business activity, or specifically commercial pursuits, as inferior to industrial activities. The problem was one of available opportunities.

5. Contrary to the situation in Eastern Europe where the Jews were very prominently represented in commerce and only faced competition later on, Jewish immigrants in the United States faced formidable competition from previously established traders right from the start. They met harsh competition from an indigenous commercial class and from other immigrant groups as well.

6. The growth of the American economy during the 1890–1914 period, reflected in the growth of internal trade and consumption, nevertheless provided immigrants with opportunities for self-employment in trade.

7. Most of the Jewish immigrants who entered the commercial sector were engaged in the trade of consumer perishables (manufactured and non-manufactured foods, cigars, stationery) and consumer semi-durables (clothing, dry goods). The only areas of consumer durables they entered (toward the end of the period) were furniture and jewelry.

8. The Jewish immigrants engaged in a broad spectrum of commercial activities; those self-employed ranged all the way from peddlers and rag-pickers to established merchants, and the employees included salesmen, saleswomen, and clerical workers.

The study *The Slums of Baltimore, Chicago, New York and Philadelphia* provides some data on the Jewish immigrants in the slum areas for the early 1890s.[19] The category of "Trade and Transportation" accounts for 34.4 percent of the total number of employed males. Thus, one could assume that roughly one-third of all persons employed were in trade. Of those, salesmen and employees accounted for up to 20 percent. Therefore, over one-fourth of the employed Jewish immigrant slum dwellers were engaged in some form of self-employment in trade. If this was the case for the largest immigrant communities, where industrial employment was relatively abundant, the percentage of those engaged in trade in the smaller Jewish communities may have been considerably higher.

A special study of one of the branches of commerce accessible to immigrants—that of the pushcart peddlers in New York—sheds some light on the process of mobility into the commercial sector.[20] The study found that among the peddlers, in Manhattan 61 percent were Jews and in Brooklyn 37.6 percent. For Manhattan, 38 percent of the peddlers had been in residence in the United States 2–4 years, 27 percent 5–10 years, and 30 percent over 10 years. Less than one-half of the peddlers owned their pushcarts, and the others rented them. The average weekly earnings of the peddlers were estimated at $15–$18 (as compared with an average weekly wage of $13.88 for Jewish immigrants from Russia in the New York clothing industry in 1909). In Manhattan, 8 percent and in Brooklyn 27 percent of the peddlers also reported other occupations. The system of licensing in New York City led to the maintenance of tight organizations by the peddlers themselves, mostly along ethnic lines; thus, even if one assumed that there were a certain number of unlicensed peddlers, entrance into this line of commercial activity would not have been without barriers. There is little comparable information about Jewish peddlers in other areas. Probably peddling in small towns or rural communities was neither controlled nor regulated as in some of the larger cities and therefore presented "lower barriers" for those immigrants who preferred self-employment.

It is my distinct impression that during the period 1890–1914 very few, if any, of the Jewish immigrants who started their activity with peddling advanced beyond perhaps a dry goods store or another type of retail establishment. This was simply not the path for Horatio Algers. I would like, however, to argue that given the growth of retail trade, there was room for the Jewish immigrants to gain a foothold in this branch of commerce. Harold Barger reports the following data for a number of branches of retail trade in which Jewish immigrants could conceivably be located. Although the enumerated branches of retail sales experienced less growth than the total volume of retail trade, some of them (such as apparel sales) grew more rapidly than the total. In any event, opportunities for entrepreneurship as well as for employment in trade clearly existed.[21]

There was obviously a category of immigrants that had to start their employment at the very bottom of the skill pyramid. These were the unskilled laborers and servants. There was a high percentage of women in this category, some of whom entered the labor market for longer or shorter periods, while some were employed in home industry or dropped out of the labor force. Over time the percentage of unskilled in the Jewish immigrant labor force tended to decline. On the one hand, their share in the immigration tended to drop off somewhat; on the other hand, both through private initiative and community support they tended to acquire skills at a relatively rapid rate. Even if we assume that in terms of private initiative in gaining skills there was no difference between Jewish and non-Jewish immigrants, collective, organized action to this end on the part of Jewish voluntary associations may have given Jewish immigrants an advantage. Already by the end of the 1890s, charitable and welfare associations in the Jewish community understood that charity for the indigent, sick, and old would not solve the problems which confronted the successive waves of immigrants; the organizations thus put greater emphasis on the type of services which would help to improve the lot of the immigrants in the long run. Assistance in the search for employment and assistance in obtaining training were made a part of the social welfare work of the voluntary associations in the Jewish communities. Emphasis upon apprenticeship programs appears in numerous reports of the local welfare agencies of the Jewish communities.

The Jewish immigrant community possessed one of the typical marks of a "young" immigrant community, namely, the miniscule percentage of professionals within its occupational structure. During the first decade of the mass immigration, not only was there a virtual absence of full-time professionals (such as physicians, dentists, lawyers) but the shortage of teachers (secular and religious) and rabbis was also marked. The difficulty of transferring specific skills, the professionals' uncertainty about the demand for their services, the fear of becoming *déclassé,* and the tremendous social distance between the average immigrant and those with a higher education, all contributed to the scarcity. It was only during the first decade of the century, when education was recognized as an alternative to other types of investment, that the number of professionals began to increase.[22]

It is my impression that more than economic factors were at work in encouraging young immigrants to overcome the various barriers blocking the way to careers in the professions during this period. For some, service to the Jewish community was a motive. Although their numbers were relatively small, their activities made a significant contribution to the health services, legal services, organization, and cultural life of the immigrants. Because of the professionals' social prestige, the demonstration effect on the community was an important influence on the immigrants' choices of roles—if not for themselves, at least for their offspring.

The previous discussion has indicated how many areas there are for future research and how much vital evidence is still missing if we are to analyze the central economic problems pertaining to the immigration of the Eastern European Jews. Is it possible at this stage to pass judgment about the adjustment and relative progress of this immigrant group? How can such progress be "measured"? The answer will obviously depend upon our criteria of progress and the relevant comparisons. The comparison of the immigrants with the ones from their countries of origin who did not migrate is almost irrelevant; the continuous migration indicated that the migrants improved their lot by comparison with those who stayed, and even more important is the fact that economic opportunities in the countries of Eastern Europe were severely limited by legislation. The immigrants in the United States suffered from disabilities and different forms of discrimination, but they had much greater freedom to seek out the opportunities that were available.

Thus the proper yardstick for quantitative comparison is either one of the other immigrant groups or the native-born labor force. Even these comparisons are difficult, however, because most of our data, which are cross-sectional for different periods, are biased; they do not indicate that the immigrants were making much progress because the immigration process was going on with increased intensity and the new arrivals depressed the averages.[23] The only way in which one could conceivably determine the rate of progress would be to follow a particular cohort of immigrants over time. It would be possible to do this with appropriate detailed unpublished census data. In their absence,[24] I will attempt to rationalize the missing evidence.

We are fortunate that we have some data for the base period of 1890, but unfortunate that we do not have comparable data for a later period. According to the 1890 data for the majority of Eastern European Jews in New York City, the average weekly wage for males was $10.13 and for females $5.80.[25] We also know that the average real wage in the clothing industry increased from about $384 in 1890 to $493 in 1914.

Using the above data as a starting point one has to turn to the time pattern which could characterize the growth of earnings and incomes of the immigrant cohorts. One could illustrate the changes over time more easily for wage earners than for those employed in commercial activity, since in the latter case the variance of the distribution of incomes would tend to be higher and most likely increase over time.

Earnings and incomes of each cohort grew over time. We can therefore assume, at the cost of oversimplification, that during the first five years of the immigrants' residence in the United States, they maintained a high rate of savings, determined by the maintenance of a largely preimmigration consumption level, and used the savings for the completion of family formation or to defray the costs of reunion and reconstruction of the family. This was also the period during which, as the data suggest, the earnings of the family head were supplemented by the earnings of the children or by incomes from lodgers and boarders. The virtual absence of net savings can also be explained by the buildup of liquidity as a reserve against seasonal variations in employment.

The subsequent period, the one of from five to nine years of residence, was accompanied by some up-grading in skills and some advancement in the employment hierarchy. Consumption expenditures tended to rise in the forms of improved housing, of more rational diets, and of consumer semi-durables. Earnings by children and non–family heads tended to decline and were replaced by some investment in human capital, represented by the income foregone when children were attending schools or learning various trades. Expenditures were made for such items as insurance and cultural and educational activities as well as for entertainment and leisure. Still, during this period of residence in the United States, the Jewish immigrants from Eastern Europe were not in a position to accumulate sufficient savings to make substantial investments, such as those required for the acquisition of an owner-occupied dwelling. It was primarily among the immigrant wage earners with a residence record of over ten years in the United States that the volume of savings permitted such investments.

The comparison of earnings of Jewish immigrants with other immigrant groups indicates that the former were earning about the average for the total foreign-born workers in most of the industries for which we have data. Since "chronologically" the Jewish immigrants belonged to the "younger" immigration, the one from Eastern and Southern Europe, we could perhaps assume that they were earning somewhat more than the other groups in this immigration and were catching up faster with the "older" immigrants from Western and Central Europe. There is no doubt that this differential can be primarily attributed to the higher ratio of skilled workers and to their general urban background.

For our purposes, the comparison of the Jewish immigrant workers with native born is more significant. Perhaps the most general judgment can be expressed in the following terms: despite their initial disabilities of language and skills, each cohort of Jewish immigrants caught up in earnings with the native American workers of the same age and in similar occupations within 10–15 years. This is a record of achievement that is all the more remarkable when we consider that the real earnings of natives were also rising during these years.

Notes

1. The decision to concentrate upon the period before 1914 was dictated by this author's conclusion that it is difficult to treat the changing economic position of the Jewish immigrants as a continuum. World War I signified not only the virtual end of mass migration of the Eastern European Jews to the United States but, equally important, it caused a major shift within the immigrant community away from wage labor and into self-employment. The impact of such developments makes it impossible to treat the pre–World War I and interwar periods as a continuum.

2. In addition to the older literature on this subject, one would like to mention the brilliant essay by Simon Kuznets, "Immigration of Russian Jews to the United States: Background and Structure," *Perspectives in American History* 9, (1975): 35–126.

3. During 1881–1914 about 2 million Eastern European Jews entered the United States, and at least 300,000 migrated to Western Europe, South America, Palestine, and South Africa. About 1–1.2 million were involved in interregional migration within Eastern Europe (a very conservative estimate).

4. See Simon Kuznets, "Immigration of Russian Jews to the United States," and Arcadius Kahan, "Toward a Socio-Economic Model of the Eastern European Jews" (unpublished paper).

5. See Arcadius Kahan, "Toward a Socio-Economic Model of the Eastern European Jews."

6. The sums of money per capita of Jewish immigrants which were reported to the immigration authorities during 1899–1914 ranged from an average of $7.31 in 1901/1902 to $24.69 in 1911/1912.

7. Serious reservations include the underreporting of employment in commerce and exaggeration of the categories of unskilled laborers and servants. For males, a misrepresentation of those formerly employed in commerce as laborers is possible, while for females the exaggeration of the category of servants was due to a "transfer" of those without occupations or skills

into the category of servants. Those biases in reporting were due to the immigrants' anticipation of what the priorities of the U.S. immigration authorities might have been. The various inquiries conducted not at the time of entry into the United States but years later, reveal that the share of those gainfully employed in commerce prior to their arrival in the United States varied between 20–30 percent of the total employed.

8. No allowances are made for the return of immigrants, and the gross figure is treated as equal to the net immigration figure.

9. The percentage of Jews among the tailors was even higher, reaching 68.4 percent.

10. One can assume as a basis for retirement the size of the labor force in the industry of about 240,000 in 1879, which would give 12,000 as a yearly replenishment, but a 15,000 yearly figure would certainly be more realistic even for the minimum assumptions of labor mobility.

11. It is difficult to assess the psychological value of being able to control when one worked—as was the case with labor in the home; clearly, this would be important in such cases as the observance of the Sabbath and religious holidays. It is relevant to note, however, that the majority of Jewish immigrants familiar with the work in clothing production came from a craft and putting out system in Eastern Europe rather than from a factory background.

12. Eventually, under the team-work system, hiring in home industry and in the smaller shops was often left to the workers themselves.

13. The level of wages in the clothing industry was related not only to the labor supply but also the rapid and significant degree of technological change within the industry during this period. The census data for 1889 suggest that the average wage in the clothing industry rose from 83.8 percent in 1889 to 90.6 percent of the average wage in total manufacturing in 1909, decreasing to 85.9 percent in 1914. The nature of the labor market in the clothing industry is perceived as a fragmented one, in which the costs of information for the immigrant workers were relatively high, while the costs of search and training for the entrepreneurs were relatively low. These characteristics of the labor market which the immigrants faced perhaps help to explain the role of unionism among the workers in the clothing industries.

The unions were probably aware of their weaknesses in view of the continuing immigration and the relative futility in attempting to drive up the average market wage. Thus, much attention was paid to combat the fragmentation in the labor market and to bring the wages of those employed in the sweatshops and smaller establishments in line with the rest of the industry. This emphasis, in addition to the experience of some immigrant groups in the countries of previous habitat, helps to explain both the high percentage of unionization and the radicalism of a segment of the Jewish immigrant labor force. Unionization on a massive scale took place during the latter part of the period, when "bread and butter" unionism substituted for much of the spontaneous strike activity which was characteristic of the early period of the immigrants' residence in the United States.

14. The above list can be extended to include such urban centers as St. Louis (Mo.) and Minneapolis–St. Paul to mention just a few in which the interdependence between the location of the clothing industry, employment of Jewish immigrants, and concentration of Jewish immigrants was apparent.

15. The case is well-known in the history of American labor and was discussed on numerous occasions in the literature. For our purposes, however, a few features are of interest since they throw some light on the general process of adjustment by immigrants to their new economic environment.

16. The earnings of Jewish male family heads in 1909 was $391 versus $426 for all foreign born. U.S. Immigration Commission, *Immigrants in Industries,* Part 6, *Clothing Manufacturing* (Washington, D.C., 1911).

17. The Jewish bricklayers had to establish their own union local to defend themselves from discrimination on the part of the general union local, in New York.

18. All the Jewish union locals in New York were chartered with the prefix "alterations," that is, alteration painters, alteration carpenters, etc.

19. Carroll D. Wright, *The Slums of Baltimore, Chicago, New York and Philadelphia,* Seventh Special Report of the Commissioner of Labor (Washington, 1894).

20. *Report of the Mayor's Push-Cart Commission* (New York, 1906).

21. The number of employed increased from 1,825,000 in 1890 to 2,460,000 in 1900 and 3,366,000 in 1910. The average earnings per week increased from $10.69 in 1890 to $12.33 in 1910.

22. The increase of professionals resulted both from the increased immigration of such, and because young immigrants with a longer residence in the United States had educational opportunities to become professionals.

23. The report on the clothing industry of 1909, for example, indicates that among Jewish male immigrants from Russia the earnings varied with their length of residence in the United States as follows:

Percentage of Immigrants Earning $12.50 per Week and Over by Period of Residence

Length of Residence	Percentage
Less than 5 years	29.6
From 5 to 9 years	55.4
10 years and over	66.0

Source: U.S. Immigration Commission, *Immigrants in Industries,* Part 6, *Clothing Manufacturing* (Washington, D.C., 1911), p. 301.

24. The 1890 original census data were destroyed and the subsequent censuses were not available when the research for this essay was conducted.

25. The Baron Hirsch Foundation collected some data in 1890 among the East European Immigrants in the seventh, tenth, and thirteenth wards on Manhattan's East Side. Their canvass included 111,690 Jews of an estimated 135,000 Eastern European Jewish immigrants residing in New York City. They found a total of 28,801 household units and 60,257 of the total population were classified as children. The children were divided in the following age groups: below 6 years—23,405; between 6 and 14 years of age—21,285; above 14 years old—15,567. They counted 22,402 employed heads of households distributed as follows for the major employment categories:

Percentage Distribution of Heads of Households (1890) by Major Employment Categories

Employment Category	Percent
Tailors and cloakmakers	30.79
Cap makers	3.19
Laundry workers	4.66
Carpenters, painters and glaziers	4.68

(continued)

Continued

Employment Category	Percent
Tinsmiths, machinists	2.50
Cigar workers	4.36
Bakers and butchers	3.04
Peddlers	10.89
Food purveyors, cigar merchants, saloon keepers	3.96
Clerks	6.17

Source: G. M. Preiss in *Nedel' naia Khronika Voskhoda* (Odessa, 1891), no. 17.

117

FIVE

The First Wave of
Jewish Immigration
from Eastern Europe to the
United States

In order to gain a thorough understanding of the problems Jewish immigrants faced in coming to the United States, we would first need to comprehend the complex world from which they came, their common ties of culture, historical experience, and shared memories, even their diverse hopes. We might find a useful framework for considering these complex problems by inquiring more narrowly into the voluntary migrations of Eastern European Jewry, and, within the category of voluntary migrations, to focus upon the external migratory stream.

By "voluntary migration" we usually mean the physical movement of populations which occur as the result of decisions freely made by individuals or heads of households with a view to improving their living conditions.[1] Although various motives might come into play here, we usually assume that economic considerations are primary. It would follow, then, that voluntary migration involves the mobility of labor under conditions of free choice. Therefore, one would have to assume among the preconditions for voluntary migratory movements the existence of wage differentials, incomes, or rates of returns to capital greater than the costs of moving the factors of labor or capital, for otherwise there would be no economic incentive to migrate. Another precondition for voluntary migrations is knowledge about imagined information that would provide a rational justification for migration. The information might be first- or second-hand based upon some recognizable authority, but it has a critical influence on the actual decision to migrate. Liberal attitudes toward migration on the part of governmental authorities at both ends of migration were of considerable importance, because such attitudes removed some impediments to mobility, thus lowering the costs of migration. In the presence of these preconditions, the possession of marketable skills would facilitate the decision to migrate by lowering the anticipated risks, and certainly not least among these preconditions is the ability to pay for the trip.

118

To the extent that one could distinguish areas (whether regions or countries) at varying stages of socioeconomic development, with different levels of income for the same occupations, there would clearly exist incentives for individuals and small groups to migrate. When such a state of affairs coincided with more spectacular processes of change, they resulted in major migrations involving large employment sectors.

Notwithstanding these objective conditions, there were doubtless elements that tended to limit and retard migratory movements. One such factor might have been the phenomenon of "rootedness," or to use the Yiddish expressions, *do'ikeit* or *farvortsetkeit.* The problem is a complicated one. Stripped of mythical notions (as are sometimes applied to the relationship between man and the "native soil," which supposedly explained the spatial immobility of an agricultural population) and of features of an ideological construct, "rootedness" appears as a form of voluntary behavior. There is no doubt that, in all lands where they had long resided, Jews demonstrated attitudes and behavior that indicated they thought of that place as their collective home. The term "home" rather than homeland or country is used advisedly, not because there are any doubts with regards to the Jews' loyalty to the countries or states that they lived in but because the term "home" better describes the whole scope and range of attitudes toward their place of residence than the terms "country" or "state," concepts that in Europe express the attitudes of a population with a territorial, statehood tradition reinforced by the modern nationalist ideologies.

Jews considered "home" as their respective communities, located in the towns and townlets of Eastern Europe where they frequently constituted a majority of the population. But even in the large cities in which they constituted a minority they most often possessed a critical mass, the population density, underscored by the pattern of settlement, that enabled them to feel "at home."

It is clear that the critical mass was not a purely quantitative characteristic, since it involved the presence of such specialized occupations as bakers, butchers, vintners, and it included within a traditional setting all the institutions that provided for the peoples' cultural or religious needs (the schools, houses of worship, ritual baths, cemeteries) as well as the multiplicity of social and charitable institutions that provided both tangible and intangible sources of satisfaction and security. And although their institutions were undergoing profound change in the process of modernization and secularization, their purpose of serving the needs of the members of the community, of providing a framework for their social interaction within the community and for facing the outside world, remained in force.

Thus, in defining rootedness and its sources, the emphasis was more upon the elements of one's daily existence rather than upon such symbolic meanings as "the graves of one's forefathers," "the place where one's cradle stood," or "my country." "Home" meant existence in multifarious forms. "Rootedness" was also a function of the preference for the known over the unknown. It was not so much familiarity with a certain landscape, although aesthetic impressions should not be ruled out. Rather, it was much more the human landscape and knowledge of the accepted behavioral ground rules that added to the sense of rootedness. The fear of the unknown as compared with the familiarity of even an adverse reality was ingrained in historical experience; evil and pain had not necessarily reached their apogee in the past; past levels could possibly be superceded in the future. Thus, given the inclination to view their place in the wider world with a great deal of pessimism, any present sense of relative security and familiarity with their milieu contributed to the Jews' positive attitudes toward their habitat.

The sense of rootedness was also stronger among those who had achieved a more elevated status within their communities and who knew quite well that their status was not automatically transferable to other, especially remote places. It is also possible that for some rootedness was nothing more than reconciliation to the fact of their virtual immobility, whether owing to poverty or an absence of marketable skills. Thus, "rootedness," regardless of its sources and forms, has to be considered as a restraint upon voluntary migration. It is difficult to assess the extent to which the positive features of "rootedness" contributed to persistence and tolerance of adversity before an individual or group decided to migrate. Obviously, we are dealing with a range and not with a fixed threshold.

Another constraint upon migration resulted from actions by the Jewish communities themselves, either as opposition to admission of new migrants, or ambivalent attitudes to new arrivals, based on assumptions of a static universe. The assumption that a city or region was static derived largely from agriculture where a particular parcel of land presumably could support only a specific number of people. In earlier centuries this had become a popular view of the state of the economy or society, and antedated the perception that an expanding economy might depend, at least in part, upon population growth. This could perhaps explain why in the past a government that might invite Jews into a particular country to perform functions which no stratum of the indigenous population could or would perform, would simultaneously prescribe and limit the number of those Jewish migrants invited. Jewish communities adhering to identical general premises of a static universe assumed that particular regions could economically support a certain limited number of Jews, especially since the latter were confined in their employment to one or two branches of the economy. Thus, Jewish community authorities took it upon themselves, even in the absence of government restriction, to limit their own size. This led among other things to the establishment of seniority principles, quota systems, and obstacles to entry for migrants. These policies of "regulating" the size of particular communities by limiting entry for migrants were effective, of course, only as long as the community authorities could enforce them. The autonomy of the Jewish communities, based originally upon the principle of collective fiscal responsibility, was lost, and they were deprived of the legal power to regulate migration and of at least a part of the moral justification for practicing discrimination against migrants. During the nineteenth century, however, the Jewish community authorities often encouraged the transit of migrants through their communities to other destinations by assisting in travel expenses or by curtailing welfare payments to needy migrants. Thus, attitudes of various local communities or regional or even national community authorities had important effects upon migration flows.

Jewish migration can be characterized usefully as "internal" and "external." However, we will define "internal" and "external" migrations not with reference to national boundaries but rather by the movement within or outside of a particular cultural area. As a cultural area we mean Slavic, German, English, Spanish, etc. The term "cultural area" has its own historical dimensions. For example, prior to the middle of the eighteenth century for some categories of Jewish migrants, the movement within the area of settlement of Ashkenazic Jewry could be defined as an internal migration. The Jews within this area shared a common culture and language and could communicate freely and easily among themselves in the territory between Alsace-Lorraine in the West and the Dnieper River in the East. This would indicate that the classification according to cultural areas has at least two dimensions. One pertains to the Jewish communities at both ends of the migration route and the degree of their homogeneity with regard to language and culture. The second pertains to the differences between regions, or the cultural boundaries between linguistic groups of the majority population inhabiting certain areas. Within the territory of Ashkenazic Jewry one encounters two major ethnocultural groups, the German and the Slavic.[2] Thus, an eastward migration until the middle of the nineteenth century would certainly require the acquisition of knowledge to operate within a Slavic milieu, while a westward migration might present less of a linguistic problem for the ones who, even in the Slavic cultural area, spoke a language (Yiddish) with many Germanic elements. But in the formal sense, movements across cultural boundaries will be defined as external migrations.

These were more easily discernible than internal migrations, not only because of their distance, higher costs, and greater demands for adjustment but also because of their visibility and the trace they left in governmental as well as private sources, literary and statistical. The problems of external migration accordingly were studied more, while some of the major internal migrations were hardly noticed by historians or, if noticed, were studied less intensively. This is unfortunate since during certain periods and places the impact of internal migration was at least as great as the concurrent external migration. But while both categories of migration had the effects of relieving the pressure of population upon the existing resources and of expanding the settlements of the Jewish population, there was a significant difference between the two migration streams. In the case of internal migration the movements were sometimes from the less economically developed to the more economically developed regions, but more often from the higher-developed to the less-developed areas where new opportunities arose. In the case of external migrations, however, almost without exception the movement was from the less-developed to the higher-developed areas. The latter was certainly true of the Jewish external migration which originated during the nineteenth century in Central and Eastern Europe. Upon their arrival at their destination the participants in that migration most often found themselves at the bottom of the skill and social pyramids, employed in low-paying jobs, largely of menial labor in the crafts, industry, or even trade. Thus, their position in terms of income, employment, education, etc., was lower than that of the local Jewish population, which might have gone through a period of economic and social advancement perhaps only a generation or two ahead of those immigrants.

This difference between the relative socioeconomic positions of the two populations created social problems and cultural tensions for both groups. For the local Jewish communities (or individuals) the problems ranged from the moral imperative to care for the immigrants to the unwillingness to be identified with them; for the immigrants the confrontation with the local Jews constituted a challenge as well as a model to which they began to aspire, and a demonstration of a behavioral pattern that promised success.

The differences in the socioeconomic positions of the immigrants and the local Jewish population created conflicts and ambiguities that became features of the immigrant experience in most countries, whether Germany, France, England, or the United States. In each of those areas and at various times the immigrants tried to work out for themselves the strategies of adjustment to their new conditions which in their opinions would lead toward an improved economic position and educational and social status. Similarly they tried to anticipate the cost-benefit ratios of such various strategies as they could derive from or attribute to the experience of the local Jewish population.

The relationship between the immigrants and the local Jewish population was determined not only by employment opportunities or the patronizing attitude that employers displayed toward the immigrants, but also by the speed and relative success of the immigrants in their process of acculturation to the value systems of their new homelands. There is no doubt that the immigrants, by and large, were willing and eager to embrace the elements of the new culture, whether for themselves or for the sake of their children, even if that embrace meant abandoning some of their previous traditions and habits.

Over time this resulted in a diminution of the differences in the social standing and economic position of the two populations. The social structure of the immigrant population and of the local Jewish population began to coalesce. The local Jewish population lost some of its anxieties of being identified with the culture of the "aliens," while the immigrants began to treat the local Jews more as mentors and role models than as the harsh critics who looked down upon the less-fortunate Jews. In other words, the emerging pattern was one of integration of both groups and the formation of larger, concentrated settlements of what was becoming a German Jewry, a French, British, or American Jewry.

None of this would have been possible without the basically active and open attitude of the immigrants as they sought to absorb useful knowledge and to change their life-styles, professions, and—if necessary—thought patterns.

This is one of the reasons why one should be wary of the tendency to equate "immigrant culture" with the "culture of poverty." It is true that the Jewish immigrants came from poorer countries and settled in the richer ones. It is also true that the telescopic memory of the immigrants themselves helped to view their state in the "old country" as one of "ultimate poverty" in comparison with the relative affluence in their new habitat. This memory was perhaps reinforced by the demands for remittances and transfer payments both to their family members, relatives, and to charitable institutions of their former hometowns. The immigrants remembered that poverty in the old country was a result of a lack of gainful employment, of total or partial unemployment, and that charity often provided the difference between the actual earnings and the minimal consumption requirement of needy households. In addition, they remembered perhaps that a contributing factor to the general squalor was the maintenance by the community of large numbers of unemployed wards.

The "culture of poverty" especially in Eastern Europe was one of the right to charity as a birthright of a member of the community. The "culture of poverty'' was also based upon the traditional belief that the affluent need charity for the salvation of their immortal souls and that the needy, providing them with such opportunities, thus participate in an equivalent exchange. But the culture of poverty, of inactivity, of resignation and despair, was alien to the immigrants. By migrating one severed the ties with one's community, thus giving up the claim to what was ''due'' to a member of the community, substituting for it activity and self-help. In addition, the mark of migration was self-reliance rather than dependence upon the community, assertion of kinship ties versus community, labor versus acceptance of leisure, but also the demand for a living wage as an alternative to the ''dole,'' and a strict saving regimen as the remedy against future uncertainty. The only claim of immigrants to what would by any stretch of the imagination be called welfare was through participation in associations of mutual assistance, in which in addition to having the share of each determined by his contributions within a contractual relationship, some benefits were perhaps general. Thus, the culture of the immigrants very quickly evolved into a culture of the marketplace; the ''culture of poverty'' was one of a mini-welfare state, to use a modern term. It did not matter whether the culture of the migrants included certain institutional arrangements continuing traditional charitable activities, along with religious and ideological elements. The monumental culture of poverty was left behind at the frontier. The immigrants, as participants in the market for labor, services, or capital, regardless of their degree of personal success, became easily socialized in the culture of the marketplace. This is not to say that the immigrants did not experience poverty as individuals, whether in their old or new homes. In fact, they were familiar with it, experienced its effects and preserved compassion for the needy and poor. But a special sensitivity to problems of poverty is not tantamount to a ''culture of poverty.''

Still another aspect of Jewish immigration which had an effect upon the immigrants' relationship with the local Jewish communities and influenced the pattern of their own adjustment to the new conditions was the presence, or emergence, of what could perhaps be called the intracommunity service group. Jewish populations everywhere, whether in old settlements or in new, required for their collective needs a group of trained ''experts,'' who served the religious-ritualistic, educational, and organizational needs of the population. There was always within a Jewish population a certain subgroup employed in those intracommunity services, supported either directly by the consumers of their services or paid for by communal funds. Jewish migrations, which resulted in population shifts and population growth required substantial investments in facilities that served the cultural and spiritual as well as health and social welfare needs of the migrants and their offspring, and thereby also required either the relocation of some of the old or the training of new service personnel for those institutions. Few of these service personnel emigrated, and some of those who migrated found it very difficult to continue in their previous role in the changed environment. On the other hand, the service group which provided for the needs of the indigenous Jewish population in the countries that received immigrants could hardly accommodate them. The cultural gulf between the spiritual leaders of the indigenous Jewish communities and the immigrants, or between the administrators of the Jewish community organizations and their immigrant clients, was too large. It took at least a generation until a new group of intracommunity service personnel arose, who were capable of bridging the cultural gap between the two communities. While this new group was evolving the two communities led a parallel existence, one under its previous leadership, but becoming rapidly a minority of the total Jewish population, and the other increasing in numbers but virtually leaderless or suffering from the absence of recognized authority. The transition had a detrimental effect upon the internal cohesion of both communities. It was only the emergence of the new service personnel that helped to restore the sense of communal solidarity and to create or activate the institutions that served the special interests of the community members.

But in addition to the tensions and ambiguities involved in the relationship between the recent immigrants and the established or indigenous Jewish community was the tension within the migrants' milieu. The root cause of the tension has to be sought in the vertically integrated employment structure of the so-called Jewish trades. Jewish migrants from Eastern Europe arriving in Berlin, Paris, London, or New York found employment in the clothing industries, leather goods, woodworking, etc., mostly with Jewish entrepreneurs, in numerous cases with other recent immigrants. These trades employed, alongside factory labor, large masses of household labor in a putting-out system. This system, known in the United States as the "sweatshop," was the purgatory through which the majority of Eastern European Jewish immigrants were introduced to the labor market and to the economic reality of their new habitat. Some of the immigrants perceived it as the antechamber to hell, some as an opportunity for a passage to a paradise; the vast majority accepted it as an unavoidable fact, albeit in the hope that it constituted a transitory phase in their existence and adjustment. The reality of the sweatshop created in the minds of the immigrants a strong tension between the myth of group solidarity and the necessity of adopting an adversary relationship to their coreligionist employers. While such tension was no novelty to the immigrants who had been engaged in various forms of class struggle in their old homes, there was, however, one difference between the old and the new. In Eastern

Europe the manifestations of a class struggle within the Jewish milieu were often mitigated by the need for communal solidarity in the defense of general human and civil rights against oppressive government and against the majority's discriminatory attitudes. In their new countries external discrimination was mostly attributed to their status as immigrants and less to their being a national or religious minority. Thus, a class struggle in the new homelands could not be mitigated by communal solidarity. The mitigating factor derived mostly from the view that the conditions of work were only a transitional phase of their immigrant experience.

While social strife within the immigrant milieu, whether on the Lower East Side of New York, the East End of London, or the Marais in Paris, was intense, it cannot be viewed exclusively from the aspects of the employment structure of the Jewish immigrants in those places. It was inextricably part of the process of social change and the changes in both the immigrants' view of the outside world as well as the self-image of the Jewish masses during the second half of the nineteenth century everywhere.

The old traditional culture was giving way to a variety of new philosophical interpretations, to the emergence of novel political doctrines, to manifestations of modern cultural forms and social interactions. This process of cultural change, sometimes described as the road from traditionalism to modernity, a difficult one under conditions of a relatively settled existence. It often created unbearable tensions when it accompanied a mass migration unrivaled in its scope in historical experience, because of the urgency of cultural adaptation and response to economic opportunities. One could argue about the degree of harmony that presumably prevailed within the traditional cultural elements in satisfying the needs of groups and individuals within the Jewish communities; but there is no doubt, however, that the process of cultural change put additional stress upon the migrants when it coincided with their efforts to get settled and to restructure their individual and collective existence.

This cultural stress coming from within and without the mass of immigrants, involving different attitudes to their old heritage and more recent experience, helped to create the great variety in cultural forms, many of them contradictory, and still a subject of study and amazement for social and cultural historians.

In the preceeding discussion, there was an implicit assumption about the social and cultural homogeneity of the Eastern European Jewish migrants. As anyone familiar with Jewish history knows, this is hardly a tenable assumption for the late nineteenth century. Regional difference within Eastern Europe provided meaning to the distinction even between such stereotypes as Galician and Lithuanian, Polish and Rumanian, Ukrainian and Bessarabian or Hungarian Jews. One could argue whether for particular purposes of sociocultural analysis the differentiation within each of the regional groups was more or less significant than the differences among the groups. But the recognition of regional differences as a shorthand description for distinct "tribes" within East European Jewry is necessary for the understanding of differing attitudes, habits, and tastes among the Jewish immigrants. Perhaps one of the consequences of the immigrants' experience was the transcendence of those "tribal" traits that appeared to their bearers to be less meaningful in their new habitat than in their original homes. Thus, the migration process helped to create a unity out of a cultural diversity, not by dominance and suppression of smaller groups but by free play of tastes and preferences growing out of the interaction of the groups within the immigrants' milieu. So, for example, different elements of the culture, which existed among the various "tribes" of Eastern European Jewry, blended to become the common cultural heritage of Eastern Europe in the formation of an American Jewry. To this extent a "melting pot" worked effectively.

The process of external migration of the late nineteenth and early twentieth centuries is without any doubt one of the most important chapters in recent Jewish history. By addressing themselves to various aspects of the migration process, historians and social scientists are broadening the scope of our knowledge and understanding. They are attempting to interpret the immigration experience and to include the immigrant generation as a link in the chain of historical continuity, in the sequence of "the generations of Adam."

Notes

1. The stress upon the *voluntary* migration aspect is topically and methodologically significant, especially in view of the frequency of nonvoluntary migration incidents in the Jewish historical experience. Much of the literature and research on Jewish migrations does not sufficiently differentiate between voluntary and nonvoluntary migrations and thereby does not distinguish between exodus and migration or between refugees and migrants. Instead we find in the literature emphasis upon a hybrid or intermediate form, one of impelled migration, which resulted from strong "push factors." In distinction from the other two types of migration which can be conceptually defined and behaviorally verified, the above third "type" is conceptually fuzzy and empirically difficult. I would suspect that, in part at least, it was formulated on the erroneous assumption that voluntary migration involved only a purely economic or psychological stress, a view totally unrealistic with regard to motives of voluntary migration.

2. One could single out some smaller regions, such as the Hungarian, etc., but their existence does not invalidate the essence of our argument.

SIX

Jewish Life in the United States

Perspectives from Economics

The contribution that economic analysis could make toward a better understanding of the present problems of the Jewish communities in the states is necessarily limited by the tools and data at its disposal. Data provide the economist with evidence that either serves to prove his theoretical propositions or suggests that his interpretation is more or less probable. Unfortunately, most of the data on economic activities collected in the United States, by either governmental or private agencies, do not distinguish among denominational or ethnic groups, and therefore leave open the field of inquiry to conjectures or, at best, to sampling procedures with different degrees of probable errors. Even the number of Jews in the United States has to be derived by a painstaking process.[1]

Of the multitude of economic problems or economic aspects of social activities, the most pertinent for our purposes are those dealing with the employment and incomes of the Jewish population in the United States. The focus on trends in the occupational structure of the Jewish population is based upon the assumption that both the levels of employment and the distribution of the Jewish labor force by particular employment categories determine to a large extent the income levels of the population in question. Data for cross-sectional analyses of the occupational structure of the Jewish community in the United States exist or could be reconstructed for

Reprinted by permission of New York University Press from *Jewish Life in the United States: Perspectives from the Social Sciences,* edited by Joseph B. Gittler. Copyright © 1981 by New York University.

The author owes a special debt of gratitude to Dr. Herbert Bienstock, regional commissioner of the Bureau of Labor Statistics in New York, who generously provided the results of his penetrating analysis of the trends in the employment structure of the Jewish population. A discussion with Mr. Joel Shinsky of the Jewish Federation of Chicago was very fruitful. My colleagues Professors Alexander Erlich, Joseph B. Gittler, Ralph Lerner, and Roger Weiss read an earlier version of this essay and offered constructive criticism. Responsibility of possible errors of judgment rests solely with the author.

different periods of the past hundred years. It would, however, be simplistic to view the changes in the structure as a continuous undirectional process.

Historical Background

The mass immigration of the East European Jews during the period between 1890 and 1914 changed drastically not only the numbers but also the occupational structure of the Jewish community. Much has been written about the Eastern European migrants and their economic adjustment in the United States. The new migrants relied to a considerable extent upon the skills that they already possessed and could utilize in their new home.[2] Even those immigrants who arrived in the United States without a definable trade, those described in popular parlance as *luftmenschen,* who could not find steady employment in the Pale of Settlement in Russia or in the towns of Galicia, possessed discernible commercial skills which they could utilize in a country with a high demand for labor of various categories. The skills embodied in the labor force, the further investments in their human capital, and their consumption and savings patterns enabled the wage earners among them to reach, within an approximate fifteen-year period after arrival in this country, an income level and life-style equal to that of the native-born wage earners.[3] The self-employed among them were also advancing rapidly in comparison with other ethnic groups among the native or immigrant population. This was, in part, owing to the greater vertical integration observed in the areas of Jewish entrepreneurship and labor.

Notwithstanding this gradual process in the advancement of human capital and financial assets, the economic life of the Jewish community was neither uniform nor continuous in its development. Although the discontinuities did not constitute a break with the evolutionary pattern of economic adjustment and gradual change in the occupational structure of the community, they accelerated growth and qualitative change. Most of the so-called discontinuities resulted when the degree of discrimination was lowered either by the business sector or by governmental authorities. This change in social attitudes brought about a considerable lowering of barriers to economic mobility and provided additional opportunities for economic activity in a variety of areas.

The first of the discontinuities can be ascribed to the period of World War I, a period during which the necessity of mobilization of resources for the war effort led to a lowering of barriers in both the governmental and private sectors. The net result, for the Jewish community, was a sharper turn away from wage labor and into self-employment and small-scale entrepreneurship. The possession of skills to organize production of scarce goods, along with the relatively modest capital requirements and liberal extension of credit, converted many Jewish wage earners into entrepreneurs and self-employed. The accumulated profits served some of them as a means of surviving the postwar period of contraction and the transition to a civilian economy. The new positions and acquired status as well as attitudes made it possible for their children to invest in human capital on a larger scale than before.

While the Great Depression had a deleterious effect upon the income of Jews and non-Jews alike, it had a peculiar effect upon those who were investing in their education. The opportunity costs of education declined because of widespread unemployment and thus encouraged the ones involved in schools and colleges to continue perhaps beyond the point of their initial intention or cost-benefit calculations based upon pre-Depression conditions. The full benefits from this protracted decline of the costs of education became apparent after World War II. After World War II the G.I. Bill provided a massive subsidy for the acquisition of skills and formal education to the many veterans who constituted a broad stratum of the American population.[4] Thus, a combination of the Depression period and the G.I. Bill raised the educational endowment and skill level of the American-born offspring of Jewish immigrants to the very top layer in American society.

World War II, as World War I, further lowered discriminatory barriers in the United States. Actually, in such areas as federal government employment, the New Deal already provided greater opportunities for Jews and other minorities. World War II also prepared the ground for a lowering of the discriminatory barriers in some branches of American business. Whether the road to the corporate structure led via science, and technology, or business administration depended upon a number of factors peculiar to the several industries.

The Great Depression and World War II also contributed to the spatial mobility of the Jewish population. Although one could assume that immigrants are more mobile than the rest of the population, mobility also depends upon the degree of acculturation of the immigrants, their knowledge of the language, mores, among other things, if their employment depends upon the communication with employers or customers outside their immigrant milieu. Knowledge of the language and facility in communication help to minimize both information costs and transaction costs. The "second generation" was certainly better equipped than the immigrants in those respects. The accompanying increase in spatial mobility, the movement away from the metropolitan areas of the Northeast to other metropolitan areas, helped not only to achieve a more advantageous regional distribution of the Jewish labor force but also contributed materially toward a more optimal utilization of the skills in the various occupations followed by the Jews.

Occupational Distribution

While a number of Jewish community studies provide data for an occupational distribution of the Jewish population in the United States, they are no substitute for national studies or reliable national samples. At best, they are only suggestive of general trends. There are only a few studies on a nationwide basis, and they can only be conducted with a great effort. I shall use here the two most recent studies, those of 1957 and 1970. Although those studies do not cover quite the same age groups and hence might suggest a somewhat misleading rate of change between the two dates, the overall structure of employment *is* reflected by the distribution of occupations in table 1. The direction of change, indicated by the data in the table and supported by community studies, suggests a growth of the professional category, a slower growth rate or perhaps emerging stability in the managerial and proprietor category, and a gradual decline in the categories of skilled, semiskilled, and unskilled workers (sometimes referred to in the literature as craftsmen, operatives, and laborers). The growth in white-collar occupations and the simultaneous decline in the blue-collar occupations is related to the retirement of an older age cohort among whom the latter were once conspicuously represented.

Table 1 Distribution of Jewish Employed Males and Females by Major Occupation Groups (1957 and 1970)

	Males		Females	
	1957[1]	1970[2]	1957[1]	1970[2]
Professional	20.3	29.3	15.5	23.8
Managers, proprietors	35.1	40.7	8.9	15.5
Clerical workers	8.0	3.2	43.9	41.7
Sales workers	14.1	14.2	14.4	8.3
Skilled workers	8.9	5.6	.7	1.5
Semiskilled	10.1	3.9	11.2	2.3
Unskilled	.8	.3	. . .	.2
Agriculture	.1	. . .	.2	. . .
Unknown	. . .	1.7	. . .	3.1

Sources: U.S. Bureau of the Census, "Tabulations of Data on the Socail and Economic Characteristics of Major Religious Groups," March 1957 (unpublished); Fred Massarik and Alvin Chenkin, "United States National Jewish Population Study: A First Report," *Amierican Jewish Year Book,* vol. 74, (1973), pp. 284–85.
[1]Employed persons 18 years old and over.
[2]Employed persons 25 years old and over.

To what extent do those occupational trends coincide with trends in the distribution of the American labor force? The general impression that one derives from the study of occupational trends in the American labor market, particularly for labor with a high endowment of education, is of a strong correlation between the shifts in the occupational distribution of the Jews and those of the general population.[5] The growth of the tertiary sector, of the role of services in the American economy, particularly of the professional technical group, coincides with the shift within employment of the Jews.[6] The relative decline of blue-collar workers, although not as precipitous as among the Jews, is certainly typical for the white labor force in the United States.[7]

In order to assess the impact of general employment shifts upon the different areas of employment of the Jewish population, three areas were selected for closer scrutiny: retail trade, wholesale trade, and some of the services.

Employment in retail trade in the United States increased from about 8.2 million in 1950 to about 12 million in 1975, while the volume of trade was increasing in both nominal and real terms.[8] But the data for sales suggest different growth patterns for some of the branches of retail trade resulting from changes in the spending preferences of consumers. The relatively modest growth of such branches as furniture, women's and men's apparel, old strongholds of high participation by Jewish businessmen, would probably cause some shift of Jews from those into other branches of trade.

The much higher growth rates of the automotive, building materials, food, and general merchandise branches, most probably attracted some of the Jewish retail merchants. While the data show a moderate growth of total employment in retail trade, we lack any direct indication that the number of Jews employed in retail trade increased. Thus, we might expect that Jewish retailers shifted from branches that were not growing to the branches that were expanding more rapidly.[9]

The situation in wholesale trade bears some similiarity to that in retail trade. The business censuses provide us with some insight into the number of wholesale merchant firms and the volume of their sales. On the one hand, the slowest growing branches in terms of employment were dry goods and apparel, groceries, and tobacco. On the other hand, the fastest growth was exhibited by the branches of electricity and electronics, metals, and automotive machinery and equipment.[10]

Circumstantial evidence supports the hypothesis that a parallel development also took place within the Jewish group of wholesale merchants, in addition to the long-term trend of movement from the retail trade to wholesale trade.[11] In addition to the problems of interpreting employment in such areas as wholesale and retail trade for which at least general information is available, there is still another problem in detecting possible shifts in Jews moving between ownership and the management of industrial, trade, or service enterprises. Increased employment opportunities for Jews, as well as for other minority groups, in the corporate sector of American business, provided the alternatives of high earnings at a lower risk than in business proprietorship. It is, therefore, possible to conjecture that, within the employment structure of the Jewish population, the category of managers not only increased secularly but perhaps also grew at the expense of the number of owners of businesses. This presupposes confirmation of the view that corporate managerial positions are somehow more attractive than independent ownership of smaller business establishments.

The most dynamic sector of employment of particular interest to us is that of professional and technical workers. Definitional and computational problems apart, this segment of employment grew very rapidly, from about 3.9 million in 1940, 5.0 million in 1950, to 12.7 million in 1975. One of the features of the growth of this segment of the labor force is the growth of female employment (from 2.7 million in 1960 to 5.3 million in 1975), thus utilizing the education of females in jobs requiring high levels of human capital.

While the totals of employment in this category are of considerable interest, representing the general growth of services in the economy, they cannot serve as a substitute for some more detailed data pertaining to subgroups of this category. The data in table 2 include a number of such subgroups chosen for illustrative purposes.[12] Among the listed subgroups in table 2, the group of business services exhibits high growth. Circum-

Table 2   Selected Indicators of Growth of Professional and Technical Employment (in Thousands)

	1950	1955	1960	1965	1970	1975
Total professional and technical	5,000	. . .	7,090	. . .	11,561	. . .
Miscellaneous business services	384	528	728	1,107	1,581	1,957
Miscellaneous professional services	270	328	466	566	798	1,016
Educational services	502	552	699	902	1,046	1,164
Legal services	234	248	297	330	385	460
Accountants and auditors	385	. . .	496	. . .	712	. . .
Editors and reporters	73	. . .	106	. . .	151	. . .
Social and welfare workers	94	. . .	124	. . .	274	. . .
Personnel and labor relations	53	. . .	103	. . .	296	. . .
Natural scientists	43	. . .	62	. . .	95	. . .
Social scientists	36	. . .	42	. . .	110	. . .

Sources: U.S. Bureau of the Census, *Historical Statistics of the United States, Colonial Times to 1970* (Washington, D.C., 1975), pp. 140–41; U.S. Bureau of the Census, *Statistical Abstract of the United States,* 1977 (Washington, D.C., 1977).

stantial evidence suggests that the participation of Jews in this category increased. The general pattern of growth of the total professional technical category suggests that the growing demand for specialized services provided opportunities for Jewish employment, both for new entrants into the labor force as well as for those who were transferring from other occupations. In addition, a policy of discrimination against the Jewish element in this segment of the labor market, even if attempted, would not be costly and difficult to administer or to maintain.

A closer scrutiny of the numerical growth of a few "prestigious" professions supports the contention that a rapid expansion was, in fact, taking place and suggests such an expansion provided opportunities for the Jewish population as well.[13]

The doubling of the size of the three professional categories (medicine, dentistry, and law) since 1950 has, without any doubt, provided employment opportunities for the Jewish population. Even if we would assume that the share of Jewish employment in those categories remained unchanged rather than increased, it would permit a numerical growth that would have affected the employment structure of the Jewish population. That assumption (minimally the preservation of the proportion of Jewish professionals in those categories) appears to be reasonable for the following reasons. First, the Jews' level of education made them eligible to study those subjects in the various professional schools. Second, given the preexisting relatively high share of Jews in those professions and the slight advantage that children of professionals have to enter their parents' professions, Jewish children might be more favorably inclined to follow suit.

The participation of Jews in the educational professions is significant but is not easily interpreted. In the past, the penetration of Jews into the area of education was made primarily by women at the level of elementary and secondary school teaching. The last two decades witnessed a very substantial increase of employment in teaching at institutions of higher learning in which Jewish males participated. Therefore, we could base our assumption about the relative stability or even growth in the number of Jews in the teaching profession, not only upon the overall increase in educational employment but also upon the rapid growth of employment in higher education, which in the case of the Jews more than compensated for their possible relative decline in employment at the elementary or secondary levels.

There is, in addition, the area of Jewish education in institutions supported by local Jewish communities. Beginning with the 1950s, an expansion of both educational facilities and employment took place here. Although this line of employment is growing slowly (given the low rate of Jewish population growth in the United States), it nevertheless provided some additional employment opportunities in education, which in all like-lihood were not accounted for by the official data upon which our previous discussion is based.

Since these groups of ''prestigious'' professional-technical employment (to which also the categories labeled ''natural scientists'' and ''social sci-entists'' belong) all have in common a relatively high education prerequi-site, it is incumbent upon us to discuss the problem of education as one of the most important vehicles of upward social mobility and as one of the factors explaining the change in the employment structure of the Jewish population.

Education

The historical dimensions of the educational achievements of the Jewish population in the United States, when viewed against all denominational groups, can be seen from the table presented by A. M. Greeley[14] on the proportion of denominational groups attending college by cohorts (see table 3).

Although an analysis of the accuracy and consistency of the National Opinion Research Center samples and Greeley's results is beyond the pur-view of this essay, the main results can be accepted as a rough approxima-tion. Not only did the Jews in his sample lead all other groups in the level of many years of education—fourteen years, a national average 11.5 years during 1973 and 1974[15]—but they also clearly overcame the disadvantage of having less-educated parents than Episcopalians or Presbyterians.[16] For somewhat more detailed data of the last two decades, which illustrate the change in the distribution of the Jewish population by years of achieved formal education for 1957 and 1970, consider table 4.

Table 3   Proportion Denominational Groups Attending College by Cohorts (in Percent)

Cohorts	Jews	All
1900–1909	17	17
1910–1919	29	18
1920–1929	42	18
1930–1939	47	23
1940–1949	69	29
1950–1959	64	32
1960–1969	88	43

Source: A. M. Greeley, *Ethnicity, Denomination and Inequality* (Beverly Hills, Calif.: Sage Publica-tions, 1976), p. 32.

135

Table 4 Percent Distribution of Years of Schooling Completed of Jewish Population 25 years and over

	Males		Females		Both sexes	
	1957	1970	1957	1970	1957	1970
Less than 12 years	37.5	15.2	39.9	16.0	38.7	15.6
12 years	21.5	22.5	35.8	35.3	29.0	29.2
College:						
1–3 years	12.6	17.3	12.8	21.0	12.7	19.2
4 years or more	25.6	41.4	9.7	24.2	17.3	32.4
Unknown	2.8	3.5	1.8	3.5	2.3	3.5

Sources: U.S. Bureau of the Census "Tabulations of Data on the Social and Economic Characteristics of Major Religious Groups," March 1957 (unpublished). Fred Massarik and Alvin Chenkin, "United States National Population Study: A First Report," *American Jewish Year Book,* vol. 74 (1973), p. 280.

While this table does not illustrate the relative change that was also taking place among the general population in the United States,[17] it represents the cumulative results of an ongoing process, which appears somewhat slower because of the increased longevity of the earlier age cohorts. There is no doubt that, historically speaking, the Jewish community in the United States is the best-educated large community in the history of the Jews. The stock of human capital that became embodied in the labor force of the Jewish population provided the basis for seeking opportunities in the areas of employment in which the highest return could be obtained for this type of capital and specific skills.

Thus we find a very high degree of correlation between the levels of education and particular types or categories of employment. Table 5, which presents a comparison between the employment distribution of all

Table 5 Percent Distribution of Employed College Graduates in Urban Areas by Major Occupation Group Total U.S. and Jewish Population (1957)

Major Occupation Group	Total	Jewish
Professional	63.2	58.2
Managers and proprietors	15.7	22.1
Clerical	8.2	8.9
Sales workers	5.8	7.8
Skilled laborers	3.2	.9
Semiskilled laborers	1.5	1.3
Other occupations	2.4	.9

Source: U.S. Bureau of the Census, "1957 Sample Survey" (unpublished data) (courtesy of Dr. Herbert Bienstock).

college graduates and Jewish college graduates for 1957, and which indicates the similarity of both distributions, illustrates this pattern of strong correlation between levels of education and employment status. For the labor force of the Jewish population with its relatively high educational endowment, a general distribution heavily weighted toward professional and managerial employment would be the one suggested by both economic theory and evidence.

The fact that the acquisition of formal education on a large scale started early in this century provided the Jews with an advantage over other immigrant groups as far as occupational mobility is concerned, and during the recent periods permitted them to overtake such "educationally minded" denominations as the Episcopalians and Presbyterians. A high level of educational achievement, which enabled Jewish members of the labor force to enter into the professional and managerial categories, has provided its bearers with a degree of social esteem. When measured, by the National Opinion Research Center occupational prestige scale, the Jews have a mean of 48.8 points (on a scale of zero to 99), or 8.5 points above the national average of 40.3 points.

The Income Profiles

While the educational data certainly support and partly explain the relationship between educational achievement, occupational mobility, and structure of populations, it is also important to examine their implications for income levels. Economic logic would suggest, on the basis of the previous discussion of educational levels and occupational structure, that the incomes of the Jewish members of the labor force should be high relative to other groups of the United States labor force in the absence of discrimination. A few exogenous factors contributed to this development. One factor was the urban character of the Jewish population with its wider opportunities and higher incomes than those of the rural population. Another factor that contributed to the economic success of the Jews in the United States was the change in demographic patter beginning with the immigrant generations. Most significant was the reduction in family size. Not only did child mortality decline and the birthrate adjust itself to the diminished death rate, but birth control practices were adopted that reduced the numbers of births even further. The decline in the size of the family led to a decrease in expenditures for goods and services and permitted either an increase in the share of savings or a greater investment in the education and training of children relative to that of the previous generations. The results were higher-quality children. While family incomes increased, per capita income increased even more owing to the subsequent reductions in family size.

Recent data for the New York boroughs provide some insight in the sizes of Jewish families or households. In the boroughs of Queens, Westchester, and Nassau-Suffolk, where the percentage of the Jewish population in the age groups between twenty and fifty-nine were 57.8, 54, and 53.9 respectively, the average household sizes were 2.85, 3.28, and 3.64 persons. Needless to say that in Brooklyn, the Bronx, and Manhattan, with high percentages in the age groups of sixty years and above (25.4 percent in Brooklyn, 34.6 percent in Manhattan, and 43 percent in the Bronx), the average size of Jewish households was considerably smaller (as low as 1.84 persons in Manhattan). Although it is clear that the two-person household is primarily an age-related phenomenon, nevertheless the fact that households have a size of fewer than four persons has a number of implications for population growth rates and for transfers of resources to younger generations. It is conceivable that under certain conditions the average size of the Jewish family could decrease somewhat further, but such a decline will have a relatively small effect upon the income position or occupational structure of the Jewish communities.[18]

Still another demographic factor, the age distribution of the Jewish population, has an effect upon the level of family incomes. The age distribution of the Jewish labor force contains a higher percentage of individuals above thirty years of age than does the total labor force.[19] To the extent that this age category contains more income earners at the peak of their earning capacity, it may raise the level of the family income. Therefore, given an age distribution which, in addition to the occupational structure, was favorable to increasing family incomes, the process of upward economic mobility continued. Although we do not know exactly when the median family income of the Jewish population reached the average for the total population, a 1956 study indicated that the median income of the Jewish urban labor force, both male and female, was higher than the median for the total U.S. population. The median income for Jewish males reported $4,773 compared to $4,472 for the total population and Jewish females earned $2,352 as opposed to $2,255 for the total female population.[20] During the subsequent period the differential tended to increase, and A. M. Greeley in his survey sample of 1974 finds the family income for his Jewish respondents to be $13,340 and $13,512 for men only compared to a national average of $9,953. Greeley estimates Jewish incomes outside the South to be $12,918 whereas they were $10,623 for the total population, and $11,204 for Jews in metropolitan regions of over 2 million inhabitants, all in 1974 dollars.[21] The data of the sample survey conducted by A. M. Greeley enabled him to indicate the rank order of a number of denominational groups in average family income in which the relative position of the Jewish group is indicated.[22]

Apart from the income position of the Jewish participants in the labor force relative to other denominational groups, it is important to place them in the distribution of family incomes of the general population. In view of the absence of direct recent data—the latest being collected for 1956[23]— one has to find in the distribution of family incomes of the general population the particular groups whose occupational distribution and educational endowment approximate the characteristics of the Jewish population described above. Such categories were found in the range between the highest fifth of the families' income distribution and between the top 5 percent of the distribution, both for occupations and education.[24] Although the results are not exact, they appear to approximate the actual range.

Both economic logic and observations, furthermore, suggest that for high income groups earnings from work do not constitute the only source of income but that property incomes constitute an important component of the total income.[25] Such property incomes might consist of dividends, interest, or rents. The holding of such assets is related both to the previous level of income or past savings, and changes over the life cycle of individuals. While for younger age cohorts current earnings from work might predominate, such earnings might peak at a certain point in the life cycle, while real estate and corporate stock holdings (both providing a growing capital appreciation) would tend to increase with age as a part of the asset portfolio. Circumstantial evidence for the incomes of the Jewish population indicates the growth of real estate in total asset holdings as a protection against inflation and an anticipation of urban growth. Accompanying the relative shift to real estate from other means to holding wealth was the active involvement of Jewish entrepreneurs in both real estate, housing, and commercial and industrial construction. Data from smaller and middle-size Jewish communities indicate the rise in these above-described forms of economic activity.

The occupational and age structure of the Jews help to explain income disparity within the Jewish community. As the average life span has extended, there has been a high degree of concentration of Jews with limited means in advanced age groups. This concentration of low-income people is a combination of demographic factors (in spite of the fact that Jews were employed more than other groups beyond the statutory retirement age) and the socioeconomic or occupational structure of earlier decades. This bipolarity of the income distribution might diminish in the future, but during the present period of protracted inflationary pressures, which tend to erode accumulated savings and affect people who depend upon fixed incomes, both the problem and the sufferings are real.

Perhaps some of this bipolarity of incomes might also be owing to the nature of income or asset transfers from generation to generation. Some of our data indicate that the cost of educating children was higher among Jews than among other groups. There is a possibility that in some cases the investment in their children's education went beyond the point of maximizing returns and might better be considered consumption expenses. There is also reason to believe that transfers of assets to their children took place not at the time of death and inheritance but earlier, during the life of the parents, in the expectation of subsequent support from the children, which might have turned out to be below expectations.

Gazing into the Future

Granted that the present Jewish generation in the United States has found itself within the upper stratum of the socioeconomic pyramid, one might inquire or speculate about their chances of remaining there within the foreseeable future. The history of minority groups within larger populations provides a number of examples which question the ability of minorities to maintain their socioeconomic status vis-à-vis either discrimination or intensified competition on the part of the majority. The problem of intensified competition deserves serious consideration; some knowledgeable scholars of the contemporary Jewish scene in the United States have begun addressing themselves to it.[26]

It has been argued on the basis of observable trends that the differences in income, status, and education between the Jews and other denominational groups (such as the Catholics) are diminishing and that competition in areas previously considered as open for entry of Jews is becoming fierce. I, for one, would not dispute such findings nor the possibility that in the longer run future generations of Jews would find it necessary to return to some of the occupations given up by their parents for what once appeared to be more lucrative or prestigious. Earnings in different occupations might change in the longer run, and adjustments will probably be necessary and will doubtless take place. However, for the shorter run, given no major shifts in society's preferences and assuming a general continuity of employment trends, one might still argue for the likelihood that the Jews will maintain their present position. It is necessary to emphasize that while we are dealing with particular categories of employment (whether defined by the census or otherwise) we are not differentiating sufficiently the composition or the scope of such categories. In other words, while concentrating upon the differences between or among the categories, we are not allowing for the quality differences within the categories.

Perhaps a simple example might suffice to illustrate our contention. If we are to measure the effects of the participation of Jews (or any other group) in the category of educational services, one general number will be insufficient because we could not differentiate between teachers in elementary schools, in secondary, and in higher education. A net decrease in the category of educational services could yield a positive result if a moderate decrease in elementary school teachers were compensated for by a small increase in teaching at the college level. Thus, the gist of my argument is the trade-off between quantity and quality. A graduate from Harvard Law School will, other things being equal, earn more than a graduate from Alabama Law School. Thus, given the high educational endowment, experience in the professions, in management and business proprietorships, it is still possible for the foreseeable future to compete in the marketplace for high-quality (and high-income) positions in a number of occupations. Our competitive model also includes an increase in the employment of Jewish women, which should help to strengthen the relative economic position by augmenting the size of family earnings. Thus while my argument does not negate my argument that there will be an increase in competition for the long run, it postpones more painful and disruptive adjustments to a later period.

While this review of some selected economic aspects of the Jewish communities in the United States is by necessity brief and incomplete, it does point to the need for a more extensive collection of data and a more rigorous analysis of phenomena which are perhaps mundane but, nevertheless, significantly touch everyone's life.

Appendix

Table A1   Percent Distribution of Employed Persons 18 Years Old and over by Major Occupation Group, Jewish, and Total Population in Urban United States (1957)[1]

Major Occupation Group	Males		Females	
	Total Population	Jewish	Total Population	Jewish
Professional	9.9	20.3	12.2	15.5
Farmers and farm managers	7.3	0.1	0.7	0.2
Managers and proprietors	13.3	35.1	5.5	8.9
Clerical workers	6.9	8.0	30.3	43.9
Sales workers	5.4	14.1	6.9	14.4
Skilled laborers	20.0	8.9	1.0	0.7
Semiskilled laborers	20.9	10.1	17.1	11.2

(continued)

Table A1 (Continued)

	Males		Females	
Major Occupation Group	Total Population	Jewish	Total Population	Jewish
Service workers	6.1	2.3	22.7	5.1
Farm laborers	2.5	0.1	3.0	. . .
Unskilled laborers	7.7	0.8	0.6	. . .
Total percent	100.0	100.0	100.0	100.0
Total white collar	35.5	77.6	54.9	82.7
Total blue collar	57.2	22.2	44.4	17.0

Source: U.S. Bureau of Census, "Tabulations of Data on the Social and Economic Characteristics of Major Religious Groups, March 1957 (unpublished).
[1]Standardized by years of school completed.

Table A2   Occupational Distribution of the Jewish and Total United States White Population, by Sex (1970)[1]

	Males		Females		Both Sexes	
Occupation	Jewish	Total White	Jewish	Total White	Jewish	Total White
Professional and technical	29.3	15.0	23.8	16.3	27.4	15.5
Managers, administrators	40.7	12.0	15.5	3.9	32.2	9.0
Clerical	3.2	7.6	41.7	8.1	16.2	18.4
Sales	14.2	7.4	8.3	36.8	12.2	7.7
Crafts	5.6	21.8	1.5	1.9	4.2	14.4
Operatives	3.9	18.7	2.3	14.0	3.4	17.0
Service	1.2	7.3	3.6	17.4	2.0	11.0
Laborers	0.3	5.7	0.2	0.9	0.3	3.9
Agriculture[2]	. . .	4.5	. . .	0.7	. . .	3.1
Unknown	1.7	. . .	3.1	. . .	2.2	. . .
Total %	100.0	100.0	100.0	100.0	100.0	100.0

Source: For the Jewish population see Fred Massarik and Alvin Chenkin, "United States National Jewish Population Study: A First Report," *American Jewish Year Book,* vol. 74 (1973), pp. 284–85. For the United States white population see U.S. Bureau of the Census, *1970 U.S. Census of Population: General Social and Economic Characteristics,* PC(1)-C1 (Washington, D.C.: Government Printing Office, 1972), p. 392.
[1]The Jewish population includes persons aged twenty-five and over; the total white population includes persons aged sixteen and over.
[2]No separate category for agriculture was included in the National Jewish Population Study data.

Notes

1. See the chapter by Professor Sidney Goldstein in this volume.
2. On the degree of congruence of the employment structure of Jewish immigrants in the

country of origin and in the United States, see Simon Kuznets, "Immigration of Russian Jews to the United States: Background and Structure," *Perspectives in American History* 9 (1975): 35–126; and Arcadius Kahan, "Economic Opportunities and Some Pilgrims' Progress: Jewish Immigrants from Eastern Europe in the U.S., 1890–1914," *Journal of Economic History* 1 (1978): 235–51.

3. It is also possible that many of the immigrant wage workers were aided by the relatively high level of unionization in their trades in localities, which provided them with a somewhat higher starting point for individual advancement and socialization in American society relative to other immigrant groups.

4. The number of World War II veterans who returned to civilian life can be estimated approximately at 11.6 million. The direct cost to the U.S. government of the educational and training programs for war veterans constituted $14,182 million between 1946 and 1952. U.S. Bureau of the Census, *Historical Statistics of the United States, Colonial Times to 1970* (Washington, D.C., 1975), 1:340; 2:1145.

5. U.S. Bureau of the Census, *Statistical Abstract of the United States, 1977* (Washington, D.C., 1977), pp. 406–11; and U.S. Bureau of the Census, *Historical Statistics*, 1:140–45. For the general trends in the occupational structure of the American labor force and economically active population, see these sources. For comparison of the Jewish occupational pattern and the general one, see tables A1 and A2 of the Appendix to this chapter.

6. The professional technical group increased during 1950–70 from 5.0 millions to 11.6 millions, while the total rose from 59.2 to 79.8 millions. See U.S. Bureau of the Census, *Historical Statistics*.

7. The decline in the proportion of the blue-collar workers in the total employed white population (inclusive of farm workers and service workers) was from 53.4 percent in 1960 to 48.2 percent in 1976. The slower pace among the general population can in part be explained by the shift of some blue-collar workers into the service workers category and by their having a lower level of education than do the Jews. See U.S. Bureau of the Census, *Statistical Abstract*, p. 407.

8. For the area of retail trade, the following table should be of interest.

Volume of Retail Trade Sales (in Billion Dollars)

	1950	1955	1960	1965	1970	1975
All retail	147.2	183.9	219.5	284.1	375.5	584.0
Durable goods:	54.3	67.0	70.6	94.2	114.3	180.7
Automotive	27.4	36.3	37.0	56.9	65.0	102.1
Furniture	8.3	10.1	10.6	13.4	17.8	26.1
Building materials, hardware	9.7	11.0	11.3	17.1	20.5	43.2
Nondurable goods:	92.9	116.9	149.0	189.9	261.2	403.7
Men's apparel	2.3	2.3	2.6	na	4.6	6.1
Women's apparel	3.7	4.2	5.3	na	7.6	10.4
Liquor	2.7	3.5	4.9	5.7	8.0	11.0
Food	31.9	42.0	54.0	64.0	86.1	131.7
General merchandise	17.3	20.1	24.1	42.3	61.3	95.4
Employment (in thousands)	8,185	8,801	9,262	9,706	10,906	11,961

Sources: U.S. Bureau of the Census, *Historical Statistics*, pp. 848–49; U.S. Bureau of the Census, *Statistical Abtract*, p. 831.

9. This assumption rests not only upon economic logic but upon scattered data on declining and increasing participation of groups of retail merchants from various branches in the affairs of some major Jewish communities, especially fund raising.

10. The total value of sales of the United States wholesale trade is given in the following table.

Volume in Wholesale Trade Sales (in Billion Dollars)

Years	Durables	Nondurables	Total
1950	37.7	54.6	92.3
1955	51.4	67.3	118.7
1960	58.6	81.3	139.9
1965	82.9	104.5	187.3
1970	112.0	135.0	247.0
1975	185.9	253.1	439.0

The data in the table and the more detailed breakdown of wholesale trade branches provide the information about the growth trends. For details for the years between 1948 and 1972, see U.S. Bureau of the Census, *Historical Statistics,* pp. 850–53; and U.S. Bureau of Census, *Statistical Abstract,* p. 829.

11. The circumstantial evidence is provided by the patterns of shifts in the charitable contributions of Jewish wholesale merchants in a number of large Jewish communities, and in the changing relationship between the numbers of retail and wholesale merchants.

12. See U.S. Bureau of the Census, *Historical Statistics,* pp. 140–41; and U.S. Bureau of the Census, *Statistical Abstract.*

13. The assumption of existing opportunities for Jewish employment in the selected categories of service professions is based upon our knowledge of the educational endowment of Jews in the labor force, a topic which is discussed later in this essay. See U.S. Bureau of the Census, *Statistical Abstract,* pp. 99, 154, 181.

14. A. M. Greeley, *Ethnicity, Denomination and Inequality* (Beverly Hills, Calif.: Sage Publications, 1976).

15. The rank order of American denominational groups on mean educational achievement (non-Spanish-speaking whites only) for 1973 and 1974 is given in the following table.

Denominational Groups	All Respondents		Men	
	Mean Years of Education	Standard Deviation	Mean Years of Education	Standard Deviation
Jews (357)	14.0	(7.1)	14.0	(3.4)
Episcopalians (320)	13.5	(5.6)	13.9	(7.6)
Presbyterians (649)	12.7	(4.6)	12.4	(3.6)
Methodists (1,535)	11.9	(4.9)	11.8	(4.6)
Catholics (5,733)	11.5	(4.7)	11.4	(5.6)
Lutherans (1,105)	11.2	(4.0)	11.3	(5.1)
Baptists (1,825)	10.7	(5.2)	10.6	(6.3)

Source: Greeley, p. 19.

16. The parental education of American denomination groups (non-Spanish speaking whites only) is given in the following table.

144

Denominational Groups	Father's Education	Mother's Education
Jews	10.2	9.9
Episcopalians	12.2	12.2
Presbyterians	10.7	10.7
Methodists	9.4	10.0
Catholics	8.5	8.7
Lutherans	8.8	9.1
Baptists	8.2	8.9

Source: Greeley, p. 20.

17. The percent distribution of years of school complted by persons twenty-five years old and over, Jewish and total population (by sex in the United States in 1957), is given in the following table.

Years of School Completed	Males		Females		Both Sexes	
	Total Population	Jewish	Total Population	Jewish	Total Population	Jewish
Elementary 0–7	23.2	14.7	20.3	16.6	21.7	15.6
8	18.5	13.1	17.4	13.1	17.9	13.1
High School 1–3	17.3	9.7	18.1	10.2	17.7	10.0
4	22.1	21.5	29.5	35.8	26.0	29.0
College 1–3	7.3	12.6	7.4	12.8	7.3	12.7
4 or More	9.4	25.6	5.7	9.7	7.5	17.3
Not reported	2.2	2.8	1.6	1.8	1.9	2.3
Total %	100.0	100.0	100.0	100.0	100.0	100.0
Median school years completed	10.3	12.5	10.9	12.3	10.6	12.3

Source: U.S. Bureau of the Census, "Tabulations of Data on the Social and Economic Characteristics of Major Religious Groups," March 1957 (unpublished).

The percent distribution of years of school completed by persons aged twenty-five and over, Jewish and total white population (by sex in the United States is given in the following table.

Years of School Completed	Males		Females		Both Sexes	
	Jewish	Total White	Jewish	Total White	Jewish	Total White
Less than 12 years	15.2	46.1	16.0	44.9	15.6	45.5
12 Years	22.5	28.5	35.3	35.5	29.2	32.1
College:						
1–3 years	17.3	11.1	21.0	11.1	19.2	11.1
4 years	14.9	7.2	13.6	5.7	14.2	6.4

(continued)

Years of School Completed	Males		Females		Both Sexes	
	Jewish	Total White	Jewish	Total White	Jewish	Total White
5 or more years ·	26.5	7.1	10.6	2.8	18.2	4.9
Unknown	3.5	. . .	3.5	. . .	3.5	. . .
Total	100.0	100.0	100.0	100.0	100.0	100.0

Sources: For the Jewish Population see Fred Massarik and Alvin Chenkin, "United States National Jewish Population Study: A First Report," *American Jewish Year Book*, vol. 74 (1973), p. 280; for the U.S. white population: U.S. Bureau of the Census, *1970 U.S. Census of Population: General Social and Economic Characteristics*, PC(1)-C1 (Washington, D.C.: Government Printing Office, 1972), p. 386.

18. Fred Massarik, "Basic Characteristics of the Greater New York Jewish Population," *American Jewish Year Book 1976* (1975), pp. 239–48.

19. Gallup Opinion Index, Report 130, "Religion in America" (Princeton, N.J., 1976), pp. 39, 49.

20. See U.S. Bureau of the Census, "1957 Sample Survey" (unpublished data).

21. See Greeley, p. 27.

22. The rank order of American denominational groups in average family income (1974 dollars) for non-Spanish-speaking whites only is given in the following table.

Denominational Group	All Respondents ($)	Standard Deviation	Men ($)	Deviation
Jews	13,340	(11,382)	13,512	(11,896)
Catholics	11,374	(8,064)	11,811	(8,082)
Episcopalians	11,032	(10,447)	12,975	(10,911)
Presbyterians	10,796	(10,265)	11,723	(10,291)
Methodists	10,103	(8,987)	10,419	(9,087)
Lutherans	9,702	(9,037)	9,725	(7,871)
Baptists	8,693	(7,985)	9,128	(8,176)

Source: Greeley, table 14, p. 27.

23. The percent distribution of persons fourteen years old and over by income in 1956 (total and Jewish urban population by sex) standardized by occupation groups is given in the following table.

Income	Males		Females	
	Total Population	Jewish	Total Population	Jewish
Under $1,000	5.6	4.1	23.2	22.5
$ 1,000–1,999	6.1	6.4	20.6	18.8
2,000–2,999	10.8	7.6	24.3	24.7

(continued)

Income	Males		Females	
	Total Population	Jewish	Total Population	Jewish
3,000–3,999	17.4	13.9	19.6	19.1
4,000–4,999	21.4	23.3	7.8	9.7
5,000–5,999	16.0	17.0	2.7	2.8
6,000–9,999	17.6	18.9	1.4	1.7
10,000 and over	5.0	8.7	.3	.7
Median Income	$4,472	$4,773	$2,255	$2,352

Source: U.S. Bureau of the Census, "1957 Sample Survey" (unpublished data) (courtesy of Dr. Herbert Bienstock).

24. The occupational distribution of Jewish males in 1970 and the occupational distribution of highest fifth and top 5 percent of the American heads of families by size of total money income in 1974 in percentages is given in the following table.

	Highest Fifth	Top 5%	Jewish Males
Professional technical:	27.5	33.1	29.3
Self-employed	4.5	10.6	. . .
Salaried	22.5	22.5	. . .
Managers and administrators:	29.9	39.7	40.7
Self-employed	4.1	4.7	. . .
Salaried	25.8	35.0	. . .
Clerical workers	5.4	3.0	3.2
Sales workers	8.4	7.6	14.2
Skilled workers	14.4	7.0	5.6
Semiskilled workers	7.4	4.1	3.9
Service workers	3.2	.8	1.2
Laborers	1.5	1.0	.3
Unknown	. . .	. . .	1.7

Sources: For the occupational distribution of Jewish males in 1970 see table A2. For the occupational distribution of American heads of families by size of total money income, see U.S. Bureau of the Census, *Current Population Reports,* Series P-60, no. 101, "Monetary Income in 1974 of Families and Persons in the United States" (Washington, D.C.: Government Printing Office, 1976), p. 29.

Percent distribution of families ranked by size of total money income in 1974 and the percent distribution of years of schooling completed by the Jewish population, twenty-five years of age and over in 1970, see the following table.

	American Families		Jews	
	Highest Fifth	Top 5%	Both Sexes	Males Only
Less than 12 years	16.6	11.8	15.6	15.2
12 years	30.8	24.7	29.2	22.5

(continued)

147

American Families			Jews	
	Highest Fifth	Top 5%	Both Sexes	Males Only
College:				
1–3	17.0	16.6	19.2	17.3
4 years or more	35.6	46.8	32.4	41.4
Unknown	. . .	. . .	3.5	3.5

Sources: U.S. Bureau of the Census, *Current Population Reports,* Series P-60, no. 101, "Monetary Income in 1974 of Families and Persons in the United States," p. 29.

25. Out of the vast economic literature on this subject, one would like to single out the volume by Lee Soltow, ed., *Six Papers on the Size Distribution of Wealth and Income* (New York: National Bureau of Economic Research, 1969). The papers by Melvyn W. Reder, John B. Lansing, John Sonquist, Dorothy S. Projector, Gertrude S. Weiss, and Erling T. Thoresen are pertinent to some of the aspects of our discussion.

26. The most interesting treatment of this issue was provided by Dr. Herbert Bienstock.

SEVEN

Vilna

The Sociocultural Anatomy of a Jewish Community in Interwar Poland

The purpose of my comments is to attempt a reconstruction of the chief characteristics of a Jewish community in Eastern Europe during the interwar period.

The Jews of Vilna (Kehile Kdoisha D'Yerusholaim D'Lita) did not consider their community typical. They legitimized their organization and activities vertically, to use the apt characterization by Dr. Max Weinreich for Ashkenazic Jewry. Five hundred years of uninterrupted communal existence and the totality of the tradition of Ashkenaz together formed the character of life in Vilna. Certainly not every Jewish community was hailed by poets as much and in such a manner as Vilna.

Moishe Kulbak, one of at least a dozen poets writing about Vilna, wrote:

You are a Psalm spelled in clay and iron,
A prayer is every stone, a chant, a melody is every wall,
You are an amulet darkly mounted in Lithuania,
A book is every stone, a scroll, a parchment is every wall,
And Yiddish is the ordinary oak garland, suspended over
the approaches, at once sacred and commonplace to the city.

The associations are not primarily poetic fantasy; they were embedded in the historic-cultural reality, and the images convey the mood and color of Vilna during the interwar period. They express the sense of austere dynamics and the transcendence of existing temporal realities.

The Jewish community of Vilna, constituting about 30 percent of the total city population, consisted of between 50,000–60,000 people, or about 10,000–12,000 families, a relatively small population by our present standards. In addition we have to remember that Vilna was an impoverished city, which explains the large share of the poor within this community. The classification, gradation, differentiation, and characteristics of various types and degrees of poverty belong to the special genius of the Yiddish language, and all I can say is that there were plenty of noble *Yordim, Nitsrokhim,* and *gefalene Balebatim,* all kinds of *kol Haminim* and *Evionim* (fallen nobility, needy, fallen househeads, all kinds of poor), but no *Kabtsonim* (shabby poor). The poverty was described as clean, concealed, or proud.

Vilna was an old city, and the Jewish quarter was originally located within the walled city. The old Jewish quarter was for a few centuries not only circumscribed but effectively enclosed by ghetto gates, which served for the protection of the Jews from their neighbors—the Polish burghers—rather than for closing off access to the rest of the city. The upper structures of the ghetto gates survived until World War II and imparted a special color and atmosphere to the old Jewish quarter. Typically for an old and impoverished city, the Jewish settlement consisted of three concentric rings, roughly coinciding with the social groupings of the population. The old Jewish quarter, the epitome of population density, where sunlight entered through small and narrow windows, through darkened panes, was populated by poor artisans, poor traders, and shopkeepers, for whom residence and workplace were almost indistinguishable. On the outer rim of this quarter, at least in two directions, were the streets of the business section or of the borders of the business center, where large-scale retail and wholesale businesses gradually extended and merged with the residences of the well-to-do among the Jewish population. The pattern of settlement of the old quarter, with its business section, streets of trade and crafts, was largely repeated in the new and more spacious residential areas (built in the Biedermeier style of the nineteenth century) where artisans and service employees occupied the inner courtyards behind the spacious facades of the residences of the well-to-do. The third ring of settlement was a broken series of extensions of the city and some suburbs (only in the sense of their location across the rivers), in many places separate, but mostly connected with the central core of the settlement by thoroughfares like spokes in a wheel. These were the residential areas of the working class, the poor, and the underworld. Here wooden structures prevailed, enclaves of Jewish inhabitants within a non-Jewish population, a complex pattern of mini-neighborhoods, some either heavily concentrated within a few square blocks or drawn out along the roads connecting the city with its rural hinterland. Few of the outlying areas had their local industry or wholesale business; thus the majority of the population traveled (or to be more precise, walked) to work in the center of the city. For entertainment and for most cultural activities other than prayers, one had to go to the center.

This pattern of concentric rings of settlement conformed to the pattern of social differentiation within the Jewish population and reflected the historical, demographic, and economic factors in the development of the community, housing costs, costs of travel to work, rates of population growth in the past, elements of discrimination, etc. Of special significance was the relationship between the periphery and its center; the access to the heart of the city enjoyed by all its neighborhoods, the material as well as cultural benefits. There was a symmetry in the distance that the inhabitants of the outlying third ring had to cover in order to congregate with the inhabitants of the inner rings, or, more specifically, in the institutions that supported them in their livelihood and other forms of collective existence. Thus, we find in the location and settlement pattern of the Jewish neighborhoods a kind of equilibrium between the forces of differentiation and forces of integration, both operating simultaneously.

The employment distribution of the Jewish population during the inter-war period in Vilna cannot be accurately presented because some crucial data were omitted from the published censuses of 1921 and 1931. A rough estimate would indicate about 10 percent of the adult population as unemployable, unemployed, or without any visible means of support. Of the rest, about 35 percent were employed in trade, mostly small-scale retail trade; about 30 percent were independent craftsmen, that is, artisans; about 25 percent were wage earners in industry and craft; and up to 10 percent were employed in services, both in communal institutions and in the professions.

In the areas of trade, Jewish merchants constituted a majority in the branches of trade in agricultural products, wood and forest products and related raw materials, and in the trade in textiles, clothing, and food products. Their participation was significant in the trade of iron and iron goods, construction materials, chemicals, and pharmaceuticals.

In crafts, the Jews constituted a two-thirds majority of all artisans and were most heavily concentrated in the garment trades, in the leather trades (with the exception of cobblers), in the metal trade, and in food and in personal services. In the construction trades they constituted about half of the artisans.

Among the wage earners, employment followed the pattern of the crafts since most of the workers were employed in enterprises owned by Jewish entrepreneurs. The average size of the enterprises was relatively small, with the exception of a few large-scale enterprises employing hundreds of workers (such as a radio factory and a fur factory). The wages of the Jewish workers in Vilna were among the lowest in Poland; the profit margins of the storekeepers and traders were slim, and competition was fierce. The workday was long; the risk of unemployment ever present.

The social differentiation in employment groups and classes was not, however, a matter of a label. It was reinforced and qualified by multifarious organizations. Every social activity—whether employment (or other means to gain a livelihood), prayer, service, education, or politics—

was excessively organized. Employment meant not only some contractual arrangement between employee and employer but also a guild (trade union), and—typically for small-scale industry or trade—involved the whole family and friends in a system of rules and regulations. To be employed meant to be socialized into a segment of organized society that possessed rituals, symbols, and traditions peculiar to each type of employment. Even the underworld had its well-functioning organizational forms, and keen observers of the streets could watch the introduction of methods of schooling and collective training in pickpocketing that superseded the previous system of individual apprenticeship in this trade.

Clearly, certain organizational forms existed in the old traditional society in Jewish communities of varying size in cities and towns. They were, however, simple and more uniform. A trade was usually organized as a guild, with its own house of worship that served as a place of prayer as well as a place to discuss and resolve the problems of the trade. Very often the place of worship had one or more study groups, and always a society of mutual financial help to assist indigent members of the trade. Obviously, apart from this type of organization one could find within the Jewish communities, depending upon their size, institutions that catered to the general material, social, religious, and cultural needs of the population at large, some of the institutions being communal, general, voluntary as well as obligatory. The new forms of organization and the focus of my comments—the voluntary organizations—were introduced to meet the requirements of changing external conditions and of the internal conditions predicated upon the disintegration of traditional values and the traditional way of life.

There were eleven guilds with over 2,000 members, a Central Artisans' Union with 2,000 members, and, almost parallel to each of these, the Workers' Trade Unions with almost 2,000 members. We find a Central Merchants' Association with 900 members and a Central Retailers' Association with 1,500 members paralleled by a union of trade employees with 650 members. Associations of wood merchants and of real estate owners actively articulated their members' special interests. The professions and service employees did not remain unorganized. The Physicians' Association with 120 members, the Dental technicians with 100 members, the Association of Engineers, a union of bookkeepers with 200 members, one of 70 musicians, a union of 100 registered nurses, and one of 230 teachers were all active.

Imagine over seventy associations of mutual assistance attached to the houses of worship (out of 100 houses of worship), in addition to the eight major associations of mutual aid, which had over 1,000 members. If we should assume only six members per board of each of the smaller, and ten board members per each of the major, associations we find 500 people actively engaged in the decision-making process of mutual assistance of those associations, in the administration of loans which averaged even for the large associations from five to ten dollars per loan.

Moreover, the social welfare voluntary associations included a society to support orphanages with 500 dues-paying members, an old-age home society with 400 paying members, a society subsidizing meals for the needy with 290 members, a relief committee with 200 members, a women's protection society with 100 members: these five associations had 1,490 dues-paying members. But this was the modern type of association, which arose parallel to and did not replace the traditional associations I will list by the traditional names, such as Hakhnoses-Orkhim, Hakhnoses-Kale, Mishmeres-Khoilim, Nikhum-Aveilim, Beis-Lekhem, Meangi-Shabos, Matzo-Umatn-Bseiter, and many others with thousands of regular contributors and many dedicated activists.

Of the educational and cultural associations, to select only seven out of a multitude, the Art Society had 200 members; ORT (supporting technical training), 237 members; Educational Society (Vilbig), 300 members; Tiferes Bakhurim, 180 members; Tarbut, 150 members; Society for Special Education, 390 members; Friends of the Yiddish Gymnasium, 207 members. Together these seven selected societies had 1,654 dues-paying members and a large cadre of active leaders.

The long lists of organizations cited above do not include the institutions proper, and their respective participants, but only a few categories of voluntary associations which represented both the group interests of various social strata of the population and supported some of the causes or concerns of the different segments of the Jewish population. The dry and incomplete statistical data conceal the identity of thousands of concerned individuals who devoted their time and effort in voluntary work in a multiplicity of organizational forms to make their labor of love more effective. If we keep in mind that the community consisted of 12,000 families, it is not difficult to conclude that there were very few Jewish families that did not participate in any form of social charitable and educational activity.

This excess or hypertrophy of organization in the Jewish community cannot be explained solely by the objective needs and demand for participation in social activities or by the purely professional interests of the various employment categories. I would suspect that the answer has to be sought primarily in the aggressive and competitive existence of the various ideologies and the zealous spirit of their adherents. I would underscore their competing nature rather than their adversary relationship not because of the lack of sharply defined ideological antagonisms (for these often created bizarre conflicts even between members of one family or household), or the lack of violence in such relationships (for ideological antag-onism was often accompanied by violence). The competitive nature of the ideologies was mostly apparent, since each tried not to propagandize its own ideas but to create its own institutions, its own systems of education, new and specific life-styles, and new types of social behavior. Obviously the most vivid and visible examples were among the youth, where each political party or group had its own uniform dress, its own party jargon, its own way of arguing, stemming from the different systems of education. But the net result of this fierce ideological competition was highly bene-ficial. The enormous volume and high intensity of energy spent on found-ing and maintaining the various competing institutions, while serving narrow ideological interests, nevertheless catered to the needs of diverse individuals. Ideological diversity stimulated a greater outpouring of creativity than a larger measure of conformity would have achieved. In today's world when we use such criteria as economies of scale and econo-mies of effort, the idea of seven or eight different groups, each separately training their members for *aliyah,* sounds strange. On grounds of cool efficiency we would choose some consensus and common denominator. But I have my doubts whether my friends Aba Kovner and Yitshak Zuker-man, leaders of the resistance in the Vilna and Warsaw ghettos, would have played their respective roles if they had been brought up on a diet of consensus rather than in a spirit of nonconformity and ideological purity.

Ideology created not only competition in institution building, a religious school next to a secular one, one in the Hebrew language adjacent to one in Yiddish, etc.; it also provided an outlet for voluntary initiative. Most of the associations and institutions were run by volunteers and not by paid em-ployees. (In all trade unions there was only one underpaid part-time secre-tary!) Voluntary work and social control made both corruption and material self-aggrandizement extremely rare. (I know of only one case of suspicion of corruption in all the institutions, communal and voluntary, and in this one case the suspicion turned out to be ill-founded.) In an atmosphere permeated by ideology, there was much more at stake than a personal reputation, namely, the risk of compromising the image of political groups; this made self-policing and control extremely thorough and effective. These characteristics of voluntarism and control provided a relatively large core of dedicated and effective activists and a broadly based training ground for social and community work.

One additional and, for our analysis, important characteristic of this "excessive" organization of the Jewish community was that ideological divisions did not always neatly coincide with social stratification and, cer-tainly for the younger generation, cut through its lines. Communists were most successful among upper-class youths, and socialists had to compete with the religious groups for the allegiance of the poor; Zionists did not have a monopoly of the lower-middle class.

But apart from the interrelation between social differentiation and ideological allegiance, there was still another important factor that worked for cohesion against the background of divisiveness: namely, the presence of discrimination and the environment of anti-Semitism. The community was used to discrimination at the hands of Polish burghers and officials; it had to face occasional outbursts of violence in pogroms, riots, and occasional outright killings, when the police and the army might stand by or help the rioters. During such moments the community would rally to self-defense with the resources at its disposal. In such moments the workers from the outer ring would come to defend the lives and property of the inhabitants of the inner rings. And it was typical that in 1937 when a ghetto was instituted for the Jewish students at the university that the socialist workers proclaimed a general strike in the city, closing all the factories and shops in solidarity with the students who fought against this humanly degrading discrimination.[1] Such actions were not lost upon the collective memory and consciousness of the total community. Regardless of social position and ideological persuasion, deeds—honest human reactions—spoke more convincingly than any prejudiced phraseology. Although the workers of Vilna did not crave the approval of their social groups, they nevertheless gained respect by their deeds on behalf of the community. And although this was not enough to override social differentiation, it created an atmosphere of communality. In Vilna no one despised a woodchopper or a water carrier for he might be one of the Lamed Vov, the thirty-six just men for the sake of whom the world will not be destroyed.

Perhaps three other characteristics of the conditions of social differentiation ought to mentioned. One was of vertical integration in the economic sphere. The fact of interdependence between the wholesale merchant and the retailer, of the craftsman and the merchant, the employment of Jewish workers in Jewish-owned enterprises, and the relationship of service and professional workers to their clients, created a sense of mutual interdependence and of boundaries within which conflicts of interest had to be contained for the purpose of self-preservation. This imposed a rational approach to conflict situations and a mode of responsibility with regard to individual and group interests. The second was the numerical balance between the different social and employment groups, giving a sense of stability which further restrained conflict. Given the conditions of economic stagnation, changes in the balance were not very likely to occur in the short run. And although changes in the economic conditions of individuals occurred as results of social mobility—some children of artisans, attending schools or universities, attained positions of professionals, and some chil-

dren of suddenly impoverished merchants found employment in the factories—they did not affect the overall balance. The third one related to
changes in the economic situation of individuals, manifesting itself in a lag
between the change in economic position and the change in social status.
Here the adjustment was not instantaneous, blurring the effect of social
differentiation since status was a form of capital, neither quickly accumulated nor quickly dissipated.

The result of the above characteristics of social differentiation and of the
constraints upon it was a community in which the social distance between
its members was the shortest that I have observed in any other Jewish urban
community. I would assert that the feeling of being at home in the various
neighborhoods, in general communal institutions, in sharing a common
culture and perhaps a common outlook upon life, was the strongest bond
and pervaded all social activities. Ask yourself about the social and cultural
distance in Jerusalem between the inhabitants of Rehavia Katamon, of Mea
Shearim and Talbiyah, and you will get the gist of the difference between
Jerusalem and Vilna. Of course, we all understand the reasons for the
social distance in Jerusalem, but I would maintain that, in comparison with
the communities of Warsaw and Cracow, Lemberg and Lublin, Bialystok
and Odessa, Vilna had the shortest social distance.

I would submit that the key to our understanding of this unity will not be
found in economic factors, habitat, and ideologies but has to be sought in
the realm of cultural heritage and in the cultural revolution at work during
this period.

The diminished social distance in Vilna was not owing to the absence of
rich Jews or to the lack of poor ones, and cannot be explained by the
general fondness for folk stories and expressions which originated either in
the houses of prayer or in the fish market. It was rooted in the emotional
intensity of the people's Jewish consciousness, in their concerted attempts
to maintain and to create cultural values.

Let me say a few words about another area of differentiation, with particular emphasis upon the role of women. If there was a Tsadik-like leg-
endary figure in this fortress of *misnagdim,* it was the cult of Dvoire-
Esther, a poor woman who lived at the beginning of the nineteenth century,
a version of Sarah-bas-Toivim, who performed miracles of charity and
human compassion. Every year, either during the holidays or on the anni-
versary of her death, the mausoleum on her grave would be adorned by
kvitlekh in which poor women would request health for their sick children,
sustenance for their husbands, perhaps even a dowry for their daughters. It
was a place of pilgrimages for the poorest women of Vilna.

In 1920, the Jewish community experienced a unique (for Poland)
event—elections to a democratic Kehila (community council) in which

women were given the franchise, voted, and were elected to the community council. Although the franchise was taken away from them later, by the combined efforts of the religious parties and the Polish government, its impact was not lost subsequently upon the range of social and communal activities in which women participated. Women who were always the most active in charitable activities were tearing down the division between the male associations and the women's auxiliaries. Women became firmly established and recognized leaders not only of charitable and educational institutions but of political parties and trade unions as well. Thus, the traditional coexisted alongside the modern: women observing the cult of Dvoire-Esther and women leading some of the largest and most prestigious Jewish institutions. The equality of the sexes was not preached but practiced, and the prominence of women in the area of professions—medical, legal, educational—was generally acknowledged. Increased participation of women was viewed as a natural development of modernity, not only unavoidable but as a constructive change.

The Jewish community of Vilna, during the interwar period, provided a demonstration that the old proverb *Im ein kemakh—ein Torah* is not valid. In fact, it almost proved the opposite, *Im ein kemakh—yesh Torah*. It is, therefore, relevant to glance at the educational and cultural institutions upon which the claim of Jerusalem of Lithuania rested.

The most outstanding phenomenon about education was the high ratio of students in secondary general education and up to the junior college level. They constituted 37 percent of the total school population of the Jewish community (3,176 out of 8,600 pupils). For an economically impoverished community such a high percentage was remarkable.

The available data indicate that of 8,600 Jewish children and youngsters about 2,600 attended schools in the Polish language, both elementary and especially high schools (gymnasium). About 2,300 attended Jewish religious schools and Talmud Torahs and yeshivas of which Remiles Yeshiva was the most famous, and the important fact here was that these were not private schools but they were maintained by various associations; over 900 attended secular Hebrew schools (elementary and high schools) or Tarbut; and 2,700 attended the Yiddish schools and gymnasiums. There were three teachers' seminaries, a Jewish vocational school, a Jewish technical Lyceum, a music conservatory, three large Jewish public libraries, a few large choirs, five Jewish sports clubs with their teams, two permanent theaters, and four local Yiddish daily newspapers apart from a half-dozen weeklies, biweeklies, etc. In addition to the famous publishing house of Romm which supplied the most popular edition of the Talmud, another 70–80 titles yearly of Rabbinical literature were published; the Yiddish publishing house of Kletskin published over 150 new titles every year of

Yiddish literature for local consumption and for export around the world; others published in addition up to 20–30 titles of modern Hebrew literature. A historical-ethnographic museum and the YIVO Institute added luster to the imposing pyramid of the institutions created in one community, literally within one generation, for itself, for its own cultural survival, and for other communities as well.

The educational and cultural institutions in Vilna were among the most modern that were created by the cultural revolution of the twentieth century within the Jewish communities. Some of the principles upon which they were built were, to be sure, borrowed from abroad, when new situations required filling in the void created by the changes in the traditional way of life. The most interesting feature was their application and integration in the life of the masses, since they were not institutions designed for an elite but to serve the interests of the broad strata of the Jewish population.

It may sound strange indeed that in 1924 in the Yiddish schools of Vilna the first Montessori classes in the kindergarten and first grades were started, at a time when in Europe such existed only in Switzerland, Italy, and Germany. In 1929 the first Yiddish school for mentally retarded and disturbed children opened in Vilna, at a time when even progressive governments considered it too luxurious an experiment. Perhaps I should mention the founding in 1934 of the first open, voluntary institution for the rehabilitation of Jewish juvenile delinquents. The ideas were imported; the success of such experiments was, however, not accidental. It was due primarily to the spiritual and social environment and the profound knowledge by the teachers and social workers of their own culture, which made it possible to incorporate the new ideas.

The crown or apex of the pyramid of the Jewish cultural institutions was the YIVO Institute devoted to social science research and training in the area of Jewish history and contemporary institutions of the Jewish communities. It was a worldwide institution in which an active group of academics and researchers were engaged, such as Edward Sapir of Yale, Simon Dubnow of Berlin, Alfred Landau of Vienna, David Jacob Simonsen of Copenhagen, Ignacy Shipper of Warsaw, and Moses Gaster of London, to mention only a few participants. Vilna was the headquarters; YIVO, however, was not just another research institution. YIVO put its services at the disposal of a broad stratum of Jewish intelligentsia and of the Jewish masses, for whom its publications became a source of their education and enlightenment. But the modernity of the YIVO was not only in its relationship with the community. It consisted of the new methods of social research and a new interpretation for the history of the Jews of the ongoing social and cultural processes. The YIVO dethroned the tradition of the German school of "Wissenschaft des Judentums" which viewed the Jewish heritage primarily as a monument of spiritual processes, a historical experience terminated by emancipation and assimilation. The YIVO considered it as an ongoing process, which can and ought to be studied not in fragments of Jewish antiquities but in the organic relationship of the elements of the process, in the mutual interrelationship and influence of social and cultural movements, through methods of an interdisciplinary analysis. The elements of the analysis included linguistics and sociology, economics and psychology, literature and politics. It strove not toward an eclectic approach but toward a set of generalizations most appropriate for the subject matter and the most modern that each of the disciplines could contribute. And may I remind you that the success of using interdisciplinary methods by the YIVO in Vilna in the 1920s and early 1930s took place prior to the time when most American universities were persuaded of the utility of such an approach.

The relative modernity of some of the cultural institutions was intimately tied to the development, modernization, and refinement of the Yiddish language. Not only did the Jews of Vilna take pride in the fact that their dialect became established as the literary language, but the language itself became more than a medium of interpersonal communication. I would say that almost a cult of the language was established there; language became an important vehicle of the cultural struggle for national continuity. Language was treated with love, care, and respect. Hebraists in Vilna loved Yiddish; Communist internationalists abandoned the assimilationist creed to participate in the process of cultivating the Yiddish language. Yiddish literature locally produced poetry and prose from one generation to another. Yiddish was the language of all communal institutions and voluntary associations. Without Yiddish one could not function or participate in the social activities of the Jewish community

How can we explain the social and cultural vitality of the Jewish community of Vilna, of its achievements and the peculiar impact it had upon a broad stratum of the Ashkenazi during the interwar period?

I would be inclined to seek the explanation in two areas. First, in the emphatic affirmative answer given to the question, Are you your brother's keeper? This necessitated the acceptance of a voluntary discipline of collective behavior and submission to the principle of general good. But because it was voluntary, it did not destroy the fabric of this society, and it provided for the transition, transfer, and transformation of ideas from generation to generation. The second area is the pattern of vertical cultural legitimization as the expression of cultural change. Nothing of importance was omitted from the historical experience.

For all its Jewish inhabitants Vilna was Jerusalem of Lithuania, Jerusholaim D'Lita, the home of the Gaon of Vilna, Reb Eliyohu, of the old and famous yeshives. In the collective memory of the Jew Vilna was the center of the Lithuanian "Haskale" movement, of the enlightenment, the place where Kalman Shulman and Shmuel Yakov Finn wrote their influential books. In the consciousness of all Jews, Vilna was also the cradle of the Jewish Socialist labor movement, of the "Bund," and an important center of the "Khovevei Zion." In Vilna the legend of the martyr the Ger Tsedek, Count Potocki, was alive. The legend and the reality of the cobbler, Hirsh Lekert, hanged for shooting the Tsarist Governor Von-Wahl in 1902, intermingled. Vilna integrated the historical traditions of martyrdom and spirit in a continuum of national and cultural survival and created a broad, colorful spectrum of social activities, permeated by the Hofets-Hakium, the will to continue, to change, and to reach the higher rungs of achievement and creativity.

We saw in Vilna the same elements of national consciousness that must have existed at various times in such chosen Jewish communities as Yavneh and Sura, Troyes and Worms, Prague and Lublin. And this is the reason why Vilna earned its name of *Yerusholaim D'Lita.* And I personally know now that in the period between both World Wars, only a generation ago, the Divine Presence, the *Shekhina,* came from above, *shel Maala,* and rested in the narrow streets of the Jewish Quarter of Vilna.

Note

1. [Arcadius Kahan, a leader of the Jewish students at the time, negotiated the joint action of the Bund and non-Jewish socialist workers.—Ed.]

EIGHT

Introduction of Czeslaw Milosz

Ordinary people have no choice as to their place of birth. But we are told that seven cities claimed Homer as their native son. Therefore, poets were granted the freedom to determine their own birthplace, and they usually listed the city where they began to write or publish their poetry. In order to avoid ambiguity, Milosz has determined that the city of Vilna was his birthplace as a poet. And this is fine, because the YIVO hails from Vilna and is happy to welcome a great man of letters. And because I was also born and raised in Vilna, it gives me special joy to introduce not only the great poet and scholar but also a fellow student at our *Alma Mater Vilnensis*.

Vilna is not only the birthplace of the poet Milosz, it is also a major theme in his poetry and prose. It was indeed a remarkable city, much more than a mere habitat, with certain, even appealing, physical features. It was a collection of symbols; as a city and an intellectual center it was in a category by itself. Located at the crossroads of Central and East European cultures and languages, it possessed the majesty of a historical capital of a Grand Duchy that occupied the plains of Eastern Europe from the Baltic to the Black Sea.

For the Poles it was an enclave of the West in Northeastern Europe, but it was a vantage point for viewing Polish culture and for contributing actively to it. It was the home of the national bard, Adam Mickiewicz, and of the national leader, Jozef Pilsudski. For the Lithuanians, Vilna was their historic capital, a necessary symbol for a reviving national consciousness, and for the Byelorussians, it was the center of book publishing and literary life.

For the Jews, Vilna was, to quote Milosz, "the Jerusalem of the North." The holy community of Vilna, with its five-hundred-year history, was one of the few truly chosen Jewish communities in the historical chain that stretched from Yavneh, Sura, Pumbeditha, Worms, Speier, to Prague and Lublin over a period of nineteen centuries, assuring the spiritual continuity of Jewish life and from which cultural creativity, learning, faith, and hope emanated throughout the Diaspora. Vilna was the home of the Gaon Eliohu, and also the cradle of Eastern European Enlightenment, of Zionism, and of Jewish Socialism. Vilna, more than any other Jewish community in modern times, possessed the whole gamut of social and cultural institutions, whether traditional, modern, or secular, that supported collective existence and provided an outlet for individual talent and initiative. In Vilna, Jewishness was active, intense, and permeated by the will to continue, by what I would call the *Khofets Hakium*. It was, therefore, natural that the YIVO Institute was founded and functioned in Vilna, in the spiritual center of Ashkenazic Jewry, the apex of a pyramid of institutions of culture and education, the center of modern scholarship.

Vilna was used by the poet Milosz as a yardstick and as a point of relative stability in a turbulent world. For myself, I must admit, when the *Shekhina,* the Divine Presence, abandoned its resting place in the narrow streets of the Jewish quarter and left on the road to Ponary to join the Jews in their last journey, Vilna ceased to exist, except only in the platonic sense of Vilna *shel Maala.*

I have mentioned Vilna as a place loved by all its inhabitants. This love transcended differences, conflicts, and animosities. It created an atmosphere in which differences could be discussed and even settled in a civilized manner. I have stressed our common experiences in Vilna because Vilna was a place of cross-cultural influences and dialogues. They started in Vilna when in the sixteenth century Jewish scholars assisted in the translation of the Bible into the local vernacular. And I find it symbolic that Milosz is now engaged in a new translation of the Bible directly from the Hebrew text. It was also in the sixteenth century that words of the vernacular[1] and the local Polish dialect began to be incorporated in Yiddish, the most intimate instrument of interpersonal relations, the daily language.

No one, to my knowledge, has yet made a cost-benefit analysis of the one-thousand-year Jewish presence in Poland. We know, however, that Milosz considered the Jews an integral part of the Polish scene and that he perceived our loss as his own. We know that one thousand years of Jewish life in Poland were a mosaic that included good as well as bad moments. And because the terms ''good'' or ''bad'' can be applied to individuals or groups but not to whole nations, always, even in the worst days of persecution, there was an uninterrupted dialogue between Poles and Jews. The dialogue concerned many topics: religious topics were discussed in the eighteenth century, solidarity in the struggle for Polish independence throughout the nineteenth century, anti-Semitism in the nineteenth and twentieth centuries. I believe that we need to continue the dialogue. We, on our part, need it not only for the study of the past, of our Eastern European heritage; we need it for our self-understanding as the largest Jewish community in the world. I would submit that Polish intellectuals would gain a better perspective on their aims and possibilities as a group that does not have a navy at its disposal, but only the power of the spirit.

The Polish intellectual elite has now raised the banner of a struggle for freedom of expression, for internal freedom of individuals, and for collective self-esteem. And to attest to the power of the word, it is symbolic that the workers of Gdansk chose a quote from Milosz for the monument erected to commemorate their fight against oppression.

Please permit me, in the spirit of our common tragedy, in the spirit of our mutual anxieties, but also in the spirit of our indestructible faith and hope, to introduce to you our dear guest, Czeslaw Milosz.

Note

1. Medieval West-Russian. Byelorussian.

NINE

The University of Vilna

The Stefan Batory University of Vilna started out as a Jesuit Academy with the aim of providing higher education, of substituting Polish and Latin for Byelorussian and Lithuanian, and of reconverting the sons of the Polish-Lithuanian nobility from Protestantism to Catholicism. It is outside of my purview to evaluate the relative success in achieving those aims. But one should not lose sight of the original objective of this institution.

The university faced a different situation during the first quarter of the nineteenth century, when it became not only the symbol but also the arena of the struggle of an embattled culture fighting for its survival against forced Russification and blatant discrimination. This was the time when the words Philomates and Philarets achieved their real as well as symbolic meaning. The university became the crucible for a generaton of Polish intellectuals of whom I will mention only Sniadecki and Lelewel, a generation that was immortalized by Adam Mickiewicz. The university became enshrined in the history of the struggle for Polish independence and cultural as well as political freedom. This is the apex of the university's long history.

The resurrection of an independent Poland and the reopening of the university provided the authorities, the faculty, and the students with a choice of aims of the university—which of the two traditions should be followed. The interwar period of the university's existence was one of tension created by vacillation between those two, often conflicting, traditions.

The hinterland of the university, the Northeastern provinces of Poland, was also one of cultural and ethnic diversity; the scene that witnessed the rise in national consciousness and cultural awakening of the broad masses of the Byelorussian, Lithuanian, and Jewish populations. The cultural aspi-

"On Edom" (p. 167 this chapter) was originally published in Hal Draper, ed., *The Complete Poems of Heinrich Heine* (Boston: Suhrkamp/Insel Publishers, Boston, 1982). Reprinted with permission.

rations of the educated of those national minorities included the recognition of their legitimate rights to obtain higher education. Was this to be perceived as a challenge and opportunity to broaden the educational horizon of the university, or as a threat to old tradition?

Hope for a positive response to this historic opportunity for a multinational cultural coexistence and cross-fertilization, at least in the area of the humanities and cultural studies, was short-lived. The murder of the first elected president of the Polish Republic, Gabriel Narutowicz, sounded the alarm of things to come. In the subsequent political development of Poland, policies toward the national minorities proved that the experience of being persecuted does not teach its victims toleration and, equally, that discrimination against minorities is no guarantee of the well-being of the majority. Those policies were reflected in the situations at the universities, and particularily in those of Lwow and Vilna, with their sizable component of national minorities. The majority of the Polish students of middle-class background subscribed to ultranationalist ideologies and viewed themselves as spearheading the drive for the polonization of the fringes (*kresy*) of the Polish state, as future cadres of civil servants, experts, managers, and intellectual elite of a cultural and economic *reconquista* of the fringes.

The student fraternities occupied a prominent and prestigious place in the student milieu; they were considered, in the words of the chaplain of the Poznan University, Father Jozef Pradzynski, ''the avant-garde of the national spirit in the institutions of higher learning in Poland, and in their internal affairs religion occupies the proper place.'' There was little of spiritual or intellectual content apart from mindless discipline, puerile exhibitionism, and religious bigotry in the Cresovia, Polesia, Batoria, Polonia, Leonidania fraternities, to mention some of those active in Vilna. For most of the time, the fraternities as the mainstay of the All-Polish Youth (*Mlodziez Wszechpolska*) dominated the Student Government (*Bratnia Pomac*), which by its statutes excluded Jewish students.

Therefore, it became increasingly common for subsequent generations of Jewish students at the Stefan Batory University to encounter a cold, haughty indifference from the majority of the Polish students, an open hostility from anti-Semitic students, and a varied but ambiguous attitude from the majority of the faculty. The ambiguity of the attitudes of many faculty members was rooted in their definition of intelligence. To be intelligent it was not enough to be bright; one needed to combine this with gentility, and this was a quality the Jews were lacking by definition. Thus, an admittedly bright Jewish student was referred to as one who had a ''*kepele*''—a fleeting quickness, a combination of superficial adaptation and dialectical skill, but any display of a skeptical inquisitive quality was deemed as incompatible with gentility, respect for tradition and status. Faculty members, especially in their discussions with Jewish students, quite often would underscore an *ex cathedra* method of transmission of knowledge and understanding.

But as much as the Jewish students suffered from those attitudes, they tried to discount them, especially when new horizons in their knowledge were opening up, when new ideas were reverberating in their minds. They were grateful and considered themselves privileged; they were drinking from the source of knowledge.

The opportunity to attend the university was enthusiastically received among the Jewish youth of Vilna. On the one hand it was the chance of social advancement, of acquiring a profession, of being able to rise in terms of income and social status. For the sons and daughters of the Jewish middle class motivated to achieve a personal career, the university provided not only access to training and expertise but also cultural enrichment which an earlier generation was seeking in faraway places and abroad. The environment of the university encouraged a whole range of new activities for Jews, such as a sports club excelling in soccer, touring, mountaineering, and boating clubs, and even imitation of student fraternities with their rituals, their colors, their playboys, and their girlfriends. Thus, the Jewish student environment was differentiated in terms of social origin, orientation, and ideals. Discrimination against Jewish students was soon introduced in some of the professions and sciences; political differentiation and polarization started earlier among Jews than among the Polish students.

While the overall enrollment of Jewish students reached its highest point around 1929–30, when 882 students declared Yiddish and eight students declared Hebrew as their mother tongue out of a total of 3,336 students at the university, the subsequent years witnessed a lessening in the number and share of Jewish students, declining to six hundred out of about four thousand by the late 1930s. The largest enrollments of Jewish students were permitted in law, where, *nota bene,* effective barriers to employment existed at the level of the bar and in the humanities.

But apart from the professional career aspects of the university training, there was the role of the university in the growth and formation of the Jewish intelligentsia of Vilna who sought new avenues of intellectual challenge and fulfillment which the old traditional religious culture was unable to provide. It aspired to the heights of European culture. Secular education in Yiddish became the vehicle. It is my contention that one has to be rather careful in defining the degree of assimilation of the Jewish intelligentsia. The old Jewish intelligentsia of Vilna was not Russified to the point of substituting the folklore of Russlan and Ludmilla or Ilia Muromets for its own folk tradition; it used elements of Russian culture and education to gain access to Europe—a window on Europe. Even in the classic case of assimilation, that of the German Jewish intelligentsia, I have doubts whether many adopted that part of the German culture I would label as that of the Teutoburger Forest. The Jewish intelligentsia of Vilna had an old tradition of seeking education and culture wherever it could be found; Salomon Maimon sought it in the eighteenth-century Königsberg of Immanuel Kant; others sought it in St. Petersburg; some succeeded in finding it in the medical school in Vilna in the first half of the nineteenth century.

Our generation was seeking it with a vengeance at the university, both in the existing curriculum and within the areas of literary creativity around the campus. I do not have to recount the numerous examples of Jewish students in mathematics attending nonobligatory courses in Polish history, or the law students sitting in on the courses of Polish literature, or the sense of excitement, the endless debates into the early hours of the morning, while reading the publications of the young local poets. *Z pod arkad* and *Patykiem po niebie* were read, reread, and recited; each new publication by Teodor Bujnicki, Czesław Miłosz, Jerzy Zagorski, Ksander Rymkiewicz, Witold Sylwanowicz, of Kazmierz Halaburda was awaited with interest and involvement. And all this at a time when we were also involved in the works and art of a large group of young, talented local poets and writers who were creating in Yiddish. One was not a substitute for the other, both were complementary, and our expanding intellectual faculties could absorb both as we enriched our inner life.

The closest neighbor of the university was the old Jewish quarter in Vilna, less than half a mile away from the office of his Magnificence the Rector of the university, or from the Sniadecki Hall, or the Aula of the Columns, where the memorable ceremonies and rituals took place.

How near in distance and how remote in understanding. For the scholars of the university it was easier to map out the jungles of the Amazon River, the deserts of Africa, than the narrow, winding streets of the Jewish quarter. They knew more about the fauna of Tibet than about the strange and alien inhabitants of this neighborhood. They did not know and they did not make the slightest effort to find out. In their eyes it was at best a vacuum, at worst a nuisance. Unfortunately some of the students showed more concern.

From the late 1920s the right-wing Polish students tried to revive the medieval privilege and ritual of a race through the Jewish quarter. But this was not a panty raid, this was a mini-pogrom. In the thirties, the university was often closed during the month of November because of the riots and violence.

The scenes during those times at the university recalled the old-time bargain described by Heinrich Heine: "Ein Jahrtausend schon und länger dulden wir uns brüderlich; du, du duldest, dass ich atme, dass du rasest, dulde ich."[1] But the worst was still to come.

In 1937, the Ministry of Education introduced a ghetto at the universities, and Jewish students had to sit down on the benches marked "B". The majority of the faculty accepted this administrative order rather passively. The names of those who did not comply, such as Professors Zygmund, Rudnicki, Kridl, and Sukiennicki will always be honored among honest people. To those Polish students who sat down on the ghetto benches as a sign of protest and of solidarity with principles of humanity, Dziewicki, Micheida, and others, we will be eternally grateful. We stood along the walls if permitted, or were absent from lectures when forbidden to stand.

But within the Polish student population the tune was called by others who demanded that the ghetto should be instituted and enforced. These students barricaded themselves in the new student dormitory on Boufallowa Street and refused to leave until the ghetto was established so that they would not be contaminated by the proximity of their fellow Jewish students. How pitiful was the sight of the official Polish community of Vilna, of the civilian officeholders, of the representatives of the church and of the media, in their pilgrimage to this Boufallowa dormitory, begging the right-wing students to come out, assuring them of their political and moral support.

The Polish right-wing students announced that their dormitory was renamed the "Vilna Alcazar." Regardless of the reality of the Toledo Alcazar, everyone who lived during the rise of fascism in Europe knows what the symbolic meaning of Alcazar was. For those who felt that perhaps the future of Europe was being decided on the plains of Estremadura, in the mountains of Asturia, the name of Alcazar put the struggle at the university in broader perspective. The demarcation lines were drawn sharper. The ghetto at the university revived the historical memories of Torquemada, the *auto-da-fé,* the burning stakes of the Inquisition.

The order of the ghetto at the university was met by the Jewish students with their own hunger strike and other forms of protest. The trade unions called a sympathy strike, and all Jewish factories, shops, and institutions were closed for a day.

The chasm between the Jewish students and the institution of the university deepened. The Jewish students had been culturally and socially alien; they were now subject to a campaign of political and ideological ostracism. The price demanded for our education became excessive; it involved a denial of our self-respect as human beings.

It was not of our doing; perhaps it was not even what the faculty and administration of the university desired; it came about as a consequence of the tragic course of government policies, and of the activities of those hate mongers who, regardless of their convictions, were working *pour le roi de Prusse.*

But in our eyes, those of us who were declared stepchildren of the institution, our university reverted to its origins; forgotten was the *phileo-arete*—for us there were no muses left on the Parnassus of Vilna—in our *alma mater.* We were saddened and we cried, out of our helplessness and because we felt betrayed. We buried in our hearts forever the gratitude for the early rays emanating from the sun of our *alma mater,* which expanded our hopes and dreams.

But today I believe that the Divine Presence who rested in the narrow streets of the Jewish quarter in Vilna glanced forgivingly at the neighboring university buildings before it left on the road to Ponary.[2]

Notes

1. [To Edom!] "For millennia now, as brothers, We've borne with each other an age; You hear the fact I'm still breathing, And I I bear your rage. But often you got in strange tempers In dark times since the Flood, And your meekly loving talons You dyed in my red blood. And now our friendship grows firmer And daily increases anew, For I too have started raging—I'm becoming much like you!"

2. Ponary—"a desolate village ten kilometers from Vilna . . . where almost half the Jews of Vilna, 20,000 or more . . . were swallowed up in death pits" in the first days of the German occupation in 1941. See Lucy S. Dawidowicz, *The War against the Jews, 1933–1945* (New York, 1975).

TEN

A Day in the Ghetto

This article was originally presented as a paper at a seminar on the Holocaust and, in that form, the introductory paragraph read as follows: I was tempted to write an essay about the fighters of the ghettos of Warsaw and Bialystok. They are a fascinating topic. They were the greatest heroes of all time, of all recorded history. Even the three hundred Spartans at Thermopylae, facing the Persian army, were well-armed, they had a hinterland, a second echelon, a reserve; the ghetto fighters had none of these. While facing the deadly enemy, they were surrounded by, at best, an indifferent world. They fought not for life, but neither were they seeking death as a suicide squad. They fought for humanity in the abstract, for human dignity, and for a world of freedom, but most of all they fought for history. With their heroic deeds they erected for themselves and for mankind a monument greater than anything created by human hands and more beautiful than anything imagined by human minds and dreams.

Although I knew many of the ghetto fighters personally, and even intimately, I realize that for the purposes of our seminars my thoughts cannot adorn their heroic deeds and their glory. I have, therefore, selected another topic, which will totally avoid subjective judgment but which might contribute to the understanding of some aspects of the Holocaust.

For many of us, the Holocaust is unreal, surrealistic at best, something that cannot be encompassed by our rational concepts. But life under the Nazis was real, it was not imaginary, even if the realities were created by sick, pathological minds.

How can we describe that reality, a day in the life of a ghetto inhabitant? For one who lacks the talent of Alexander Solzhenitsyn, it would be best to read and analyze the available literature, the dry and impartial evidence, in order to reconstruct the reality of the ghetto, and not to rely upon subjective judgment, to suppress one's own emotions and view the subject from a distance that obliterates names and faces and deals only with abstract categories, with types.

I shall focus on the experience of two large ghettos in Poland in order to reconstruct the daily routine of their inhabitants: the ghetto of Warsaw with approximately 370,000 inhabitants, and the ghetto of Lodz with about 160,000 inhabitants, together over half a million Jews in the two largest cities of Poland. The patterns observed in those two ghettos can be considered as representative of many other ghettos in the large Jewish population centers of pre–World War II Poland (see tables 1 and 2).

The term "ghetto," for the period of the Nazi occupation, denotes the quarter within an existing city inhabited solely by the Jews, whose mobility was restricted to movements within that quarter and whose contacts with the world outside were either prohibited or tightly controlled by the German authorities. Unauthorized contacts with the outside world were severely punished; the German authorities established a virtual monopoly that controlled not only the "import" of food and raw materials into the ghetto but also the goods and services produced for "export" by the inhabitants and institutions within the ghetto. The "terms of trade" established by and controlled by the German authorities were clearly discriminatory against the ghettos, and had as their aim the ruthless exploitation of ghetto labor and resources by forcing the standard of living below the minimal level of subsistence.

Although the objectives of the German administration were consistent throughout occupied Poland, the methods of application differed between Warsaw and Lodz, and those differences in turn affected the organization and to some extent the ways of life of the ghetto inhabitants of those cities.

In both cities the Nazis had as their point of departure the expropriation

Table 1   Age and Sex Distribution of the Warsaw Ghetto Population (January 1, 1942)

Age (years)	Total	Male	Female
0–10	51,458	25,759	25,699
11–19	75,073	35,283	39,790
20–29	55,788	19,747	36,041
30–39	70,047	29,155	40,892
40–49	51,780	21,128	30,652
50–59	35,570	14,758	20,812
60–69	21,216	8,881	12,335
70–	7,970	2,899	5,071
Total	368,902	157,610	211,292

171

Table 2 Age and Sex Distribution of the Lodz Ghetto Population (July 12, 1940)

Age (years)	Male	Female	Total
0–8	10,711	10,115	20,826
9–14	9,602	9,131	18,733
15–19	7,284	8,078	15,362
20–25	5,812	8,440	14,252
26–35	11,392	15,380	26,772
36–45	10,077	13,329	23,406
46–60	10,747	13,395	24,142
61–	5,602	7,307	12,909
Total	71,227	85,175	156,402

of as much capital of the Jews as possible. Confiscation of real estate, bank savings, capital equipment, commercial inventories, and raw materials was followed by further expropriation of jewelry, fur coats, and other personal effects of value. All that was left was an actual or potential labor force (see table 3).

The German authorities of Lodz (a city incorporated into the German Reich) imposed a tightly administered and controlled economy on the ghetto, in which all the labor resources (ten years of age and above) were used for direct work for the German army, supplying raw materials and some food as a payment for labor in exchange for manufactured goods. The result was a hermetically sealed ghetto, a conglomerate of large workshops, where the means of production were common ghetto property, and in which labor services were paid for at rates determined by the food supplies available to the ghetto and distributed among the employed and their families by the appointed ghetto authorities.

The organization of production in the Warsaw ghetto was different. Only a part of the labor force was directly employed by German firms

Table 3 Economically Active Jewish Population in Warsaw (October 28, 1939)

Agriculture	200	Trade:	
Industry:		Independent	14,450
Owners	730	Wage earners	13,100
Wage earners	7,170	Peddlers	9,850
Crafts:		Transportation	5,700
Independent	21,100	Education, cultural	5,800
Wage earners	53,300	Health services	3,200
		Social services	1,600
		Other	20,500
		Total	156,700

working for the military. The larger part produced for civilian use, for the gray and black markets through German and Polish firms. A part of the production was legally transferred from the ghetto, a part smuggled out. This particular sector of ghetto production employed tens of thousands of craftsmen and workers through a system of subcontracting, and a large proportion of this labor force was officially registered as unemployed, and therefore not entitled to the additional food ration given to workers who were officially working. This mixed system—working for both the military authorities and private firms—required that the Warsaw ghetto not be hermetically sealed off and left room within the ghetto for private business initiative.

The above description is significant for our understanding of the "rationality" of a system in which the Jewish population in the ghettos was considered as a virtual resource of the German state, administered by the SS and Gestapo, which would lease the resource to either the military or to civilian firms for a price that exceeded the cost of maintaining this resource by a large margin. Under the circumstances, the actual depreciation rate of this resource was very high, as witnessed by the deterioration of its quality and the mortality rate. To put this in economic terms, one could say that the realized return on this resource in the short run was so high, at a minimum of costs, that within a period of 6–7 years the resource would be used up; the ghetto population would be dead in the absence of extraordinary violence (tables 4 and 5).

These "rational" aims of the German authorities might explain their stress on the role of work and production in the major ghettos and upon their "usefulness" for the German war economy. The widespread assump-

Table 4   Natural Deaths in the Warsaw Ghetto (January 1940–June 1942)

	1940	1941	1942
January	1,178	898	5,123
February	1,179	1,023	4,618
March	1,014	1,608	4,951
April	1,044	2,061	4,432
May	865	3,821	3,636
June	650	4,290	3,356
July	563	5,550	
August	525	5,560	
September	489	4,545	
October	457	4,716	
November	445	4,801	
December	581	4,366	
Total	8,990	43,239	26,116

Table 5　Mortality by Age Groups in the Lodz Ghetto

Age (years)	May–December 1940			January–December 1941			January–July 1942		
	Male	Female	Total	Male	Female	Total	Male	Female	Total
0–1	484	338	872	83	71	154	72	52	124
1–8	190	148	338	148	158	303	156	157	313
9–14	39	41	80	105	97	202	78	74	152
15–19	107	71	178	470	213	683	310	185	495
20–25	84	83	167	411	196	607	341	160	501
26–45	401	454	855	1,487	956	2,443	1,402	851	2,253
46–60	673	619	1,292	2,084	1,130	3,214	2,223	1,202	3,425
61–	1,470	1,599	3,069	2,168	1,663	3,831	2,191	1,819	4,010
Total	3,448	3,403	6,851	6,956	4,481	11,437	6,773	4,500	11,273

tion of the German's "rational" intentions in exploiting the labor resources of the ghetto explains the incredulity of the Jewish response to evidence of the violent and systematic destruction of the ghetto working population.

The conditions of organization of the ghetto of Lodz created a beehive society. At the apex of the social pyramid was a bureaucracy that managed the workshops and the distribution of work and of food, performed the functions of a police, and was the most powerful and opulent group in the ghetto. Below this group was the mass of workers, not very differentiated, without any voice in decision making; they took orders and performed tasks. The lowest on the social ladder were the refugees resettled from other cities or ghettos, who did not have any roots in the community and any ties to the existing network of kinship and group relations that helped

Table 6　Mortality of Western European Jews deported to the Lodz Ghetto
(October 1941–July 1943)

Deported from:	Number	Died	Mortality (%)
Berlin	4,054	1,257	31.0
Frankfurt	1,186	357	30.0
Emden	122	30	24.6
Vienna	5,000	1,140	22.9
Hamburg	1,063	214	20.1
Luxembourg	512	99	19.3
Prague	5,000	871	17.4
Cologne	2,012	337	16.7
Dusseldorf	1,004	164	16.3
Tota	19,953	4,476	22.4 (average)

the natives to mitigate the harsh effects of their personal existence (table 6).

The social stratification in the Warsaw ghetto was only a little more complex than that of Lodz. At the apex of the social pyramid we find a group that perhaps accounted for 10 percent of the population. It consisted of (1) former members of the old bourgeois class who managed to save a part of their wealth; (2) the "new" ghetto bourgeoisie, a new class engaged in dealings with German and Polish firms and with German authorities, acting as subcontractors or experts on shady deals; and (3) the leadership of the ghetto administration and ghetto police.

We find a very broad stratum of the trading and working population which managed to survive in the ghetto by combining work, trade, and dissaving. The lowest group in the socioeconomic pyramid consisted of paupers, disabled, and those resettled from other cities and towns.

I have selected as my object of inquiry a day in the life of an ordinary person, a worker in the ghetto—an undramatic day, one of ordinary toil. The driving force was the desire to survive the day. One might begin the description of a day in the life of a ghetto inhabitant or ghetto household with an imaginary siren, which announced in the early dawn the end of the police hour and awakened the population to its twelve-hour workday; perhaps a more realistic sound instead of the imaginary siren would be the one of wooden shoes on the cobblestones of the street announcing the return of the nightshift of workers to their homes.

The awakening of the people at the gray dawn helps us to glance at their sleeping arrangements and at the conditions of their night's rest. The beds and other improvised or makeshift sleeping arrangements—on chests and boxes, or on the floor occupied an inordinate share of the space of a room. Six or seven (average for the Warsaw ghetto) inhabitants, not necessarily belonging to the same household, slept there. At dawn they would get up and rearrange the room for daytime activities. The absence of closet space or even of cupboards made the task difficult and was compounded by the variety of bedding or pieces of clothing often serving as a substitute for bedding, in disrepair or simply absent; no questions asked. Moving the bedding, airing the room, sweeping and rearranging the room for daytime activities was not a matter of routine but depended on the plans for the day, the work assignments of the inhabitants, and therefore required some degree of consensus, since it had to be negotiated by a number of people with different obligations, habits, and tastes.

Washing oneself created additional problems. The lack of privacy was cast aside long before and nobody paid much attention to such considerations. Given the average diet, many of the men were impotent, and many of the women had ceased to menstruate. Sex belonged to memories and fantasies. There were abundant excuses to skip daily washings once so routine: the water supply was part of the problem—frozen pipes, disrepair of plumbing, lack of tubs or washbasins; in the absence of running water, water had to be carried from the still-functioning wells in the neighborhood, and, last, there was either apathy or the hurry to get to work.

Washing and shaving, bathing and disinfecting the body and clothing became a barometer of one's will to survive in the longer run and of one's self-discipline. The degree of personal care, previously cultivated and followed by habit, or enforced by family authority, became, in view of the erosion of both, an indicator of the degree of consciousness and the ability to exercise good judgment. People differed with respect to will-power and readiness to make the physical effort to keep themselves clean and their ability to do so. Access to toilets in working condition was an even more serious problem. Physical exhaustion, a watery diet, diseases of the digestive tract and of the kidneys and and bladder made it extremely difficult to stick to a schedule for using the available toilets. Some household members would either queue up at the toilets of friends on the next block or wait until they would reach their workplaces.

Getting dressed was the next item of business. It was not a consideration of aesthetics that created the problem but the expected activities for the day that dictated a choice of clothing. The one who expected to work outside of the ghetto walls needed baggy pants, or a long heavy coat, so that a piece of bread, or a few potatoes, or a few handfuls of peas could be obtained and smuggled in on the way back from work. Work inside a building did not create much of a problem, but street cleaning or outdoor construction work required special clothing. In most cases, unfortunately, there was not much of a choice. The "surplus" clothing was either worn-out or sold or donated to somebody even more needy. Depending on the season and the nature of one's work, people tried to "keep warm," in view of the increased sensitivity to temperature changes of an undernourished organism; thus the tendency to be overdressed, as we might describe it. Fur coats, fur collars, sheepskins, etc., had long been confiscated by the German army, and cloth substitutes, shawls, and sackcloths had to be worn to protect oneself from the elements. Usually it was the mother in the family who would inspect the clothing ahead of time and make the necessary repairs or patches. The results were combinations of materials and colors, in comparison with which Joseph's coat of many colors was only a pale prototype.

Footwear was perhaps more of a problem than clothing, because of the overall wartime shortage of leather. Given an infinite variety of choices in the abstract, the inhabitants of the ghetto chose the Dutch fashion of footwear. The Dutch fashion spread with unbelievable speed, and the wooden soles and heels held together by a few leather or linen strips crowded out all prewar fashions of footwear. It is true that the fashion was not perfectly suited for the late autumn or winter seasons, especially if one had to walk to work or school. In fact, school absenteeism was often caused by the lack of footwear, but life had its imperfections, as the ghetto inhabitants had learned earlier.

To start the day with prayers was an old custom among many of the Polish Jews. Some continued it in the ghetto; some dropped it quietly. Another custom in Eastern Europe was to have breakfast before going out to work: Was it maintained or disposed of, like prayers?

Breakfast in the ghetto was no longer a household decision; in most households it was left to individual "tastes." Those who managed to save some bread from the previous day (or from the last distribution) would have a piece of bread with the brew from roasted grain which was imaginatively called coffee. Those who did not have any bread had to be satisfied with "morning coffee" and the memories of bread. As a rule no meal was cooked in the morning; shortages of fuel and food dictated cooking only one meal daily at most. Hardly any cooked food was kept overnight; too much temptation for hungry stomachs and the risk of spending a sleepless night in the vicinity of cooked food instead of sweet dreams about ambrosia and nectar, or the more familiar vision of the promised feast of the time of the Messiah.

Thus, breakfast did not last very long, just long enough to gulp down the hot water with the bitter taste, a foretaste of the day to come. And thus began the day of work. As the Bible says, "In the sweat of your face shall you eat bread." There was sweat upon many brows. Was there enough bread to go around? We'll follow our ghetto inhabitant and see.

In the room a new commotion started after those who had to leave actually departed. A workbench, a sewing machine, or other tools of trade were moved over to the window or to the light and the craftsman sat down to work, to his minimum twelve-hour workday, or to as long as he was able to work. No one believed in long-term contracts, either with one's fellowmen or with the Creator; and when work was available, one had to put in the maximum hours and have endurance to finish it. A similar situation existed in the shops or on the construction sites; the irregularity of arrangements, the difficulties in obtaining raw material supplies, and the tight delivery schedules made for irregular working conditions, while Jewish labor was treated as an abundant and expendable factor.

Therefore, whether in one's routine activity or in the search to survive the day, in order to find sustenance for oneself and family one had to mobilize the maximum of one's mental faculties and physical energy. One had to be alert, to react instantly to opportunities as well as to the threat of danger, of injury, and of death.

The advantage of working in a German shop outside the Warsaw ghetto was the ration of two soups and a pound of bread; but over and above that was the chance of purchasing some additional food from a Polish foreman or a German official or of bartering something valuable for food. The danger of being searched and punished while leaving and returning to the ghetto was great. Not infrequently the punishment was death, but this did not stop many.

Work in shops inside the ghetto supplied two soups and no bread over and above the general food ration, but with it came the presumption that one would be spared during the early waves of deportations, since one was presumably "useful" and making a productive contribution.

We all know about the drudgery and disutility of labor; textbooks tell us all about it, and many of us have experienced it. We are told by wise men that it is the expectation of reward that makes labor palatable or acceptable. For our ghetto inhabitant there were no expectations of a yearly or monthly bonus or cost of living wage adjustment. The expectation of reward had a very short time horizon; the expectation of a soup within a few hours was enough. It was this expectation that kept the people at work for the hours before the meal break.

My documents reveal clearly that a nutritional deficiency existed (see table 7). There are a certain minimum number of calories that are necessary for the support of life, and this minimum could be obtained only by working; however, even then the energy expended in working was not compensated for. After death carried off the paupers, the disabled, and the elderly,

Table 7   Monthly per Capita Food Consumption of Jews in Warsaw (1940–42)

	Authorized Rations (kg.)	Actual Rations
Bread	7.50	2.50
Flour	.75	. . .
Macaroni	.45	. . .
Cereal	.45	. . .
Meat	.40	. . .
Milk	3.75	. . .
Eggs (no.)	4.00	. . .
Fat	.30	. . .
Potatoes	15.0	. . .
Vegetables	3.75	. . .
Sugar	.75	.18
Coffee (roasted grains)	.45	. . .

an increasing number of the working-age population were afflicted by "hunger disease" and other illnesses, which added to the death toll. The survivors could see the writing on the wall as a collectivity; they refused, however, to accept it as individuals.

Let us for a moment take leave of our workers and turn to some of the nonworking members of their families. Nonworking mothers or their substitutes might be taking their small children to the soup kitchens set up for the children. They were maintained by the ghetto authorities although administered by the welfare department or welfare institutions. They were often located in the neighborhood, and the children were each registered in one of them. There was a conscious effort to save the children from a hunger death. The children's soup kitchens were not only food distribution centers, when the schools were closed, but substitutes for kindergarten and elementary schools as well. The soup was not only a bribe but also a source of energy to overcome the apathy of hunger, to get the children to respond to the educational challenge; they became more receptive, alert, and alive in the presence of other children and responded to their teachers. What interested the children most? Apparently, the description of nature in prosaic and poetic forms. For little children in the stone jungle of the ghetto the sight of a pine tree was as alien and exotic as the biblical description of palm trees and the cedars of Lebanon; it was to be found only in books and in songs. The sight of a cow in the Warsaw ghetto by accident created more commotion and uproar among the little children than a first visit to the zoo.

The clandestine school activities in the children's soup kitchens were subversive, given the aims of the Nazis not only to exploit the ghetto inhabitants but to degrade them and to turn them into brutes.

The mother left the little child in the soup kitchen and hurried back home. On the way she stopped in front of the bakery to join the long queue of women waiting for the distribution of their bread ration. In the queue the women talk about bread, Will it have more bran and potato admixtures than last week? Today's ration is doughy, small and moist; the bread is worse than the most pessimistic expectations. The mother hides her bread in the inside pocket of her coat, watching tensely the swarm of beggars and particularly the beggar children standing around on their swollen legs. She turns her back to the beggar crowd and holds on tight to the bread in her pocket. There is not much time to be lost, since at the soup kitchen in the next block there was to be a distribution of potato peels. Not everybody is privy to the news, but in front of the kitchen there is already a crowd of women. The lucky ones can get a pound of peels, which they put in bags, aprons, or whatever they can fit it in, and carry the treasure home. They call it "vitamins" in the ghetto, and it makes a valuable addition to an evening meal. It will be carefully washed, cut up into little pieces, boiled, and together with the frozen turnips it will turn into a sweet, filling meal, the first cooked family meal this week (table 8).

After having deposited the bread and potato peels in a hiding place in the room and throwing a tender glance at the husband slouching over his work, the woman runs down a few flights of stairs to the apartment of a neighbor where a meeting of the house committee is taking place. Under her arm she carries a little package, a pair of socks knitted from the thread of an old torn sweater. This is her contribution to the refugee family that moved into the lower cellar of the house. The house committees are not a part of the ghetto administration; they exist independently in all major buildings of the ghetto. They are elected by the inhabitants and deal with mundane problems: sharing of water and fuel, hygiene and voluntary sanitation inspections, child care, help for the needy and cultural activities. Here they share poverty. They have no official authority, only moral authority and social pressure and the demonstration that one can be his brother's keeper and not an animal in the jungle. At today's meeting they discuss the problems of the new family, the secretary reports on the death of the older girl and the illness of the little boy, the possibility that it might be typhoid fever and the need for a quarantine, but they also discuss food supply and clothing for the other family members inhabiting the dark and wet lower cellar. The present committee members make up a list of proposed food contributions and clothing donations. Our woman puts the socks on the table; the donation is being duly recorded by the secretary. After the meeting, the person in charge of book circulation hands over to the woman a package wrapped in paper and whispers: "You've got to return it in three days; twenty people are waiting their turn, this is the real thing." A glance into the package convinces the woman that it *is* the real thing, *Forty Days of Musa Dagh*— the novel by Franz Werfel about the Turkish massacre of the Armenians. This is the most popular novel among the adults in the ghetto. They'll read it aloud this evening, if there is electricity. It has been a good and lucky day. The husband is at work, the sister and the older son are at work, she got bread, potato peels, and a book, the little one in the soup kitchen is

Table 8 Estimated Daily Consumption for Various Ghetto Groups in Warsaw (December 1941)

Judenrat employees	1,665
Shopkeepers	1,429
Independent craftsmen	1,407
Workers in German shops	1,229
Resettled from other ghettos, living in barracks	805
Beggars	785

learning some songs for the holidays; a good and peaceful day. Perhaps she can afford now to go home and have her one hundred grams of bread for brunch; after all, she earned her reward when she donated the socks to the refugee family. All she asks in return is peace and health for today.

The son at the construction site outside the ghetto also has a normal day. He is good at carrying the bricks to the upper floors of the large storage facility they are building. He is handy, alert, and, especially after the hot soup, energetic. He also makes a deal with his Polish foreman. He sells him a dozen wrist bands for watches, which he got on commission from their neighbor, and gets not only a loaf of bread and a piece of bacon for the neighbor but also three hundred grams of bread for his share of the transaction. It would have been a nice and uneventful day, except for what happened in the afternoon. Somebody stole two large pieces of coal from the coal heap, and the head of the guards, the new one, not yet broken in, noticed it. He blows his whistle and assembles the whole group of workers for a line-up. The verdict is announced: a general body search of the whole group, and three days' confinement in the ghetto jail for the whole group, or the culprit gives himself up and receives twenty-five lashes. For a while there is general silence, until an elderly man in a gray coat steps forward and admits to stealing the coal. At this moment a young man in the traditional garb of the Polish chassidim, with his long earlocks hidden beneath his cap, runs up to the head of the guards. In fluent German he explains that he, and not the old man, is the real culprit. In addition, he admits that this is not the first theft and he is responsible while all the others are innocent. The head guard is both astonished and furious. He orders the flogging of the young man and counts each lash in a loud, unhurried voice. When the flogging is over, and the two guards who were the executioners have poured water on the bleeding back of the young man, the head guard asks him, ''Why did you do it?'' ''I guess that I can survive the flogging; the old man wouldn't,'' was the quiet answer. The head guard takes out a pack of cigarettes, and shouting, ''Stupid bastard! I won't take you anymore to work!'' throws them to the young man. The young man has a faint smile on his face. ''I don't smoke, thank you,'' he says, as though to himself, as he joins the ranks of the group, but his words are drowned out in the shout of ''Stupid, proud bastard!'' At the proper hour, the column of workers are marched back to the ghetto under guard.

At one of the ghetto gates the group is met by the ghetto police, who take them into the guardhouse. A police officer lines them up and demands ten zloty per head. Everybody complies; the young man with the earlocks beneath his cap pulls out a pack of cigarettes. A short exchange follows: ''Money,'' barks the police officer. ''I need cash for the Polish police and for the Germans.'' ''I haven't got any—only the cigarettes.'' ''Damn it, stupid bastard, you won't go out to work anymore, if I can help it.'' Some people in the group exchange glances; the policeman's shouts have a familiar ring.

The police officer collects the money and knocks at a side door, from within some men and women can be heard. He enters the darkened room and places a roll of banknotes on the top of the desk. "Buy me some oranges," demands a drunken female voice from the corner of the room. The police officer turns around, leaves the room, and closes the door. Through the guardhouse the group enters the ghetto street, and the son notices his mother among the waiting crowd. He waves at her and with difficulty makes his way through the crowd. When he reaches her, he can see that she is happy he has come home safely.

The traffic, always heavy, at this hour creates bottlenecks. The ghetto rickshaws can hardly move, pedestrians overflowing the sidewalks and onto the pavement. Our pair move slowly, making their way through the crowds. When they turn the corner of their street, they all of a sudden find the sidewalks empty. On both sidewalks small groups of German soldiers are walking and taking pictures of the crowd compressed on the pavement. They obviously are having fun. Mother and son quickly get off the sidewalk. A shot rings; a young German soldier has fired his pistol into a second-floor window. The crowd runs into the nearest entrances, trying to hide and to avoid an encounter with the soldiers. Mother and son together with others get into a staircase of the nearest house. After a while, the noise of the street returns to its normal level. They come down, walk another half block to their house, and begin climbing the stairs. The son is in a pensive mood. "It was a hard day," he says to himself. Mother does not ask for any details but watches his stooped shoulders.

Both families occupying the room make preparations for the evening meal. The table is small; they have to eat in shifts. During the meal, everybody is busy counting the pieces of turnips and potato peels in his neighbor's dish. The registration of one's own portion was automatic and did not require any effort, and any discrepancy would result in an immediate argument. But no complaints today; the bread rations are neatly cut and put in front of everyone. The option to dry the bread on the stove is left to each individual. Mother has cheated; she hid one hundred grams of the bread her son brought for his breakfast. "He had a hard day; tomorrow is another day; it might also be hard for him," she reasons to herself.

After the meal, which is followed in its minutiae by the hungry eyes of the other family in the room, everyone among the lucky ones pretends that it was filling, knowing well that within a few minutes the gnawing hunger, hardly subdued, will be felt again.

There is light in the room and still time before the police hour. The father opens the book and begins to read aloud, while mother makes preparations to put the child to bed. The neighbor girl pulls out a book of her own, and while the grown-ups listen to the gruesome details of the massacres the girl plugs her ears with her fingers and takes flight into the romantic world of de Amicis' *The Heart*. It is a tale of the life and struggle of Italian children in the nineteenth century. The son, wide awake from listening to the account of the massacres, feels all of a sudden that he has to share today's experience with some of his friends. The young man on the construction site, the head guard, the ghetto police, the German soldiers . . . all begin to fall into a pattern. No use listening to *Forty Days of Musa Dagh;* it does not offer any solutions; perhaps one ought not to seek solutions in books but rather in real life. He gets up and, to avoid interrupting the reading, whispers to his father, "I am going to see some friends. I'll be back before the police hour." When the son disappears, the mother's mind starts to wander; she cannot concentrate and listens intently. "We had a good day; we survived. Tomorrow is another day," she mutters.

This poorly rendered description of a day in the life of ghetto inhabitants was benign, with a minimum of violence and drama, and consciously avoided mentioning issues that could raise the blood pressure of an unprepared audience. I did not portray, after all, how an orphan lived in the ghetto, how a young man had to face the choice between his siblings and his parents, or how parents chose who among their children should be given the chance to survive, when the overall scarcity became obvious. I didn't ask how children reacted when they perceived, rightly or wrongly, that their parents could not or would not protect them from starvation or death. I did not raise a thousand other questions that people of the ghetto asked of the Creator of the Universe and to which the leaden heavens did not respond.

What I have to say—and the data support my claim—can be put in one sentence containing two figures. The conditions created by the Nazis resulted in the natural death (over and above the prewar mortality rate) of 19 percent of the ghetto population of Warsaw up to July 1942, and almost 35 percent of the ghetto population of Lodz from May 1940 up to 1944 (tables 9 and 10).

This was a death rate unacceptably slow for the proponents of the final solution and, to accelerate the process, Chelmno and Treblinka, Majdanek and Auschwitz were outfitted with speedier forms of genocide whose methods and results are all too well known.

Their names were obliterated; the holy letters returned to heaven in a fiery holocaust, and our subjects became the numbers that were quickly adding up to the frightful total of six million.

Table 9   Deportations and Death in the Warsaw Ghetto (July 22–September 30, 1942)

	Deported to:					
	Treblinka	Labor Camps	Shot in Ghetto	Died in Ghetto	Suicides	Total
July 22–31	64,706	1,812	498	1,022		68,038
Aug. 1–31	134,070	7,403	2,303	2,303	155	146,988
Sept. 1–12	51,969	2,100	2,621	339	60	57,089
Sept. 13–30	2,196					2,196
Total	243,941	11,315	5,422	3,664	215	274,311

Table 10   Changes in Population in the Lodz Ghetto Caused by Deportation and Death

	Male	Female	Total	Population by End of Month
Deported to Chelmno, 1942:				
Jan. 16–29	4,263	5,740	10,003	151,000
Feb. 22–Apr. 2	12,847	21,266	34,073	110,806
May 4–15	3,657	7,257	10,914	104,470
Sept. 1–12			16,500	89,446
Deported to Auschwitz, 1942:				
June 23–July 14			7,910	68,516
August			67,000	1,500
Total dead from ghetto			145,680	

ELEVEN

Forces for and against
Jewish Identity in the USSR

It is difficult to encompass within a short presentation the basic elements of national identity and national self-consciousness of the Russian Jews in view of the radical changes that have taken place during the last hundred years.

At the turn of the century Russian Jewry constituted the most culturally homogeneous and the most dynamic and creative part of the Jewish people. Not only in number, with its population of over 5 million, but in terms of its inner vitality, it constituted the backbone of Ashkenazic Jewry. It derived its legitimacy from the Talmudic and Rabbinical traditions, and to use Zangwill's apt phrase, "It had its roots on Mount Sinai and its eyes turned toward the millennium."

There were no identity problems among them. The sons of Baron Ginsburg, serving in the cavalry guard regiments, or the children of the Rabbi of Moscow, the offspring of the tea, sugar, and lumber merchants, or of the tailors and cobblers of Lithuania and Byelorussia, of the itinerant peddlers and agricultural colonists of the Ukraine, of the weavers and spinners of the Polish textile cities, or of the Odessa waterfront gangsters à la Benia Krik—all were Jews, thought of themselves as such, and behaved accordingly.

Does one need a better witness than the Russian population census of 1897 which reported 97.5 percent of the Jews spoke Yiddish as their mother tongue, or even more amazing statistic that 157 members of the Russian nobility listed Yiddish as their mother tongue? This overwhelmingly homogeneous response was based not upon a negative identity imposed from the outside but upon the deep sense of the objective and subjective value of their autonomous tradition and culture. This deeply ingrained set of values and pride of heritage were not only held by the traditionally religious, but, in a remarkable continuity, they lay at the root of human values that formed the modern ideologies of Jewish social movements.

Among the many wrong clichés that accompany our own blurred image of our not-too-distant past, among our uncritical and misleading use of such terms as ghetto, *shtetl,* etc., we have also inherited the mistaken notion of traditional Jewish society as one of stagnation, impervious to change. Nothing is more remote from the truth. It was the genius of our traditional society that it had a mechanism for absorbing the new and adapting to it; the process of adaptation was a selective one, a slow and gradual one, but it was at work: witness our survival in the Diaspora for 2,500 years. At the end of the nineteenth and in the twentieth centuries, the pace of traditional adaptation became slower and its bearers perhaps too inflexible. This was when the process of weakening of the old life-style and orthodox precepts began.

The new ideologies called for national and social modernization and even secularization. Emphasis shifted from the elements of the religious community to elements of a national community. But the idealistic and heroic Jewish nationalists and socialists were expressing the old messianic dream and the revival of Maccabean courage. Assimilation was the route of the few; national and cultural self-emancipation was the pattern for the vast majority.

Even when Russian Jews tried so hard to obtain access to Russian schools, to secular education, and to the professions, it was rarely in order to escape their identity or to abandon their less-fortunate brethren. In most instances the goal was to serve their own community. Their example raised the aspirations and the quality of life of the other members of the community and prepared them for the transition to modernity.

Along this road, Russian Jews created lasting monuments of their emancipation, a truly modern Jewish intelligentsia, the modern Yiddish and Hebrew literatures, Jewish schools, the Jewish press and the Jewish theater, all expressions of an autonomous community life, of a spirit of new creativity within a framework of inherited ethical values that have guided Jewish behavior through the ages.

Modern scholarship created by Russian Jewry viewed Judaism as a national history, a nation preserving not only religious treasures but also the genuine complexion of its diversified dynamic life of a living social organism. All this created a rich culture which not only helped the community in its spiritual survival, reaching out to its multifarious sources, traditions and aspirations, but it also satisfied the individual who could find in the multitude of cultural expressions the ones that served his needs or that agreed with his tastes.

This period of cultural "Sturm und Drang"—which coincided with but also reflected the upheaval of pogroms and revolutions, of migrations gigantic in their scope, and external conditions that undermined not only stability but often sheer survival—had its spillover effect both in space and in time, and continued for a while even during the Soviet period. We know well how such poets like Hofshtein, Der Nister, and Markish were silenced, we know the fate of hundreds upon hundreds of poets and writers, artists, and teachers whose creative voices were silenced in the snows of Siberia. We also know their crimes, which consisted in expressing their thoughts and their feelings in their own people's media, in their attempts to continue a glorious tradition. We have not forgotten the noble resistance of simple Jewish craftsmen, who under the guise of the artisan cooperatives would enlist a rabbi, a *shohet,* or a melamed to teach their children the Bible during the dark years of Stalinist terror. Nor have we forgotten the often nameless simple Jews who supplied kosher meat to the patients in the hospitals, thus earning a double reward for the old mitzvah of Bikur Holim.

I have mentioned such instances because they clearly indicate both the nature and scope of resistance. The subsequent rise in national sentiments was not only a response to external factors but also a continuity of a suppressed sentiment, not a *deus ex machina* but an expression of a will to live and exist as Jews.

Since in my previous comments I dealt indirectly with elements of tradition and heritage, with cultural community based upon language and creativity, reinforced by the conscious will to survive, let me mention two more factors, one of which reinforces the sense of group identity: this is the pattern of settlement. As long as the Russian Jews constituted the majority population of the towns in the Pale of Settlement, of large concentrations in the cities of the Pale, with what we would call in our American parlance "ethnic neighborhoods" in those cities, the elements of common lifestyles, the characteristic features of their culture provided both a feeling of security and a stimulus for continuity. If, in addition, we encountered a high degree of concentration in particular branches of industry, craft, or commerce, their opportunities for continuous interaction, the knowledge of the symbols of interaction and behavior, strengthened the bonds between the members of the group whether in the marketplace, in the shop or factory, or during their leisure time.

In this respect, important changes took place during the Soviet period. First, there was the opening up of opportunities for social advancement for those who were literate into the various government institutions; there was an opening up of educational opportunities as one of the most important channels of upward social mobility, to which the Jews as an urban element availed themselves. In addition, there was a conscious governmental policy of transferring Jews from small-scale craft to large-scale industrial establishments. All these elements caused a major migration from the towns of the Ukraine and Byelorussia to the rapidly growing cities of Moscow, Leningrad, Kiev, Kharkov, and others. But the Soviet system of control did not permit the exercise of free choice or of spontaneous formation of ethnic neighborhoods. In fact, it was one of the objectives of the state to atomize the population, to mix them up so that none of the elements of solidarity in subgroup culture would survive, and under such circumstances the bonds began to break. World War II, the destruction of the Jewish population in the occupied regions of the Ukraine and Byelorussia, and unwillingness to readmit the survivors back into the areas of their previous settlement, radically changed the pattern of settlement, the territorial distribution, and the social composition of Soviet Jewry. Great Russia became the territory, the large cities their habitat, professions and services the areas of their predominant employment.

There is one more factor that was of crucial importance for manifested identity: the sense of solidarity among Jewish communities in times of adversity. There was no problem up to the end of the eighteenth century; all Ashkenazic Jewry from the Ukraine to Alsace and Holland, from the Dnieper to beyond the Rhine, constituted one extended community. But the nineteenth century, with assimilation in Western and Central Europe, and with the growth of national states, put Jewish communities on trial. Fortunately, by and large, the Jewish communities rose to the challenge. Do I have to recite the response of Western European Jewry to the exodus of the Jews from Moscow, to the pogroms in Rumania, or the protest of American Jews against the massacre of Kishinev? It is important to remember that the old biblical dictum, "I am my brother's keeper," was reaffirmed. Let us remember that the Jewish population in Eretz-Israel was maintained by the help of the other Jewish communities, an age-old custom that was crucial to sustaining an uninterrrupted Jewish communal life there. Let us also remember that American Jews not only sent remittances to their relatives back home in Russia but supported the synagogues, the schools, the burial places, the hospitals, and the welfare functions of the communities in the old country.

This awareness of the Russian Jews that they have a cousin in Brooklyn or a nephew in Chicago provided them with a greater sense of security at times of adversity. Fortunately, very few American Jews have encountered the sensation of European Jews during the times of the Holocaust when in the vale of tears, the *Emek Habocho* of total destruction, two hunted individuals exchanged among themselves the magic word "Amkho," to have their spirit uplifted in the knowledge that there existed another brotherly soul in this jungle of inhumanity. The greater the physical separation of

Jewish communities, the greater their feeling of isolation, the more crucial the sense of solidarity for their will to survive.

What is the essence of the Soviet attitude of policy toward the Russian Jews? Many students of the subject believe that the Soviet policy is one of wavering between two extremes: on the one hand, a denial to the Russian Jews of their status as a national group; and on the other hand, treating them as a collective hostage in the game of power politics. I personally feel that the Soviet regime has not made up its mind with respect to a systematic or consistent policy that can lead to a solution of the Jewish problem. For Communists there is the requirement of a theory that dictates or justifies practice in the old Leninist sense, that there is no revolutionary practice without a revolutionary theory. However, up to now we do not have any thorough, authoritative Soviet analysis of the history of the Jewish presence. We are confronted instead with contingency measures based mostly upon short-term political expediency. And in this sense we cannot speak about Soviet solutions of the Jewish problem. We can and we ought, however, to review the intentions of the various policies. In my humble opinion they add up to a consistent set of measures, using the carrot or the stick, but designed to destroy the national and cultural identity of the Jews.

Language assimilation, destruction of all autonomous institutions, religious, educational, literary, artistic, were the means by which not only the bonds to traditions but also the tools of interpersonal communication were to be rendered inoperative. Atomization of society was the overriding goal of the regime and was applied to all Soviet citizens, but with a particular consistency to the Jews. Their identity was stripped of religious, cultural, social, and ethical attributes, and was left only as a mythical, almost mystical quality incomprehensible to their environment and one that could become incomprehensible to themselves.

Fortunately, this design did not produce its desired effect for a number of reasons; to mention only three—the Holocaust, the birth of the State of Israel, and the will to survive.

What are the chances of the Soviet Jews maintaining their identity, or regaining it? My own sense is that the odds are in favor of survival. There is one institution usually outside the field of vision of even trained analysts. This institution is the Jewish family. It has been less affected than the others. This is still a treasure box of many tangible and intangible traditional and cultural values. Given this base, provided that we continue to demonstrate our concern and help, to demonstrate our own Jewishness, it should be possible to revive and rekindle the spirit of Russian Jewry.

We are an old people; we do not measure our adversity or success on the scale of years, perhaps not even of decades. The Russian Jews are our brothers, and we are our brothers' keepers. We would be forsaking our sacred tradition if we were to forsake them. We have to help them stay alive as Jews. Our objective is not to subvert the Soviet system but to demand that the Soviets live up to their promises under the Helsinki agreement, a minimum statement of human rights, of civilized behavior. Among human rights there is the right to exercise one's religious beliefs and to maintain one's national identity and choice of place of residence. This is the minimum that we demand for the Soviet Jews. Of all the nationalities inhabiting the Soviet Union, the Jews are the only ones whose national life is not secured by a territorial base. For their survival, contact with other Jewish communities is essential.

TWELVE

Religion and Soviet Policy

The Case of Judaism

Religion, both as a set of traditional beliefs and as a personal need, was very important in prerevolutionary Russia where being Russian was equivalent to being Greek-Orthodox. The official emphasis on religion was so strong that in his legal documents a convert had to state both his present and his former religion. Thus, the Jews who did convert would usually undergo a double conversion, first into a more liberal Christian denomination, and then to Greek-Orthodoxy. Many St. Petersburg Jewish converts were labeled *provoslavnye iz liuteran*. And while, for identification purposes, the Provisional government and later the Soviet government stated nationality instead of religion on identification papers, in the popular mind religion survived for a long time as the criterion for differentiating and describing individuals.

The case of the Jews is special in the sense that, for Russians, nationality meant Greek-Orthodoxy; however, Greek-Orthodox included other nationalities as well. In the case of the Jews, the national group and the religious group were identical. And while subsequently one would distinguish Jewish nationality as including both religious and secular Jews, government policies might affect individuals in several ways as they would deal with religion, nationality, or culture.

Perhaps something ought to be said about the several policies of the Soviet government with respect to the three-faceted problem. The formulation and the application of policy indicate, if not a high degree of sophistication, at least a sense of realism. A government that engaged in the task of combating or suppressing the Jewish religion or the religious community, given the legacy of previous regimes, would lay itself open to the accusation of anti-Semitism. It could be expected to behave differently when dealing with the church of the majority of the population, or even when dealing with a worldwide church which is the official church in foreign countries (e.g., the Catholic Church) than when dealing with the religious institutions of a small minority.

In addition, the influence of the Bolsheviks among the Jewish masses in 1917–18 was absolutely minimal. (There were hardly any that could write in Yiddish, and it took repatriated emigrants from the United States to provide the minimum human resources even to publish one tabloid newspaper by the Commissariat of Nationalities.) It was the price of at least 100,000 victims of brutal massacres of the pogroms in the Ukraine in 1918–19 that had made the Jewish population view the Red Army as the lesser evil, in spite of the pogrom-like conduct of such army detachments as Budenny's cavalry. Thus, the Soviet government was aware of the very tenuous hold it had even upon the groups who "had no choice" but to accept Soviet power as the lesser of two evils. It appears to me that these two elements, the memory of religious persecutions and the weak hold over the loyalty of the Jewish masses, had a constraining effect upon anti-religious propaganda directed against the Jewish religion.

Therefore, a positive emphasis was put upon the features of national and cultural work in order to strengthen the position of the secular versus religious elements within the Jewish community. It should, therefore, be no surprise that the Soviet strategy relied upon the secularized Jews to weaken and, if possible, to destroy the religious institutions.

Secularist tendencies were not new; they accompanied the rise of enlightenment, of the *Aufklärung* or, to use the more pertinent term, of the *Haskala,* the Hebrew-Yiddish term: they were accompanied by the rise of nationalist and socialist movements in Eastern Europe and Russia. But there nevertheless was a difference between a secularism that claimed freedom of conscience, internal autonomy from organized, religious traditionalism, and a combative secularism of the militant, godless type, of a militant atheism, ready to apply force to suppress the practices and beliefs of their religious neighbors, relatives, etc. It appears there are two possibilities: one of doing the job as a result of conviction, the other of doing it for appearance sake. The possibility of doing it to others is illustrated by the anecdotal case of the Russo-Tatar village *zakryt' tserkov sdelat' klub pravul'no; zakryt' mechet' i sdelat' club* [close a church to make a club: close a mosque to make a club]. To do the job by conviction involves not only atheistic fanaticism but also the disintegration of the family, the social structure, and the complexity of socioeconomic networks. All of the above happened at a time when the economic disintegration and decline of the small towns sent tens and later hundreds of thousands into the factories, offices, and schools of the large cities.

The campaign against religion in the Jewish milieu as well as in the

Russian started after the famines of 1921, after dependency upon foreign food supplies diminished.

The experience of 1921 indicated the relationship between antireligious policies and foreign policy: whenever foreign policies required the antireligious campaigns to be silenced or suppressed, in 1921 and in World War II, would be done.

Thus, official governmental strategy consisted of a discriminate application of policies directed at different targets. The policies directed against religion and the religious community reached their peak in the late 1920s and during the 1930s, when they gave way to the policies of cultural discrimination, later to be replaced by policies of national discrimination (cultural discrimination—proassimilationist language and educational policies; national discrimination—moving away from the idea of national autonomous regions, etc.).

The policies directed against the religious community went in two directions: first, to create obstacles and raise the cost of religious practices to the observants of religious rituals; second, to prevent the training of competent religious scholars, rabbis, and men versed in areas of religious law. The first involved not only taxation, closing houses of worship, shutting down ritual baths, making it difficult to perform marriages, circumcisions, funerals, and to obtain food prepared according to the ritual laws, but also adhering to a strict application of labor law that made it difficult to observe the Sabbath. The second was promoted by closing down all Talmudic academies, closing down all elementary private religious schools and prohibition of private instruction, by banishment of scholars and religious leaders, even sending some abroad (others for a handsome ransom extracted from foreign Jewish communities, e.g., the case of the Rabbi of Lubavitch). The Soviets understood the peculiar importance of scholarship in the maintenance and development of Jewish religious life, and they paid a great deal of attention to this aspect. They could be more lax with respect to the ritual and permit some synagogues to continue, closing and opening up opportunities; they were, however, adamant with respect to the continuity of religious training and scholarship, which had to be halted. It is not at all obvious that the religious community at the beginning behaved defensively. Correctly or incorrectly, it assumed that much of the antireligious zeal could be ascribed to the intentions of the Jewish Communists more than to the intentions of the government and the non-Jewish members of the party. The religious community tried to use its contacts abroad, acting through their contacts with the Narkomindel and Narkompros, to persuade the government to moderate the virulent campaigns of the Yevsektsii (the officers of the Jewish sections). It also used loopholes of the New Economic Policy economy to have a mass of liturgical and religious literature printed and distributed and to maintain a supply system for meeting the needs of the religious community.

After a while it was realized that the perceived dichotomy between the Jewish party members and the party did not exist; the NEP came to an end, the industrialization drive began; the exodus from small towns followed, and the economic and social composition of the Jewish community changed and affected religious life independent of the policies, though in the same direction. Within the religious community there was no unanimity on the chances or on the strategy of survival. There were some who would disregard the prohibition against work on the Sabbath. Thus, the minimalists were ready to reduce the requirements of religious observance in order to save the faith, a pattern which could be described as "modern Marrano." On the other hand, we have a clear development of a maximalist attitude, one of internal resistance, especially within the Hassidic milieu; a tendency that went in two directions, one toward renewed mysticism, which was particularly strong among the Hassidim of Bratislava, a sect that had had no leader since 1810, and the other an activism that for obvious reasons of security had to be carried out under clandestine or semi-clandestine conditions. Perhaps a few examples of such activism in the 1930s and 1940s would illustrate the style and range of such activities.

In order to avoid working on the Sabbath, religious Jewish craftsmen did not enter the factories but organized themselves into craft cooperatives. The work schedules of such cooperatives, which also included some non-Jewish members for security reasons, would permit observance of the Sabbath. In smaller and medium-size towns, such craft cooperatives would include some of the religious service personnel, sometimes a rabbi, a slaughterer, or a teacher, whose primary role would be to continue their functions in religious services but who nominally would be employed as craftsmen. The premises of such *artels*—craft cooperatives—would be used as places of worship and study. By the preservation of parts of the previously existing network of social contacts, the economic aspects of such cooperatives would be secured either in the supply of critical raw materials or in the sales of finished products (even during the war a critical supply of raw silk was diverted from the NKVD silk factory to a silk-weaving *artel* operating in Audizhan). The same network tried to provide a livelihood and protection to the members of the religious community who insisted on remaining observant. The maximalists persisted not only in their own observances of religious laws but even in the continuity of charitable work. (Let me give as an example the supply of kosher food for patients in a number of civilian hospitals in Central Asia during the war and the attempts to penetrate some military hospitals in Siberia and the Ural regions to supply wounded Jewish soldiers with kosher food.) A daring exodus of groups of Hassidim from the Soviet Union was, by and large successfully organized and carried out in 1945 and 1946 under the guise and cover of repatriation of Polish citizens. This involved at least 2,000 members of activist families. But the war experience, whether under the Nazi occupation or within the Soviet Union, was not conducive to strengthening religious convictions.

In addition, evacuation and reevacuation, the destruction of the area of the traditional settlement of the Jews in the Ukraine and Byelorussia, the concentration of Jews in large cities, the tremendous educational and social upward mobility among the Jewish population, the passing away of the earlier generation with prerevolutionary memories and experiences—all weakened the religious, cultural, and national resistance of the Jews.

But then we all witnessed the unpredictable, the sudden and strong rise in national consciousness among the Soviet Jews. I would like to underscore the national rather than the religious, despite certain symbolic acts related to religious observances (e.g., Jews congregating in the neighborhood of the Moscow synagogue is a case in point). The nationalist revival is in the forefront of the civil rights and freedom of emigration movements; it is supported by large groups for whom emigration is a way to escape the consequences of diminished upward mobility and discrimination which would make large parts of the young generation of Jews déclassé. A purely religious revival has not yet emerged, although I predict that it will in time. Given the yearning for religion on the part of some young Soviet intellectuals, one could expect a revival of Jewish religious observance. But it is difficult for Jews after the Holocaust to gather under the messianic banner of a religious movement, and therefore I would not expect the Soviet Jews to follow the example of the Moslems. The rise of mysticism occurred within the religious community at an earlier stage.

In 1965, in a lecture about the problems of the Jews in the Soviet Union at a conference of the American Jewish Committee, I stated that for the Bolsheviks there exists a unity of theory and practice, and one could not make any firm predictions with respect to the government's solution of the Jewish problem in the Soviet Union until we can read in the appropriate literature a basic evaluation or examination of the history of the Jews. Old Leninist or Stalinist quotes will not do the trick. We have not yet seen any general reappraisal of Jewish history coming in the Soviet Union. But I am glad to report that I was mistaken in 1965—a mistake of omission. I treated the Soviet Jews only as objects of policies, but they have risen to the position of actors in a historical drama. It is therefore possible that they may become activists in the area of religious observance.

THIRTEEN

The Soviet Jews

On the present territory of the Soviet Union the Provisional government in 1917 granted the Jews equal rights and abolished the centuries-old discriminatory legislation that was typical of the Tsarist regime. The Jewish existence under Soviet rule, however, was far from idyllic; it was a saga of a hard struggle for survival. During the 1920s, after the Soviet rulers destroyed the more wealthy members of the Jewish community, there followed a brief period of relative freedom for small-scale businesses and crafts, combined with land grants for settlement of pauperized Jews in agricultural colonies. But from the latter part of the 1920s, this innocuous attempt to restructure the social composition of the Jewish population turned into a policy of direct labor mobilization for the build-up of Soviet large-scale industry, in the process of which the former craftsmen and traders were transformed into blue- and white-collar industrial workers, into managers, officials, and technical specialists. The previous relative freedom of private decision making was subordinated to direct job assignment and labor mobilization by the state. Being an urban element with a relatively high rate of literacy, some of the Jews could perhaps adjust quicker than their neighbors. They could participate in the process of upward mobility, moving out or being moved out of the traditional regions of settlement, or out of the typical Jewish trades.

The children of those who were given and those who seized such opportunities were admitted to the institutions of higher learning, and for them education became the major vehicle of social advancement. Some of them, subsequently, made their way into the technical, literary, artistic, and academic elites of Soviet society. The route into the elite of high technical skills was also the safest from the political point of view and was therefore preferred by most of the younger Jewish generation.

However, such opportunities were not granted without a price, or as my colleague Milton Friedman says, "There ain't no such thing as a free lunch." The price was conformity, outward acquiescence, and assimilation. The regime demanded obedience as it strove toward a modicum of homogeneity in the population as a means to assure its own continuity.

The majority of the parents of the present generation of immigrants paid the price under duress. The ones who did not were severely punished or disadvantaged. Their struggle is one of the glorious unwritten chapters of our common martyrology. But no one has the moral right to judge those who, under the conditions of Stalinist terror, adjusted themselves to reality.

It is true that due both to the process of linguistic assimilation and under the impact of official indoctrination the spiritual continuity of our traditions, both religious and secular, cultural and national, was broken for numerous Jews. One of the basic values, however, was preserved and is still in operation. Religious and national consciousness were always crucial in assuring our Jewish continuity, but they could endure only as long as the basic social unit—the primary cells of our communities, the family ties among individuals and between generations—was preserved. The Soviet Jews have kept the basic unit and fundamental set of attitudes that characterized Jewish family relations. And this involved not only the nuclear family but also the extended family. Therefore, whenever the problems of self-identification and differentiation from their neighbors or their adverse environment arose, they could fall back upon the syndrome, which I will for the lack of another term define as "the cousin in Brooklyn" syndrome. This, more than anything else, reflected both the myth and the reality of their situation.

At present, threatened with the real prospect of reversal in their social postions, suffering from both popular and official anti-Semitism, becoming once again a discriminated-against minority, the Soviet Jews have fallen back upon this fundamental, real familial relationship, and thus hundreds of them have come to the United States. Thereby, their fate becomes not only a challenge to their ability, as immigrants, to adjust to the United States as new Americans but is a test of our capacity to welcome, to assist, and to absorb them as new members of our Jewish communities.

In order that we should better understand their problems as immigrants as well as our task, permit me to characterize the general population of the Soviet Jews from which the immigrants are recruited.

The most important sociodemographic characteristics of the Jewish population in the Soviet Union, according to the census data, are the following:

1. There is still a substantial imbalance in the sex and age composition of the Jewish population, with women exceeding men, and about a quarter of the reported population over sixty years of age.

2. At least half of the Jewish population is located in areas outside the former Pale of Settlement. It is predominantly urban with a high degree of concentration in major cities. About half of the population (988,115) lives in eleven major cities.

3. In contrast with the pre–World War II situation, however, only in one of these cities (Kishinev) do the Jews make up over 10 percent of the city population; in the other cities the percentage is much smaller (2–3 percent).

4. The size of the nuclear family is somewhat over three persons, which reflects the tendency to have one child per family.

5. The typical household is a three-generation one and includes the parents, a child, and usually one grandparent.

A few additional features reflect the situation of employment:

1. A typical household has two wage earners, since the wages or salaries of one would be insufficient to maintain the family at a desired level of income.

2. About one-half of the gainfully employed among the Jewish population has the equivalent of a college education.

3. This high rate of participation of women in the labor force can be explained by the high level of schooling of females, which, while somewhat lower (about 5 percent) than males in higher education, nevertheless exceeds the male rates in unfinished higher education and in special schooling, a euphemism for vocational schools.

4. About 40 percent of the employed Jews were working in positions that require higher education.

5. Therefore, reflecting the demand for skilled specialists with advanced schooling, the size of such categories as engineers, physicians and academics is quite conspicuous and includes women as well as men.

6. About 10 percent of the employed are classified as scientific workers (including academics), those employed in research institutions or doing research in industrial laboratories.

7. About 25 percent are employed as highly-skilled technical specialists who, although lacking higher education, perform important tasks within industry.

Although the data about the population from which the immigrants are recruited, is important, qualitative indicators should be considered as well as quantitative ones. These might be implied through a brief review of the system of education that ''produces'' the specialists and the mechanism of allocation within this segment of the labor force.

The Soviet educational system is polytechnically oriented and emphasizes practical experience as well as job-relatedness. It provides two tracks for secondary and higher education. One level leads directly through general secondary to higher education. The other follows, through a special secondary education, a program of vocational training of skilled workers and foremen for industry and other branches of the economy. The decision to separate pupils along the two tracks is reached at an early phase in the pupil's life. Followers of the second track, however, can still acquire advanced degrees while on the job through enrollment in evening or correspondence courses. Since over 80 percent of the gainfully employed have secondary schooling, theoretically at least, many can upgrade their formal education during their working life.

Once the formal schooling is finished, a Soviet citizen usually expects either to be placed on a job or given the chance to find one. While jobs and job security do not constitute any major problems, the quality and location of the job and the benefits it bestows vary widely. The location of the job could make a difference in the whole life-style, quality of housing, consumer goods, and of cultural milieu for the employed. Thus, competition for the more desirable jobs might be fierce, and trade-offs of various kinds between benefits and costs take place constantly.

Since the development pattern of Soviet industrialization places heavy emphasis upon the capital goods industries, machine building and heavy manufacturing, stressing volume rather than quality of production, an inordinate number of engineers were trained relative to other professions. The training of engineers and other technical personnel is narrow and highly specialized, sometimes geared to specific tasks or types of products. For example, since machine tools are mass produced and models change at infrequent intervals, engineers might be trained to produce particular models or types of machinery. The Soviets, while imitating the German and American patterns of specialization, pushed it to the extreme. By breaking up technological processes into their components and by using workers and engineers for routinized tasks, the Soviets hope to achieve the maximum volume of production.

In this centrally planned system, the factories submit their long-term requests for specific skills, and the schools attempt to supply the labor market with the desired number of specialists within the narrow ranges of specialization.

Because of the inefficiency of the system, however, frequently misallocating trained specialists, or because of necessary changes in the technological processes on the job, engineers and other technical specialists might acquire a much broader experience than their training or assignment intended. In fact, the technical specialists are often forced to use all their ingenuity and inventiveness to meet the planned production targets and thereby have a chance to broaden their experience.

Soviet technology, except for some military hardware, is inferior to

American technology in spite of the supply of translations of foreign technical literature in the Soviet Union among scientists and engineers; their daily practice has to rely on their own resources to resolve many of the problems that are resolved in American industry by our system of subcontracting and consultation.

Needless to say, immigrants from the Soviet Union are expecting to find in the United States employment commensurate with their education and job experience. That this maximum of expectations is not always possible is due to a number of problems, some of which are beyond our control (e.g., differences in technology, etc.). However, there are problems that we together with the immigrants are capable of resolving and thereby help them in achieving a realistic level of satisfaction at the least cost. Such problems can be classified in a few broad categories as follows:

1. Language training, including the technical vocabulary and terminology pertaining to their skills.

2. Opportunities for a certain amount of retooling, acquisition of additional skills, learning about American work methods and job performance criteria.

3. Opportunities to find permanent employment.

4. Social and psychological adjustment.

The language training as it stands involves only instruction in conversation and a smattering of civics. I am suggesting that in an immigrant's area of concentration additional courses in technical English be instituted, which ought to furnish them with the rudiments of the terminology they will have to use on their jobs.

The problem of retooling clearly suggests that the first job would most likely be one below the technical competence of the immigrants and might be explained to them as an investment in their training and skills application within the American context. This trade-off between present income and future opportunities ought to be understood, explained, and presented to them, and a mutual understanding made with their approval. I am very much aware of the psychological obstacles facing immigrants in understanding the workings of our economy, the complexities of the job market, and the whole value structure of our society. For they come to us from a society in which no one trusts anyone; in which ordinary people do not trust the authorities, the media, or even their friends. To use an apt phrase of a friend of mine: you kiss your wife, but you do not confide in her. They are conditioned to mistrust anyone in authority, and they see us as members of the establishment. The idea of providing services without personal benefit at the expense of the client is alien to many of them. The idea even of an equal exchange, that one man's meat is not necessarily the other man's poison, might be foreign to the popular culture of Soviet citizens.

And there is something else. The Soviet society, popular beliefs not-withstanding, is the most rigidly stratified society that I know. Social status, with all its symbols, is jealously guarded, because it is a co-determinant of income and a substitute for wealth. Our immigrants are no exception. Anyone watching them closely is struck by the subtlety of their stratification, by their insistence on titles, by the attempts to preserve the pecking order within their small groups. After all, many of them were moved to emigrate when they faced the danger that their children would become déclassé and that they would be pushed down the social ladder as a result of anti-Jewish discrimination. We have to be aware of all the problems of their background and sensitive to their acquired attitudes, even when they appear to us somewhat idiosyncratic, but we must, nevertheless, insist upon rational decisions and rational behavior. We have to keep in mind that they have a risk aversion. Perhaps many of them cannot afford risks and uncertainty; they lived in a world of guaranteed employment, of meager but guaranteed services, and did not enjoy the freedom of private decision making. Their adjustment involves a learning process, and we are there to assist them in learning by doing.

The most difficult problem is the one of finding suitable permanent employment for them. This involves our knowledge of the relevant segments of the American labor market. It is my perception of this market that opportunities for the employment of immigrants from the Soviet Union might be more abundant outside of New York or other large Jewish communities; that the optimal choice might require their diffusion over a wider territory in areas of growing industrial employment rather than in areas of shifts from industry toward the services. Opportunities in our declining industry, academia, might still exist on the periphery rather than in the major population centers. This problem of organized diffusion of immigrants for the sake of employment opportunities is not a new problem for our welfare agencies and relief organizations. During 1901–14 tens of thousands of Jewish immigrants were directed away from New York, Philadelphia, Baltimore, and Boston into the American heartland. It was not an easy task to induce them to move, to entice them to abandon the familiar East Side, to separate them from their friends, their *landsleit,* and the milieu of which we were recently reminded by Irving Howe's *The World of Our Fathers.* Nevertheless, in historical perspective, and in terms of the long-run benefits for the immigrants, the policy of organized dispersion was the right approach. I believe that with respect also to this most recent immigration group, a planned effort of dispersion, when necessary, might work. Perhaps we need a better clearing-house of available job opportunities, perhaps more preliminary communication with their relatives and friends, perhaps even a committee of experts to help our devoted social workers to evaluate the diplomas and job experience of the immigrants in order to better match the jobs with the applicants. These are organizational problems that can be discussed and resolved.

As an economist I cannot resist making one comment with respect to the costs of our joint effort on behalf of the immigrants from the Soviet Union. My tentative figures indicate that in real terms, in terms of the estimated future costs of relief expenditures for this population, the per capita expenses for those immigrants will be lower than for any immigration cohorts with which the Jewish communities in the United States had to deal. This does not mean that we have achieved the maximum efficiency, but one is certainly entitled to suggest that in terms of even the conventional cost-benefit type of analysis—and as an economist I am not embarrassed to use the concept when human and moral values are involved—our costs are relatively low.

The problem of social and psychological adjustments of the immigrants do not end even with a job and a place to live; we all realize that "it is not by bread alone" that people reconstruct their existence. Thus, the elements of their own social integration and of their children's loom high in their minds. We have limited means to deal with special aspects of this problem. But this is exactly the area of concern for the local Jewish communities. Their role is crucial in making available to the immigrants the various education, religious, and cultural activities in which they could participate.

The immigrants from the Soviet Union have a special need that singles them out from among the earlier cohorts of immigrants: the need for a community. While the early immigrants had a highly developed sense of community and collective activities, an attachment to and the capability of recreating the Sabbath, whether the traditional religious one, which elevated them from their drab existence, or the belief in a Sabbath for the Jews, provided them with a variety of spiritual uplift. The Displaced Persons had a strong sense of continuity after World War II and were busy reconstructing their own psyches, depending upon the inner resources of their group and upon the commonality of their nightmare experiences.

The immigrants from the Soviet Union are sorely in need of a sense of community, of being accepted by the Jewish community and sharing in the experience of Jews and Americans. This is a tall order for many of us, but it is required as an act of duty and love. I hope we can approach the Soviet immigrants without condescending and censorial attitudes, as brothers and friends. Through true understanding and effective assistance we can make their dreams of happiness, peace, freedom from intolerance and discrimination a reality.

Table 1   Jewish Population of the Soviet Union (1970 Census)

Republic	Total Population	Males	Females
USSR	2,150,707	988,099	1,162,698
Ukraine	777,126	345,048	432,078
Byelorussia	148,011	67,483	80,528
Moldavia	98,072	45,110	52,962
Latvia	36,680	17,659	19,021
Lithuania	23,564	11,389	12,175
RSFSR[1]	807,915	378,902	429,013
Uzbekistan	102,855	48,417	54,438
Georgia	55,382	26,094	29,288
Azerbaijan	41,288	18,761	22,527
Kazakhstan	27,689		
Tadzhikistan	14,615		
Kirgizia	7,680		
Turkmenistan	3,494		
Armenia	1,048		

[1]RSFSR: Russian Soviet Federated Socialist Republic.

Table 2   Distribution of Gainfully Employed Jews

Education	Male	Female	Male	Female	Male	Female
Higher	486	447	286	279	251	240
Higher, unfinished	45	37	42	36	37	34
Secondary, special	163	185	200	230	189	231
Secondary, general	123	159	218	255	186	230
Secondary, unfinished	110	115	148	137	200	193
Primary	57	. . .	81	45	110	57
Total	984	943	975	982	978	985

Table 3   Specialists with Higher Education Employed in the National Economy (December 1, 1960)

	Total	Jews
USSR	3,545,234	290,707
RSFSR	2,083,306	160,732
Ukraine	685,851	83,689
Byelorussia	110,177	12,632
Uzbekistan	108,936	8,161
Moldavia	33,284	6,206
Kazakhstan	124,818	4,148
Azerbaijan	73,213	4,110
Latvia	40,807	3,611

Table 4   Number of Students (in Thousands)

| | VUSy[1] | | Special Secondary | |
Year	Total	Jews	Total	Jews
1962–63	2,944	79	2,668	47
1963–64	3,261	83	2,983	51
1965–66	3,861	95	3,659	52
1967–68	4,311	110	4,167	47
1968–69	4,470	112	4,261	43
1969–70	4,550	110	4,301	41
1970–71	4,581	106	4,388	40
1971–72	4,598	. . .	4,421	. . .
1972–73	4,630	89	4,438	37
1973–74	4,671	. . .	4,448	. . .
1974–75	4,751	. . .	4,478	. . .
1975–76	4,854	. . .	4,525	. . .

[1]VUSy: Vysshie uchebnye zavedeniia (Institutes of Higher Education)

Table 5   Number of Scientific Workers

Year	Total	Jews
1950	162,508	25,125
1955	223,893	24,620
1958	284,038	28,966
1959	310,022	30,630
1960	354,154	33,529
1961	404,126	36,173
1963–64	565,958	48,012
1964–65	611,964	50,915
1965–66	664,584	53,067
1966–67	712,419	56,070
1967–68	770,013	58,952
1968–69	822,910	60,995
1969–70	883,420	63,661
1970–71	927,709	64,392
1971–72	985,200	. . .

Table 6   Distribution of Jewish Students in VUSy (1960–1961)

	Total	Females	Day Program	Evening Program	Correspondence
USSR	77,177	31,564	. . .	. . .	. . .
RSFSR	46,555	19,018	21,483	6,268	18,804
Ukraine	18,673	7,441	7,007	3,545	8,121
Byelorussia	3,020	1,068	1,416	669	935
Uzbekistan	2,902	1,270	1,238	317	1,347
Moldavia	1,225	556	570	113	542

Source: TsSU SSSR, Vysshee Obrazovanie v SSSR, Stat Sbornk, Gosstatizdat, (Moscow, 1961).

Table 7   Married Persons per 1,000 of Each Age Group

Age	Ukraine		Byelorussia		Moldavia	
	Male	Female	Male	Female	Male	Female
16–19	14	57	10	34	21	63
20–29	409	569	394	510	448	606
30–39	882	825	898	819	922	873
40–49	946	791	960	785	965	853
50–59	949	604	959	602	962	697
60–	788	571	767	575	818	784

Table 8   Age Distribution of the Jewish Population in the RSFSR

Age	Number	Age	Number
0–10	56,002	30–39	121,675
11–15	34,335	40–49	129,563
16–19	31,375	50–59	131,592
20–29	88,006	60–	213,379
		Total	807,915

Index

207

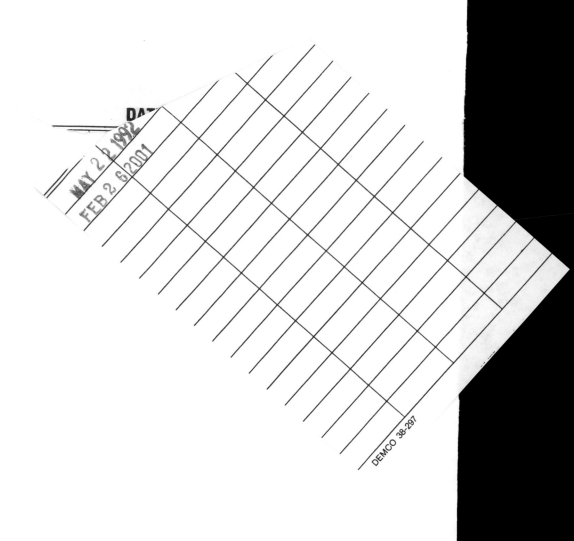